NON-STOP

NON-STOP

A TURBULENT HISTORY OF NORTHWEST AIRLINES

Jack El-Hai

University of Minnesota Press
Minneapolis · London

The Fesler-Lampert Minnesota Heritage Book Series
Funded by the John K. and Elsie Lambert Fesler Fund and Elizabeth and the late David Fesler, the Fesler-Lampert Minnesota Heritage Book series publishes significant books that contribute to an understanding and appreciation of Minnesota and the Upper Midwest.

Published by the University of Minnesota Press
111 Third Avenue South, Suite 290
Minneapolis, MN 55401-2520
http://www.upress.umn.edu

Design and production by Mighty Media, Inc.
Interior and text design by Chris Long

Library of Congress Cataloging-in-Publication Data

El-Hai, Jack.
    Non-stop : a turbulent history of Northwest Airlines / Jack El-Hai.
    Includes bibliographical references and index.
    ISBN 978-0-8166-7445-9 (hc : alk. paper)
1. Northwest Airlines Corporation—History. 2. Aeronautics, Commercial—United States—History.
I. Title.
HE9769.U5E4 2013
387.706'573—dc23

                                                                                    2013010388

Printed in China on acid-free paper

The University of Minnesota is an equal-opportunity educator and employer.

20 19 18 17 16 15 14 13   10 9 8 7 6 5 4 3 2 1

CONTENTS

PREFACE

Few businesses originating in the Upper Midwest wobbled between the extremes of Northwest Airlines. At different times in its history of more than eighty years, Northwest led its peers in daredevilry, effective war production, safety, weather forecasting, profitability, technological prescience, international relations, and smart efficiency. At other times, it sank to new depths of labor acrimony, hazardous operations, debt accumulation, parsimony, cynicism, and bad luck.

More than a simple chronicle of the evolution of transportation and technology, Northwest's tale sheds light on food, fashion, advertising, heroism, and catastrophe, to name several topics in these pages. The company's history presents many contradictions. Within a few years of each other, for instance, one Northwest employee received a Congressional Air Mail Medal of Honor, and another a criminal conviction for contempt of the U.S. Senate. How did this happen? How could a podunk mail carrier without a single airplane to call its own grow into the envy of the airline industry, and then decline into the company that aggrieved passengers and employees loved to call "Northworst"? If the airline deregulation of the 1970s was supposed to make the industry more competitive, why did it eventually push every one of the largest carriers like Northwest closer to—and often over—the precipice of bankruptcy?

Those are the sorts of questions I tried to investigate. But as I researched Northwest's history, I grew interested in the countless individual stories of passengers, employees, and others who together form the web of Northwest's company biography. What was it like to pilot a crippled airliner, pioneer the new profession of stewardessing, and ride in the cabin of a luxurious Stratocruiser for the first time? I hope readers will enjoy following those smaller stories in this big picture of an airline's turbulent history.

I referred to this narrative as a company biography. Unlike one person's life story, Northwest's narrative lets us speculate on the opportunities, motivations, and ambitions of a tangle of individuals, groups, and the nebulous corporate entity that they comprised. What a rich stew of complexities—and what an overpowered human drama! Northwest's eighty-year story covers the length of a human lifespan, and it burrows deep into the psyche of people and organizations.

CHAPTER 1

THE ROMANCE OF AVIATION, THE PERILS OF A BUSINESS

MOST ACCOUNTS OF AVIATION HISTORY BEGIN AT THE DUNES OF KITTY HAWK, NORTH Carolina, where the Wright brothers made their first flight in 1903. Commercial aviation became a possibility, however, some forty years earlier in the Upper Midwest. There, during a seemingly inconsequential stop in his travels, a German army officer on tour of the United States germinated an idea that soon grew into an obsession. From his fixation evolved passenger air travel and the exploits of modern airlines.

The visitor to St. Paul, Minnesota, who carried a letter of introduction from President Abraham Lincoln, was a twenty-five-year-old representative of the King of Württemberg named Ferdinand von Zeppelin. Zeppelin's purpose in America was to observe the Union Army in action during the Civil War. After sampling the fields of battle, Zeppelin had ended up in Minnesota in August 1863 as part of an excursion into the American frontier. He must have wondered how such a sparsely populated region could contribute to his investigation of military strategies.

Two days after his arrival, he crossed paths with the locally celebrated balloonist John H. Steiner. Their meeting would transform Zeppelin's life. Although Zeppelin had already seen how the Union Army used manned balloons to strategic advantage by surveying Confederate positions, he had not yet experienced an ascent. Steiner, himself German by birth, gave him that opportunity. Carrying Zeppelin and other passengers, Steiner's balloon soared to the full length of its tether, about seven hundred feet. Zeppelin gazed down at the Mississippi River, the rocky bluffs rising from its banks, and the barracks of Fort Snelling. The view, and the sensation of flight, set his imagination aflame. What if such a balloon could be freed from its tether, propelled, and steered? "While I was above St. Paul," he later wrote, "the idea of aerial navigation was strongly impressed upon me, and it was there that the first idea of my Zeppelins came to me."

Aloft in the sky above Minneapolis's Lake Calhoun in 1911, pilot Hugh Robinson embarks on the region's first airmail flight.

It took more than thirty years for Zeppelin to patent his design for a gas-filled passenger airship and begin its construction. In 1909, while the Wright brothers were still trying to prove to the U.S. Army that their two-seat biplane was airworthy, Zeppelin had overcome repeated setbacks to launch the world's first passenger airline. Soon the skies of Europe were filled with the cigar-shaped aircraft that bore Zeppelin's name. Not long after Zeppelin died in 1917, his airships were making trans-Atlantic passenger flights. They remained a common, if expensive, form of international travel until 1937, when the fiery destruction of the *Hindenburg* at Lakehurst Naval Air Station in New Jersey ended the era of Zeppelin travel.

RIGIDLY ALOFT

Decades after the Upper Midwest was the scene of Zeppelin's first visions of flight, the region again served as a stage for the development of commercial aviation. But it was a slow evolution. In 1911, a thirty-year-old aviator named Hugh Robinson, a veteran of three thousand hours in the air who had already been the first to skydive from a balloon and

Passengers in a horse-pulled wagon contemplate the new age of airmail service that dawned in the Twin Cities during the early 1920s.

drop bombs from an airplane, loaded a bag of U.S. Mail into his hydroplane and took off from Lake Calhoun in Minneapolis, bound for Rock Island, Illinois. He delivered and picked up letters in Mississippi River towns along the way, making his trip one of the nation's earliest commercial flights. By 1920, advancements in airplane design and the availability of experienced pilots after World War I allowed the U.S. Post Office to continue the airborne delivery of mail on a stronger footing.

That August, the Twin Cities gained its first commercial air link: a daily airmail connection with Chicago. Commanding an assortment of war-surplus biplanes, single-engine craft, and decommissioned twin-engine bombers, pilots struggled against dangerous weather, poor navigation, and the perils and discomforts of primitive airports to deliver the mail. Flights terminated on the somewhat level strip of a facility called Speedway Field, south of Minneapolis, which despite a new shed erected for the airmail deliveries would not be recognizable as an airport under today's standards. Flights often terminated in other ways as well, with terrible results—four pilots died and eight aircraft were wrecked in crashes during the nine months the Twin Cities–Chicago airmail route remained active before the Post Office pulled the plug.

That left the region without any kind of commercial air connection with the rest of the country, a humiliating state of affairs that hurt business as well as civic pride. The airborne efforts of bootleggers aside, how long would Minneapolis–St. Paul, with its combined population of more than six hundred thousand in 1920, have to go without this vital lifeline?

THE RETURN OF AIRMAIL

The hiatus ended in 1926, soon after the federal government began allowing private aircraft operators to bid for airmail contracts covering service that the Post Office had previously handled on its own. Up stepped Charles "Pop" Dickinson, a pioneering aviator whose successful bid on Air Mail Contract No. 9, the Twin Cities–Chicago route, briefly made him a local hero. Scraping together five planes—two of which had been built by hand by pilots—Dickinson restored airmail deliveries on June 7, 1926.

A postal official weighs parcels en route to Chicago from St. Paul after the resumption of airmail service in 1926.

Charles "Pop" Dickinson *(center)* confers with his staff between airmail runs in 1926.

Unfortunately, the route remained dangerous and subject to some of the nation's worst weather. By summer's end, Dickinson was down to a single beleaguered pilot, the legendary Eddie Ballough. An experienced navigator of the clouds who had taught piloting to one of Minnesota's most heroic figures in aviation, Speed Holman, Ballough declared that no amount of guts and experience could compensate for the risks of airmail flying. He told Dickinson of his intention to quit, leaving the airmail impresario no choice but to give the Post Office notice that he was bailing out of the contract effective October 1.

During his travails, Dickinson confessed his troubles and his plans to close shop to a close friend. Colonel Lewis H. Brittin listened and took action.

Two years past the end of his brief airmail experiment, Charles "Pop" Dickinson (right) poses with Northwest pilot Charles "Speed" Holman.

A SURPRISING AVIATION MOGUL

Brittin unexpectedly stepped into the part of airline founder at a time when the romance of aviation was peaking. In less than a year, an obscure twenty-five-year-old Minnesota pilot named Charles Lindbergh would stun the world with his solo nonstop flight, the first of its kind, from Garden City, New York, to Le Bourget Field in Paris. Overnight Lindbergh became one of the most famous people on earth, and the story of his intrepid flight continued to captivate Americans for decades.

Little in Brittin's background hinted that creating an airline was in his future. A Connecticut-born industrial engineer, he spent no time in the air during his World War I service and eventually settled in the Twin Cities to manage an innovative industrial park and railroad hub called the Northwest Terminal. He went on to direct the business development activities of the St. Paul Association, a predecessor of the city's chamber of commerce. In that role, Brittin helped St. Paul buy a plot of land previously known as Riverview Flats near the Mississippi River and develop it into a municipal airfield, later called Holman Field. Once the airport was open, he persuaded the organizers of the

BRITTIN'S BRAINS 🕐

Lewis H. Brittin, who earned the rank of colonel during World War I and retained his officer's title for the remainder of his life, was the sort of enthusiastic booster every enterprise needs in its fledgling years. His appearance—gangly at six feet three inches, bespectacled in rimless glasses, fatherly and stern, a bit academic—gave no hint of his drive to get things done and persuade others to help his cause. Without the plain-talking Brittin's willpower and fervor, Northwest Airlines would never have lifted off the ground.

Born in Connecticut in 1875, Brittin was orphaned as a youngster and attended boarding schools before studying science and engineering at Harvard. He served as an artilleryman in the Spanish-American War and as a member of the Quartermaster Corps during World War I, but his military experience never introduced him to the cockpit of an airplane. Eventually Brittin settled into a career as an engineer who worked on construction projects in Mexico and the planning of new factories in the United States for General Electric. On assignment for GE, he arrived in Minneapolis–St. Paul around 1920, and his commercial zeal quickly made him a favorite among local businessmen. They stole him away from GE, in fact, to become the industrial director of the St. Paul Association, a precursor of the city's chamber of commerce, to manage the construction of a transportation complex and wholesale distribution center called the Northwest Terminal, which yoked together railroad lines and manufacturing facilities.

Apparently not yet busy enough, Brittin took business and law courses at night at the University of Minnesota. His energy and the success with which he handled the complex Northwest Terminal project impressed a cadre of Twin Cities manufacturing leaders, who asked the colonel to lead additional business develop-

Lewis Brittin in 1929, by which time the airline's general manager had declared the air carrier industry unlike any other form of transportation.

ment activities. Brittin's networking talents paid off handsomely when he persuaded carmaker and aviation advocate Henry Ford to send the Edsel B. Ford National Airplane Reliability Tour—a demonstration of new aircraft and their commercial potential—to the Twin Cities in 1926, and then Brittin delighted everyone by convincing Ford to open a $23 million auto assembly plant in St. Paul. (That plant continued to benefit the region until Ford closed it in 2011.) Soon after, he helped orchestrate a municipal bond issue that enabled St. Paul to develop a plot of land near downtown into the airport that was eventually called Holman Field.

So Brittin was already a Minnesota business hero, a dynamo who combined visionary thinking with winning persuasiveness, in the late summer of 1926 when "Pop" Dickinson spilled his woes to him about the imminent demise of his airmail service connecting the Twin Cities with Chicago. Dickinson could no longer make a go of it, and Brittin took action. When he could not interest any other aviation firms in taking over the airmail line, Brittin made the perhaps irrational decision to start his own company to seize the opportunity, resulting in the hasty birth of Northwest Airways.

Brittin's concern over the consequences of the Twin Cities losing its airmail connection with the world led him to take such a great business risk. But his ability to make others enthusiastic about the future of the enterprise kept Northwest Airways from becoming just another slapdash airmail carrier with a questionable future. His Ford connections drew a pool of funding from Detroit before the airmail contract expired. Brittin and St. Paul postmaster Charles Moos personally loaded the first airmail delivery that Northwest carried.

Brittin knew the difference between launching a business out of enthusiasm and building one that could survive. Only two years after Northwest's start, when the young airline still faced formidable challenges, Brittin wrote about the airline evolution already underway and the challenges that Northwest had to overcome to thrive. "Commercial flying must develop its own business techniques," he declared. "Aviation accounting and aviation organizational methods will constitute a special field of modern business. . . . In this industry, rigid economy in operating costs is absolutely essential." That conclusion, which he might have expressed with industry approval in the 1990s as easily as the 1920s, signaled Brittin's conviction that aviation must transform from a novelty to a well-oiled enterprise.

As Northwest's longtime vice president and general manager, Brittin battled the Great Depression, fickle government officials, competitors, and creditors to hack out a path of efficiency for his company's entry into the uncharted territory of passenger aviation. He battled for route expansions, attained profitability, and looked after the airline's interests in Washington, D.C. Under his watch, no staff member could spit on the floor, and mechanics complained that the overall uniforms he required to instill professionalism were so heavily starched that the wearers could not bend over.

Years later, one employee remembered during the 1930s seeing Brittin stalking the company's main hangar days, nights, and weekends "to make sure every tool was in its numbered cabinet, everybody was wearing clean coveralls, and anything not in use was put away properly." He wasted nothing—not even a live lamb that Montana livestock breeders gave him when he arrived in Helena to show the feasibility of a route ending there from the Twin Cities; he had the lamb dressed in a diaper, brought it home aboard the return flight, and presented it to an employee's daughter. Brittin made it his mission to obtain for Northwest a route connecting the Twin Cities with Puget Sound, and with the help of general manager Croil Hunter, he eventually cajoled and wore down the competitors and government bureaucrats standing in his way.

Once the airline was financially sound, Brittin helped the company most as a lobbyist who looked after Northwest's interests in Washington, D.C. In addition to introducing the company's route requests to government officials and securing influential community support for them, he waded into the notorious airmail scandal, which he called "the battle of Washington." As Northwest's only representative at the Capitol, he was outnumbered by an army of lobbyists representing larger airlines. Protesting what he called "the monopolistic hold the three big groups [United, American, and TWA] have on the nation's domestic airmail service," he characterized Northwest as the last independent operator still standing.

Brittin's tireless work in Washington on Northwest's behalf even landed him in prison, albeit briefly. In 1934, President Franklin Roosevelt canceled all federal airmail contracts on the suspicion that corruption and favoritism had led to contract awards. Alabama senator Hugo Black (soon to become a U.S. Supreme Court justice) began an investigation. He called scores of witnesses and sent agents of the Senate's Interstate Commerce Committee into airline offices to capture potentially incriminating documents. Northwest employees stood by helplessly as the agents confiscated papers from the company's headquarters in St. Paul. "How we hated those men," a switchboard operator later remembered.

One of the committee's subpoenas demanded papers from the Washington office of William Mac-Cracken Jr., a lawyer representing Northwest and several other airlines. Brittin kept in MacCracken's office most of his daily business notes—including his candid and unflattering impressions of the intelligence, amiability, and character of various Washington politicians—and he did not want these personal papers to fall into Black's hands.

Immediately after learning of the subpoena, Brittin went to MacCracken's office, sorted out the files that he wanted to keep private, and tore them up. Unwisely, he dropped the shreds in the trash. Suspecting such a circumvention, the Interstate Commerce Committee's investigators rummaged through three hundred pounds of garbage and succeeded in piecing together some of Brittin's documents. Although the papers shed no light whatsoever on the airmail controversy, Black wanted Brittin to pay for disregarding the subpoena. Northwest apologized to Black for Brittin's mistake, but the senator was unswayed. Along with MacCracken and two other airline representatives who had removed papers from the office, Brittin faced a rare trial on the charge of contempt of the U.S. Senate. The tribunal remains the last time that the Senate has tried anyone on contempt charges.

Black introduced Brittin's reconstructed papers as evidence in the contempt trial. Voting in a secret session, the senators found Brittin and MacCracken guilty and sentenced them to ten days in prison. Before serving his term, Brittin, then fifty-seven, denied his guilt and took sole responsibility for his acts. Northwest then announced that he had resigned from his position, but Brittin told one reporter he had been fired.

Reporting to prison on February 15, 1934, he took a cot "between a bootlegger and a burglar," he said. He told reporters that he felt no malice for Black and his committee, and he was confident that the Post Office would fairly reorganize its system of awarding airmail contracts. He remained proud of his accomplishments for Northwest. "Anyway," he ruefully noted, "we carried the line to the coast."

One U.S. senator characterized Brittin's conviction as "a damn shame," and Northwest issued a press release reminding Minnesotans that "it would be ingratitude for the city and [state] to forget that his enterprise and energy were largely responsible for the building up of this new industry in the Northwest." (At the same time, the company called Brittin's crime "extremely foolish; he should have been aware that such an action would be open to the worst possible construction.") For the first time in its history, Northwest Airlines had to move ahead without the guidance and gusto of its founder.

Brittin continued to work as an airline consultant and board member of the aviation section of the New York Board of Trade. Northwest's founder died in Washington, D.C., in 1952 at the age of seventy-seven. In 1989, he joined the other luminaries in the Minnesota Aviation Hall of Fame. •

Edsel B. Ford National Reliability Airplane Tour to make a stop at St. Paul, and he became acquainted with several of Ford's leaders in Detroit. Famously social and respected, Brittin easily forged professional connections.

Dickinson's failure to profitably operate Contract Air Mail Route No. 9 alarmed Brittin. No way, Brittin thought, should Minneapolis–St. Paul again lose its airmail service. The region's business health and prestige were at stake. He appealed to Twin Cities businessmen and investors to keep the airmail line going, but its dismal history and the approach of fearsome winter weather fired nobody's interest.

Brittin could not let the matter drop there. "If nobody else will keep this thing alive, then I'll do it myself," he told his friend Bill Kidder, who owned a Curtiss airplane dealership, had managed Dickinson's airmail effort, dusted crops, took airborne student pilots and adventurous sightseers, operated his own airfield in St. Paul, and had helped in the development of the city's new municipal airport. Brittin invited Kidder and Brittin's secretary, Camille "Rosie" Stein, to join heads in a brainstorming meeting, thus merging the talents of Brittin's two most valued associates. The purpose of the meeting, Kidder recalled, was "to discuss ways and means of fulfilling our obligation to the Twin Cities and keep the airmail line running."

The group quickly concluded that only a large infusion of cash could support such an expensive and low-earning enterprise as the transport of airmail. "We tried to figure where we could raise the money in the Twin Cities in a short time, but selling stock in a losing venture that might eventually pay off would be a slow process and our money would run out before we could get the proper financing," Kidder remembered. A silence fell over the threesome.

Stein suddenly admonished the others. "Colonel," she said, "don't get down yet. You have promoted some pretty big deals, and Mr. Kidder has airplanes and knows aviation people. If you two can't put it over, you should be ashamed of yourselves." Thus upbraided, the men stewed some more, and Kidder later said his glance fell on a photo of the Ford Dam hanging on the wall of Brittin's office. "I said to Brittin, 'Almost through your efforts alone the Twin Cities gave Henry Ford that dam, and now you are up against it. He ought to help you out, anyway temporarily.'" Within a minute, Stein was on the phone to Ford's office in Detroit.

Ford himself was unavailable, but Brittin spoke with William Mayo, Ford's chief engineer. Brittin made his pitch and succeeded in scheduling a meeting with the business leaders in Detroit. With their financial support from that city, which brimmed with money from the booming automobile business, it was barely possible that Brittin could assemble everything necessary—planes, pilots, facilities, Post Office approval—to launch an airline before Dickinson's airmail contract expired at the end of September. Kidder accompanied Brittin to the meeting to contribute his aviation expertise.

At the meeting that Mayo organized at the Detroit Athletic Club, Brittin delivered his investment appeal with all the passion and urgency he could muster. By the end of the meeting, he had secured $300,000 from twenty-nine Detroit businessmen—just enough to get his airline off the ground. (Kidder remembered, though, that he and Brittin had to cash in their life insurance policies to support the airline until the Detroit investments actually arrived.) The investment group included Harold Emmons, the airline's new president and a lawyer well known in Detroit for his long service to the city's automobile industry; Frank Blair, a bank president; Eugene Lewis, another bank president who became acquainted with Ford executives in his earlier career as a sales manager of ball bearings; and William Stout, designer of the Ford Tri-Motor airplane. Except for Brittin, who held the title of vice president and general manager, all the company's officers lived in the Detroit area.

NORTHWEST TAKES SHAPE

Now came an important moment: the naming of the new airline. According to Kidder, he asked Brittin to somehow acknowledge Kidder's crucial assistance in the company's name. He suggested that Brittin adapt the name of his aviation dealership, the Curtiss-Northwest Airplane Company. "I've pioneered this business," Kidder said. "The name of my company means a lot."

A surprised Brittin replied, "But we can't call it the Curtiss-Northwest Airplane Company." Kidder agreed and recommended simply dropping "Curtiss" and using Northwest Air Service, Northwest Air Transport, or anything that included "Northwest." Brittin—who had previously created the Northwest Terminal transportation facility—liked the term because of the vast stretch of territory it evoked. On September 1, 1926, he incorporated the business in Michigan as Northwest Airways, Inc.

The pace of events accelerated under what Brittin later called "emergency conditions." Nobody else had been rash enough to apply for the airmail contract, and the Post Office Department approved Brittin's bid on September 4. Although that was good news, the quick approval must have thwacked Brittin with a sickening realization. His contract with the government mandated a starting date of October 1, 1926—leaving just three weeks for Brittin to start flying. Suddenly the task ahead seemed outrageously complex: To fulfill the terms of Northwest's contract, Brittin would have to carry off—in all types of weather and flying conditions—a twice-a-day, four-hundred-mile mail route, something nobody in the Upper Midwest had ever previously managed. In addition, the financial control of his company lay hundreds of miles from company headquarters in the Twin Cities, an awkward situation. "The company had only 40 days in which to organize, finance itself, secure the contract, acquire the equipment and organize its personnel," Northwest later cautioned in reporting its shaky first quarter of operations.

Brittin's most urgent task was to acquire aircraft. The company's investors had approved the purchase of three Stinson Detroiters—not coincidentally, manufactured with capital many of them and their Detroit Athletic Club friends had raised—which could cruise at 125 miles per hour, at a cost of $37,500 (about $480,000 in today's dollars). Even though Brittin paid extra to leapfrog over other waiting buyers, the three-passenger biplanes would be available way too late for the start of Northwest's airmail schedule, not until November 1926. To the rescue came Kidder. For $4,312.50, he offered a month's rental of a pair of open-cockpit airplanes from his inventory, one a Thomas Morse Scout of World War I vintage, and the other a gold-winged, 90-horsepower Curtiss Oriole.

The planes could not fly, however, without pilots and someone to manage them. Brittin brought in Charles "Speed" Holman, a daring stunt flier who had helped keep Pop Dickinson's airmail line going, as the airline's chief pilot; he quickly moved into the job of operations manager. But it is hard to know whether Holman was truly the airline's first pilot. David Behncke, who went on to cofound what became the world's largest pilots' union, the Air Line Pilots Association, claimed that distinction for himself. "I definitely know that I was the first pilot to be hired by Northwest Airways," Behncke asserted seventeen years later in a letter to the airline's publications editor, J. A. Ferris. Behncke stated that Kidder had asked him to fly for Northwest during Kidder and Brittin's earliest days of planning. When Behncke agreed to the proposition, Kidder replied, "Well, consider yourself hired." Behncke then asked whether any other pilots had been engaged, and Kidder said, "No, but I'm going to talk with Speed Holman about going to work for us this afternoon."

Unquestionably a good hire, Behncke possessed piloting experience that went back to aviation's early years, when "you made a living by risking your life," he once declared. Like Holman, he had flown Dickinson's airmail routes. After flying for Northwest for two years, Behncke became a pilot for United Air Lines, where the long hours and difficult working conditions—much like those at Northwest—inspired him to start thinking about the usefulness of a pilots' union.

Robert Radall and Chester Jacobson also joined Northwest's piloting staff, earning, like the others, $75 per week. At the beginning, the airline's entire payroll numbered nine people, not counting Brittin himself, who worked without pay. (For several months, he continued receiving paychecks from the St. Paul Association.) The top dog in the office was Rosie Stein, who Brittin immediately pilfered from the association's staff and grew into Northwest's soul and brains. She was in charge of ticketing and reservations, public relations, advertising and promotion, secretarial and clerical functions, cash disbursement, and dispatching. In a pinch, she helped the mechanics. Stein accomplished virtually everything necessary to keep the airline running, especially, as Kidder remembered, "doing everything that had to be done when no one else happened to be around to do it." She later evolved into a company director, the first female corporate executive in the American airline business, and the creator of Northwest's stewardess training program.

Other early Northwest employees made up a colorful collection of aviation pioneers and characters. There was James "Big Jim" LaMont, the chief mechanic with a voice like a loudspeaker, who had learned to pilot within a few years of the first successful powered airplane flights and soon became a toolbox wizard and built Glenn Curtiss's first ship. George Miles, unofficially titled "general factotum," assisted with paperwork, maintained the payroll, took reservations, ordered gasoline, sent airmail arrival times to the Post Office, and cleaned up, among other duties. Julius Perit, hired as a clerk, sometimes had to heat engine oil on the office stove when the cold made it too stiff to pour. The sum of the paychecks issued to Northwest's staff in November 1926, the company's second month of operation, was only $838.

In rapid succession came agreements to give landing privileges and the free use of hangars at the airfields of the cities on the route, including Wold–Chamberlain Field in Minneapolis, the Milwaukee County Airport, and Maywood Field in Chicago. Although Wold–Chamberlain had been the home field for Dickinson's airmail line, it was still a primitive facility. Landowner Guy Thomas and auto-racing promoters had originally developed the 342-acre Minneapolis property near Fort Snelling before World War I as a 2.5-mile concrete-paved oval track. They hoped the Twin City Motor Speedway would enable Minneapolis to become the next Indianapolis on the car-racing circuit. It hosted only one major race, a noisy five-hundred-mile marathon featuring drivers Eddie Rickenbacker and Barney Oldfield, before the track went broke in 1917. The land reverted to crop and hog farming, and the track's bankruptcy left the Snelling Land Company in possession of the property. Soon, however, the Minneapolis Civic Commerce Association leased it as a landing field. The U.S. Post Office built a lone hangar there and used it for airmail operations during 1920. The construction of a few more hangars preceded the official dedication of the airport in 1923 with the names of Ernest G. Wold and Cyrus Chamberlain, sons of prominent Twin Cities bankers, and flyers killed in France during World War I. Eddie Rickenbacker returned for the dedication ceremony, this time as a pilot, to drop memorial wreaths on the field.

Eventually it became a publicly owned airfield. When Northwest began using the airport, the abandoned racetrack still circled the airstrip. "Northwest's maintenance and overhaul hangar was a wooden building, also inside the track, with a dirt floor, canvas curtains for doors and potbellied stoves for heat in the winter," recalled early mechanic Louis Koerner, "while the engine shop was a lean-to against the side of the hangar."

On October 1, 1926, at Speedway Field, Brittin's leased plane was loaded with postal sacks—with each letter bearing ten cents in postage per half ounce—and received the go-ahead to take off. It headed into the east toward Milwaukee, with Chicago as its final destination. (There were hundreds of letters aboard for this historic flight, and most of them have been discarded or lost. Northwest later acquired one of these envelopes for its archives: a letter from the Odds & Ends Shop, 377 W. Seventh Street, St. Paul, to one Albert A. Pollard of Chicago.) Nobody knew it at the time, but Northwest's inaugural flight marked the initial moments of an airline that for decades would rank as the air carrier with the longest history under a single, continuous name.

The next week, pilot Behncke filed the airline's first known expense report. His initial entry, probably for Northwest's first flight, listed $1.50 he spent on taxi transportation and $0.85 for dinner. He also reported $1.25 in expenses on October 5 and 7. With these modest expenditures, Northwest pilots began nearly eight-five years of layovers.

ROUGH LANDINGS

Within two weeks, Chester Jacobson crashed Kidder's rented Thomas Morse ship. (Jacobson escaped without injury, but the discomfiture he felt from the accident compelled him to resign.) Brittin suddenly had only the Curtiss Oriole to carry out the remaining weeks of scheduled deliveries until the arrival of the Stinson Detroiters. Brittin begged another rented aircraft from Kidder, a Travelair monoplane.

When Northwest would at last put the long-awaited Stinson Detroiters to use, it would become the first commercial airline ever to fly a closed-cabin plane. Brittin had an inspired idea. Why not combine the delivery of the new planes to the Twin Cities with the promotion of a board-approved effort to raise stock subscriptions among Minnesotans? Four of the Detroit investors gamely agreed to hop aboard the Stinsons—which had enclosed cockpits—as passengers to draw attention to the delivery and stock opportunity. They probably wished they hadn't volunteered. A blizzard compelled two of the three pilots, including the builder Eddie Stinson, to seek shelter in Milwaukee. But the snowstorm did not delay the christening of the Stinsons by Mrs. George Leach, wife of the Minneapolis mayor, and their maiden scheduled flights on November 2. Brittin soon repainted the Detroiters in gold, red, white, and blue.

The earliest of Northwest's Detroiters served the airline well into the 1930s, with one eventually flying 435,000 miles, carrying nearly fifteen thousand passengers, and hauling 178,000 pounds of mail before the company donated it to the Minnesota Historical Society.

Unlike Dickinson's airmail line, Northwest experienced no loss of life or injuries during its inaugural months. From October 1, 1926, through the end of the year, the airline reported red ink totaling only $897, much less than Brittin had anticipated. (The airline's board cited him for "splendid results achieved during these exceptionally difficult months.") Northwest completed 122 trips covering 46,260 miles at an average ground speed of seventy-nine miles per hour, carried thirty-five pounds of mail per flight, and lost only 11 percent of its scheduled miles to bad weather and mechanical problems. This kind of reliability gave the Post Office no reason to hand out Air Mail Contract No. 9 to an unproven upstart competitor.

Dave Behncke (*left*) on the ground after he piloted this new Stinson Detroiter through a blizzard in 1926 to convey it to Minnesota. Lewis Brittin and Bill Kidder examine the aircraft.

A Northwest Stinson Detroiter outside the company's Wold–Chamberlain hangar.

HAZARDS IN THE AIR

The arrival of winter and its accompanying hours of darkness increased the danger of the airmail flights. The airports had no snowplows—only huge rollers that could pack down the drifts. Storms and dense clouds often forced the cancellation of flights, in which case the mail moved by train or truck. Pilots wore leather coats and eye goggles in the open-cockpit planes. "We flew part of the route to Chicago almost completely after dark during the winter months," remembered early pilot Behncke. "There were no emergency fields and no radio—no aids of any kind except one revolving beacon atop the Milwaukee

Lewis Brittin *(left)* with one of his first Stinson Detroiters.

AIRMAIL FOLLIES

Although Calvin Coolidge never flew in an airplane during his presidency, he worked to enact legislation that organized the postal chaos that reigned in American skies during the 1920s. Among several fed-

eral aviation laws he supported was the Contract Air Mail Act of 1925, which ended the government's dangerous experiment in the delivery of airmail by allowing private air carriers to bid for routes that the U.S. Post Office had calamitously handled on its own.

The resulting opportunity to get rich by flying the mail excited Charles "Pop" Dickinson, a sixty-seven-year-old seed dealer, aviation fanatic, and Santa Claus look-alike from Chicago. Six years earlier the Post Office had abandoned as too hazardous its Chicago–Twin Cities airmail line after four pilots died and eight planes crashed during nine months of attempted mail deliveries in 1920–21. (Dayton's Department Stores had also briefly flown freight between Minneapolis and New York during a railroad strike in 1920.) But Dickinson, himself the nation's oldest licensed pilot and so infatuated with flying that he disdained the comparatively bland experience of driving a car, submitted a bid to service the route at a rate of $2.75 per pound of mail. It is unknown whether Post Office officials considered Dickinson courageous, enterprising, or foolhardy, but they awarded him Contract Air Mail Route No. 9, which became effective in the spring of 1926.

Having already lost airmail service once, Twin Citians did not want to see it slip away again. The press campaigned for the venture, and the business community supported Dickinson's enterprise with the collection of thousands of airmail letters for the first eastbound flight. Those were perhaps the last good omens the new service received.

On June 7, 1926, pilot Elmer Lee Partridge took off for Chicago under the Dickinson Airlines name in a plane Partridge had built, loaded with the pioneering sacks of mail. A gale promptly swatted down the aircraft, and Partridge died in the crash. Cancellations of flights, forced landings, and incursions of cows onto the airfields grew so frequent—despite Dickinson's company motto of "Celerity, Certainty, Security"—that he saw public opinion, and even the Minneapolis postmaster, turn against him. He was losing money and had to make a flight himself because of a shortage of pilots. By August, he had one plane left, and all of his pilots had quit or given notice to

Northwest's pioneering airmail efforts were part of a growing network of routes moving the U.S. mail during the 1920s.

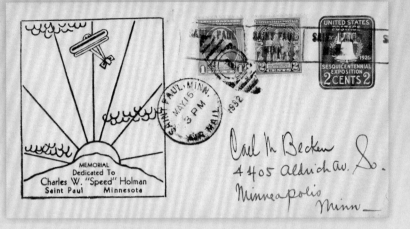

An envelope cover honoring the life of early Northwest airmail pilot Charles "Speed" Holman, who died in a crash in 1931.

operation, the airline transported an average of only thirty-five pounds of mail per flight, which brought in a paltry $96.25. Within a year, though, the payload and income nearly doubled.

The airline sometimes boosted its airmail revenues through borderline dishonesty: on one occasion, it packed its planes with old, one-hundred-pound propellers, varnished and lettered with the words "Use Air Mail," for display at far-flung post offices. Each of these shipped propellers yielded an immediate $100 profit for Northwest. (When passenger service started in 1927, the airline took in just $40 per person for each flight, so airmail revenues remained an essential part of the company's balance sheet for a long time.) Within a couple of years, the company expanded its airmail deliveries to Duluth—using hydroplanes that landed on Lake Superior—as well as Milwaukee, Appleton, and other Wisconsin communities. (As the planeloads of letters

leave out of concern for their safety, and Dickinson had no choice but to inform the Post Office of his withdrawal from the airmail business.

He discussed his predicament with Colonel Lewis Brittin, then an officer of a business alliance called the St. Paul Association. Brittin tried to convince several Twin Cities aviation firms to leap into the void, but they all refused. Brittin scraped up financing and planned a transfer of the airmail contract that played a crucial part in the creation of Northwest Airways. October 1, 1926, marked Dickinson's last day in the airmail business and Northwest's first. An airline—one without any immediate plans to accept passengers—was born.

Northwest suffered its share of problems in the initial months of airmail service. Nearly 40 percent of the early flights encountered bad weather, while crashes and close calls produced delivery delays that limited the profitability of the enterprise. The Post Office gathered airmail letters, priced at ten cents for the first half ounce, from a modest network of red, white, and blue collection boxes scattered throughout the Twin Cities and Chicago. Over the first dozen weeks of

Pilot L. S. "Deke" DeLong (right) collects letters in Green Bay, Wisconsin, along a newly established Northwest airmail route in 1929.

A cover marking the start of the Rock River route, carrying mail between the Twin Cities and Chicago, 1930.

A first-flight envelope from the start of service between the Twin Cities and Mandan, North Dakota, 1931.

increased in value into the 1930s, pilots received Colt .38-caliber pistols, which got in the way during the loading of mail sacks.) Northwest had succeeded where Pop Dickinson could not.

The airmail service was so much a part of Northwest's early identity that Brittin's own design for the company's first pilot insignia included "U.S. Air Mail" combined with an image of a globe with outstretched wings. Captivated by this graphic design, the Post Office received Brittin's permission to appropriate the insignia for the uniforms of all airmail pilots nationwide, banners that promoted airmail service, and a series of airmail postage stamps. For years, retiring Northwest captains passed to new pilots the gold wings pins that symbolized the airline's identity.

This enthusiasm over an insignia was a rare bright spot in a rough relationship between the Post Office and Northwest, as well as other airlines, during the 1930s. Walter Folger Brown, the U.S. Postmaster General under President Herbert Hoover, grew dissatisfied with the practice of paying carriers by the pound, and he suspected that the modest resources of some aviation firms put the U.S. mail at risk. He threw his support behind the McNary-Watres Act, which gave the Postmaster General the power to redraw routes and strike down airmail contracts when he thought it was in the public interest. He invited representatives of the largest airlines to a meeting at which airmail contracts would be redistributed, and he snubbed smaller firms like Northwest. (After his reassignment of contracts, Northwest retained only 5 percent of the $1.2 million that the Post Office allocated for airmail carriers.) Brown also threw out the old weight-based payment terms in favor of new ones based on space and mileage.

Lewis Brittin's airmail insignia won widespread acceptance during the 1930s and appeared on U.S. airmail stamps.

In addition, Brown believed the new law empowered him to order carriers to take up airmail routes to unserved cities, as in 1930 when he declared that Northwest must provide service between the Twin Cities and Omaha. The route proved a money loser.

Members of Congress heard allegations of the Postmaster General's abuses of power and formed a committee to investigate accusations of the stifling of free competition in the bidding process for airmail contracts. U.S. Attorney General Homer Cummings pronounced the recent route awards to be "highly irregular," and President Franklin Roosevelt responded in February 1934 by taking drastic action: He tossed out all airmail contracts then in force and handed the delivery of the U.S. Mail to the flyers of the Army Air Corps.

Protests from Charles Lindbergh, the airlines, and editorial writers of the business press pointed out that the president's order left many airlines in financial peril and would result in the layoff of hundreds of workers in the depths of the Great Depression. Overnight 80 percent of Northwest's income vanished, and it lost money continuing its passenger service. Northwest issued press releases claiming that the loss of these contracts would drive the airline out of business. "In the event of the cancellation of these contracts," said one Northwest official in February 1934, "we simply cannot go on. We will pay our employees up to the first of next month, after which it will be goodbye."

Roosevelt would not change his mind. For nearly two weeks, there was no airmail delivery. When the Air Corps finally gathered together a geriatric and poorly equipped fleet of planes and organized itself to carry the mail, disaster followed. A series of fatal crashes shocked the public and prompted the famed aviator Eddie Rickenbacker to decry the new airmail system as "legalized murder." Northwest offered to carry the mail for free along its routes until the Air Corps made its flights safer, but FDR's appointed Postmaster General, William Farley, did not respond. Instead, he suspended airmail delivery for another week in March 1934.

To Farley fell the job of fixing the airmail mess. With the Air Corps doing the flying, the cost of transporting airmail had quadrupled. Farley's only choice was to return the airmail routes to commercial operators. He reopened the service to bidding from private companies—with the stipulation that the carriers who had won contracts under Postmaster Brown, including Northwest, had to reorganize and restaff their ranks with untainted company officers. Many of the carriers consequently changed their names, and Northwest Airways was reincorporated as Northwest Airlines, Inc., on April 16, 1934.

In May 1934, Northwest reclaimed its Twin Cities–Seattle mail route, but it lost the valuable airmail contract to Chicago and had to cancel passenger service to the Windy City. The U.S. government eventually paid Northwest $51,365 in partial compensation for the loss of airmail income. Through government lobbying and the acquisition of contracts from other airlines, Northwest eventually regained many airmail routes. In later years, airmail subsidies became a less important part of Northwest's financial picture, but the mail fiascos of the 1930s wounded the company for several years. •

airport hangar." An emergency landing required luck and assistance. "When bad weather trapped me at night, I circled a farm house and the farmer would come out with the family car, light up a field with his headlights, and down I'd come." During dangerous weather, Behncke grew to rely on his own parents, who lived on a farm strategically located along the route in Cambria, Wisconsin. "I had ended up as an airmail pilot over the very stretch of sky where, as a boy, I had watched the hawks fly and dreamed of flying myself," he wrote. He sometimes made unscheduled stops there to pick up dinner. On one such occasion, Brittin, always keen for free publicity, tipped off the local newspaper that a Northwest pilot would be dropping in. The resulting published photo showed Behncke's aged mother waving good-bye as the pilot took off from the farm's field.

Another winter night over the Wisconsin Dells, Behncke was riding as a passenger with Robert Radall piloting when a blizzard reduced visibility and made it dangerous to continue. "You know this country much better than I do," Radall shouted. "So far as I'm concerned, I am all caught up, and it is your airplane." They switched positions, and Behncke took the controls to land the Detroiter on the family farm. Radall, later killed in an accident as a United Air Lines pilot, "could never understand how I found the farm on this particular night," Behncke recalled. Warm weather, though welcome, brought its own problems. Trapped in a cramped cockpit, pilots stripped to their underwear to stay cool.

Decades later, Kidder, eventually an inductee in the Minnesota Aviation Hall of Fame, compared the chanciness of Northwest's early operations with the practices of modern commercial aviation. "Every time I go to the airport, I am pleased with the lack of congested traffic, the ease of parking my car, the cleanliness of the surroundings, and the lack of difficulties that make other kinds of transportation [less attractive] when starting a trip for pleasure," he said. "I usually go forward to the pilot's cockpit to see and marvel at the hundreds of gadgets, and I am assured the pilot has the answer to any problem right in that little office of his. What a far cry from the days of our little 'kites' with about three instruments and when you had to guess right the first time."

PASSENGERS IN THE SKY

Even in the days of Pop Dickinson's short-lived airmail service, unticketed passengers—often Dickinson himself—had sometimes hopped aboard flights, and this practice continued into Northwest's operation of the airmail line. The construction of emergency landing fields between Minneapolis and Chicago and the arrival of tolerable weather, however, made ticketed passenger service along the airmail route a comfortable and attractive possibility. Brittin planned July 5, 1927, only a few weeks after Charles Lindbergh's thrilling solo flight across the Atlantic, as the inaugural date of this service, the first scheduled passenger flights between Minneapolis and Chicago, and points between. He chose St. Paul mayor Laurence C. Hodgson to receive the honor of becoming Northwest's first official passenger. Hodgson would fly with the city's council president and ordained minister L. R. S. "Doc" Ferguson.

Hodgson canceled at the last moment. At 2:00 P.M. on July 5, Brittin had a plane and pilot Speed Holman ready to fly from the grass runway of Speedway Field, and a crowd of onlookers present, but an open seat. He surveyed the crowd and selected a young St. Paul laundry executive he knew, Byron G. Webster, to replace the mayor. "Come on, Byron," Brittin called out, "let me write you the number one ticket on Northwest Airways." Web-

ster needed no persuasion to join Ferguson on the historic flight. He shook hands with Brittin, who quickly wrote the ticket and sent the excited passenger climbing into a seat in front of the pilot's. With a spin of the Detroiter's propeller and the deafening roar of its engine, Holman piloted the plane southeastward.

Able to communicate with Holman only through gestures because of the thunder of the engine, Webster later recounted that the flight initially went smoothly as they followed the meanderings of the Mississippi River. At the Mississippi's skirting of Minnesota's border with Wisconsin, where the big river

Dated July 5, 1927, Byron Webster's ticket to ride made him Northwest's first official passenger.

merged with the St. Croix near Hastings, however, "the engine suddenly went deader than a smelt," recalled Webster. Now piloting a crippled glider, Holman in eerie silence steered the Detroiter toward an open field and made a flawless landing.

As Webster and Ferguson waited, Holman produced a tool kit and poked around the engine. Soon he had repaired the clogged fuel line, but the shortness of the landing field would not permit a takeoff with passengers and sacks of mail. After phoning Brittin from a farmhouse, Holman told his passengers they would have to wait for the arrival of a truck from St. Paul for the ride back to Speedway Field. While they were on their way north, Holman flew the plane to Minneapolis for a new start. Webster was game to try a

PIONEERING PASSENGERS ⏱

Although Byron Webster deserves credit as Northwest's first ticketed passenger, several other travelers earlier hopped aboard the airline's flights more informally. Their intrepidity should not be forgotten. They include the following:

W. P. STEWART, CHIEF OF THE MILWAUKEE WEATHER BUREAU

Northwest's archives record that this veteran government meteorologist signed an agreement on January 24, 1927, granting him permission "to ride upon an airplane operated by the Northwest Airways, Inc.," in exchange for assuming "all of the risks incident thereto and hereby release[s] said Northwest Airways, Inc., . . . from any and all claims or liability for injuries or damage suffered or received by me . . . whether resulting in death or not."

JOSEPHINE LEHMAN AND WILLIAM LEHMAN

On June 10, 1927, Lehman and her three-year-old son flew in an open-cockpit, two-seat Northwest airmail plane, with Speed Holman piloting, from Chicago to St. Paul to comfort her husband, who had suffered an attack of appendicitis. The two had been on their way to Europe to buy mushrooms for Lehman's fungus supply business. She had received a telegram about her husband's sudden illness while she rode a train passing through Canton, Ohio. "It was represented to us as a matter of life and death," Lewis Brittin noted two weeks after the flight. "We do not ordinarily carry passengers on our line but in view of the circumstances did so and brought her through to St. Paul in time to reach her husband at the hospital." The impromptu air trip had its rough moments. "It got a little bumpy once or twice," Lehman recalled. "But Speed told me not to worry. And I didn't. I had a lot of faith in him." Her fare was $40, although it is unclear whether the airline charged to carry the child. "My mother used to make the comment that she and I were the first passengers to fly with Northwest Airlines," William Lehman noted nearly a half century later. Lehman's husband survived the appendicitis.

LAWRENCE A. DARE

This editor and publisher of the Elk River (Minnesota) *Star-News* said he flew in a Stinson Detroiter between Chicago and Minneapolis for a weeklong vacation on June 18 (or perhaps June 24), 1927. Holman was at the controls. Northwest's sales department "was rather casual, then, and no ticket was issued," he said. The flight so fascinated him that he immediately began flying lessons. Dare remembered that two other people, Minneapolis sportswriter Dick Cullum and boxing promoter Jerk Doran, accompanied him on the return flight. He observed that flying in the four-engine DC-4s of the 1950s was "vastly superior, but not as thrilling."

FRANCIS J. GAST

Gast, a Minneapolis druggist, maintained that he was Northwest's first paying passenger. In July 1927 he heard that the airline was about to begin passenger service, and he took a train to Chicago. There he bought a ticket from Holman, who had just flown Byron Webster from the Twin Cities. Gast was the only passenger on the July 6 flight that left at 5:55 A.M. from Chicago, arriving in Minneapolis at 1:40 P.M. Later that same year, he flew Northwest to Chicago to see Jack Dempsey fight.

HOMER J. ARMSTRONG

In 1951, Reverend Armstrong, pastor of the United Baptist Church in Duluth, wrote a letter to Northwest recounting flights he made with Northwest in 1927. One day the deacon of his church called to say he had to turn down an offer from Northwest to ride free to Minneapolis on the mail plane, but that Armstrong could take his place. "I went to the Duluth airport (then only a vacant field) and got aboard a small plane (probably a Stinson) and rode to Minneapolis," Armstrong remembered. "I sat right back of the pilot and enjoyed my riding immensely. After attending a pastor's conference for several days I rode back on the same plane." Armstrong presumed his distinct place in Northwest history: "I may have been the first minister to ride to the minster's conference via plane, and maybe one of the first clergymen to ride a Northwest Airlines plane." •

Decades after becoming Northwest's first official ticketed passenger, Byron Webster was still the airline's customer.

An early Northwest passenger plane receives a flapper's christening, circa 1927.

second takeoff; it is not known whether Ferguson continued on the flight. Holman and Webster made it 120 miles to the rain-soaked airfield at La Crosse, the first stop. A group of drenched onlookers witnessed the historic landing. Next came a special stop to pick up mail in Madison, also sopping, and then Holman and his intrepid passenger made their way to Milwaukee. Now delayed by the inclement weather, they flew through heavy wind and another rainstorm at low speed, spilling their meal on the plane's deck because of the turbulence. Webster scanned the midnight darkness as they approached Milwaukee, where the airfield had little lighting. "He must've had cat eyes," he commented on Holman's soft landing. The waiting crowd, including Milwaukee's mayor, had long gone home to bed. Bolstered by hot coffee, Holman and Webster decided to press on to Chicago.

At last, at 2:30 A.M. on July 6, more than twelve hours after taking off in Minneapolis, Northwest's first ticketed passenger flight, 370 miles long, ended. (Webster, who retired decades later as a vice president at Merrill Lynch, Pierce, Fenner, and Smith, remembered his flight as a highlight of his life; he died in 1971 at age seventy-seven.) Later on July 6, Northwest carried more customers—including Hazel Hart of Brooklyn, New York, who became the airline's first woman passenger—on the flights between Chicago and Minneapolis. Before winter weather put a temporary end to passenger business at the end of 1927, Northwest sold tickets to 106 customers that year. That added an important $4,000 to the company treasury. By the spring of 1929, Northwest would have 9,200 sold tickets on the books and boasted one million miles flown, ending only a small number of flights because of bad weather or mechanical problems. Most importantly, it delivered all passengers to their destination without injury or death. By that time, the airline was charging $50 ($631 in today's inflation-adjusted dollars) for a round-trip between Chicago and Minneapolis, $30 one way.

These numbers are impressive because the speed of early air travel improved little on conventional rail transportation, and trains offered far more luxury. Airliners sometimes flew just high enough to clear wires, trees, and buildings, hitting much turbulence along the way. Northwest's early flight steward Joe Kimm (later a long-tenured pilot) took a creative approach to one of the unique perils of flying that passengers faced. He brought some relief, or at least greater cleanliness, to many by providing the first motion-sickness bags—paper bags that he bought from grocery stores. "I'd give the bag a whip, you know, like they do in grocery stores, give it to the passenger, take it back after a brief interval and run for the door," Kimm remembered. "If I was lucky I'd get it tossed out before the bottom fell out. . . . You could usually tell when a passenger was ready to let go because he'd get pink behind the ears." All other trash also went out the door, including glass bottles.

ADDING TO THE FLEET

With the uptick in passenger traffic, Northwest needed new planes capable of holding more people and moving them faster. In mid-1928, a pair of seven-passenger Hamilton Metalplanes—nicknamed "Silver Streaks" and boasting heated cabins and leather seats that made them "comparable to the better type of limousine," according to Northwest's advertising—joined the fleet, and the company again turned to Detroit for an additional ship, the first of six Ford Tri-Motors that Northwest eventually acquired. Brittin quickly ordered maintenance workers to paint over the Ford logo emblazoned on the fourteen-passenger planes, noting, "Ford doesn't own them anymore."

Passengers long remembered the Fords with affection as the "Tin Goose." Like the Hamiltons, the Fords had heat and bathrooms, but, at a cost of about $65,000 each, they were more luxuriously equipped with comfortable wicker (later metal) seats, good lighting, call buttons, headphones that carried locally broadcast AM radio to customers, and passenger windows that could be opened, a nice perk in the days of eighty-five-mile-per-hour cruising and low-altitude flying. (Airsick passengers sometimes used the windows to evacuate their stomachs, a problem if the window behind was also open.) Northwest's promotional literature declared the Fords the equal of "the finest Pullman cars." Built of aluminum alloy and producing 1,230 horsepower from its three motors, the Ford was also acrobatic; Holman sometimes rode it through rolls and loops during air exhibitions. The arrival of the Fords gave Northwest a fleet that was still mostly made in Detroit.

The Northwest passenger terminal at Wold–Chamberlain field in 1927.

Passengers board a Hamilton aircraft in Milwaukee
for a flight to the Twin Cities, circa 1928.

A squadron of Northwest Hamilton planes, circa 1932.

With pilot Charles "Speed" Holman, passengers board a Northwest Hamilton Metalplane, nicknamed the "Silver Streak."

(Left): The interior of a Ford Tri-Motor plane, looking toward the cockpit.

(Right): This Northwest Ford Tri-Motor featured wicker seating.

A Northwest Ford Tri-Motor flies over the University of Minnesota campus in Minneapolis in 1930.

A Northwest Ford Tri-Motor in the snow at Wold–
Chamberlain field, 1930.

THE AIRLINE MOVES ITS MONEY

Until this point, Northwest's financial control remained in Detroit as well. Brittin disliked the awkwardness of the five-hundred-mile distance between his operations and corporate headquarters. He was pleased in 1927 when a few Twin Cities investors, fewer than he had hoped, bought shares in the company, including Holman, who sunk into the business a sum equal to almost half of his annual salary. The following year, though, Brittin realized his dream of bringing financial control of the airline back to Minnesota. At a meeting of the board of directors, St. Paul bank president Richard C. Lilly proposed creating a pool of Twin Cities shareholders who would buy a majority interest in the company. Well-familiar with Minnesotans' heretofore feeble enthusiasm for investing in the company, the directors were dubious. "What they didn't know," a company historian observed, "is that when Dick Lilly charged into action, he could make a buzz saw appear to be standing still."

Using every business connection and all the charm he possessed, Lilly commanded investments from his friends and associates. In some cases, he dictated the amount of money he expected each person to pony up. To the astonishment of the Northwest board, Lilly reported back in 1929 with a collective commitment of $160,000 from the Twin Cities, enough to buy all the Detroiters' shares at $400 each. (This largesse would not have been possible a few months later, after the stock market crash that launched the Great Depression.) The stunned board discussed the offer and issued a recommendation for all Michigan investors to accept the Minnesotans' money. When most followed that advice, virtually the entire company—except for some shares retained by t.a.t. and Universal Airlines—moved to the financial control of people living near Brittin's operating headquarters. The new board of directors included only one man from Michigan, William B. Mayo of Ford, serving alongside a collection of influential statesman and capitalists of Minneapolis and St. Paul (including a Nobel Prize winner, former U.S. secretary of state Frank B. Kellogg). Lilly became the airline's president, and he quickly pushed through his initiative to sell a hundred thousand shares of the airline on the open market. In no time at all, Northwest was internationally owned.

SKETCHING A NETWORK OF ROUTES

Although only eleven airmail collection boxes occupied the street corners of Minneapolis in 1928—each marked on a map that the Twin Cities newspapers printed daily—Brittin eventually expanded the delivery of airmail from five days a week to seven. He also began an ambitious enlargement of Northwest's route map. He had announced his intentions the previous year: "Northwest is the only operating commercial air line today in the states of Wisconsin and Minnesota," he wrote, "and this territory with North and South Dakota, which is the field for logical extension of this line, can never be served adequately by a flying organization that operates only between Chicago, Milwaukee, Madison, La Crosse, Minneapolis and St. Paul." Brittin offered free help to any community in the region interested in building airports and hangars, a service "offered as a practical contribution to stimulate commercial aviation in this state," he said. Rochester, Minnesota, took up Northwest's offer, establishing the "Mayo Clinic Special" as a stop on some Chicago-to-Twin Cities flights. Many other towns followed suit, including the Minnesota communities of Little Falls (Charles Lindbergh's hometown), Faribault, Mankato, Duluth, Red Wing, Hastings, and Redwood Falls, as well as Superior, Wisconsin, and Bismarck, North Dakota, which named its airport Brittin Field. Soon the airline was operating a second daily flight between Minneapolis and Chicago.

Lewis Brittin *(right)* gives his good wishes to the pilot of Northwest's first night airmail flight, 1929.

Airmail bound for Chicago leaves the St. Paul airport in 1929 on a ski-equipped Northwest Waco aircraft.

To Speed Holman fell the job of greasing the way for air travel in many far-flung cities. Along with advising airport planners on technical matters, he often gave talks at social gatherings of aviation enthusiasts. Holman loved entertaining them by drawing from his deep well of feel-good stories. "One of his favorites was about two drunks who were tossed out of a saloon," one Northwest historian wrote. "After picking themselves out of the gutter, one of them said to his friend, 'I'm going back in and clean out the place. You stay here and count them as I throw them out.' A few seconds after the tough one reentered the saloon, a body came flying through the swinging doors, and the drunk outside shouted, 'One!' Struggling back to his feet, the other yelled, 'Don't count yet. It's me!'" With such yarns, Northwest conquered the Upper Midwest.

Northwest became the first North American airline to operate an international route when it opened a route between Minneapolis–St. Paul and Winnipeg, with stops in Brittin's hometown of Fargo and Pembina, in February 1928—the line foundered after three months because of low patronage and the apathy of the Canadian government—and it rolled out a Fox River line serving such Wisconsin towns as Green Bay, Oshkosh, and Appleton. In 1929 it began regularly scheduled overnight airmail service. This rapid letter carrying made possible the mind-boggling arrival of overnight airmail deliveries between New York and Minneapolis.

Northwest's early ledgers offer confusing reckonings of income and expenses that would infuriate a modern accountant. The organizationally challenged company, which could have failed anytime with only a little worse luck during its first four years, "didn't have a Personnel department," Joe Kimm remembered. "No departments at all that I recall. Hardly any paperwork." But financial books make it clear that Brittin's efforts to stretch the airline's route map and improve flight frequencies made a big difference to the bottom line. For the first time, the company found itself with regularly occurring monthly profits by 1929. Airmail and passenger revenues amounted to only part of the take, however. The airline made smidgens of money through a variety of other ways. It flew sightseeing trips at $5 a head, earning as much as $500 on a busy day, which put otherwise inactive pilots to work and convinced the public that flying could be safe and pleasurable. In addition, tuition flowed in from students attending Northwest's flight school in Minnesota. Some student pilots who completed the program received reward trips to Chicago alongside the airline's pilots. One remembered the thrill of flying next to legendary pilot Walter Bullock, only to be handed a terrifying responsibility later during the flight. "When Walter decided I was to be trusted," the greenhorn pilot remembered, "he took a nap. I had to wake him up to find out where Maywood airfield was."

The perils of seat-of-the-pants navigation by light beacon at night and referring to landmarks on the ground during the day could never allow Northwest to expand its routes

LINDBERGH BRINGS HIS LUCKY NAME

During the late 1920s, when Northwest Airways' survival depended on every dollar it could scrounge, General Manager Lewis Brittin cooked up a variety of money-making schemes. His plan to coordinate his airline's routes with the schedules of passenger and freight trains—to move people and packages to places they could not travel by plane alone—stands out as especially intriguing. To promote it, Brittin enlisted the world's most famous aviator.

The air-rail plan evolved from the limitations of commercial flying during Northwest's first years. The airline at first landed at only a few airports in Minnesota, Wisconsin, and Illinois, and the lack of radio and scarcity of visual beacons for pilots made night flying risky. Planes could carry express cargo and passengers during the day, and trains could operate at night. Brittin reasoned that cooperation between Northwest and the railroads of the Upper Midwest could vastly enlarge the airline's range and service hours. This marriage of commercial air and rail would be a first in the history of American aviation.

Brittin brought in Charles Lindbergh, ostensibly to head a committee to negotiate the technical challenges of this effort. Lindbergh, who had crossed the Atlantic nonstop alone in the *Spirit of St. Louis* two years before, single-handedly boosted the profile of aviation and had generated the public interest that made commercial aviation possible in the years that followed. Brittin had little real use for the aviator's technical assistance, but attaching Lucky Lindy's name to the air-rail project added tremendous publicity.

With the Great Northern, Northern Pacific, Chicago, Milwaukee & St. Paul, Baltimore & Ohio, and Pennsylvania railroads signed on as partners, the service began on September 1, 1928—barely a year after Northwest's initial flights of ticketed passengers. Fargo's mayor, J. H. Dahl, won the honor of making the first passenger connection by materializing in New York City via rail from Fargo to Minneapolis, air from Minneapolis to Chicago, and rail as he advanced farther east. Once in Manhattan, Dahl gave newspaper interviews that spread word of the service.

Brittin put the airline's Ford and Hamilton planes to work mak-

Anne Morrow Lindbergh and Charles Lindbergh with Northwest operations vice president Fred Whittemore, 1935.

A Northwest aircraft transports freight to a Rock Island Railroad train.

ing the first connections. The Fords, which fed trains along the Twin Cities–Chicago route, were nicknamed Grey Eagles, following the rail tradition of naming routes. The Hamiltons became Silver Streaks. Two months after the inaugural connections, Northwest's Stinsons became Black Birds as they serviced a third route to northern Wisconsin. These air and rail connections lasted for three years, by which time air route expansions and the increased safety of night flying made the service unnecessary.

Lindbergh never again professionally associated with Northwest, although he gave public support to the airline and its competitors in 1934 when President Franklin Roosevelt canceled all airmail contracts and ordered the Army Air Corps to deliver the mail. •

Charles Lindbergh *(center)* with Lewis Brittin *(second from left)* and other Northwest staffers, circa 1928.

Northwest's St. Paul terminal, 1930.

or customer base. The 2.5-million candlepower beacons, spaced along Northwest's flight paths every ten miles, could vanish in bad weather. "If you couldn't find the next light," a company publication noted, "you were lost—it was as simple as that. In that case, you looked around for a good cow pasture, made an emergency landing, and waited for daylight." One pilot reported aiming at what he believed was his next light beacon, only to find his target steadily receding. It turned out the pilot was following the taillight of a freight train that was moving faster than his plane. In 1929, Northwest solved this recurring problem by setting up its Ford and Hamilton passenger planes with primitive radio equipment that could receive directional beacon information as well as hourly weather reports. These receivers picked up signals from stations along the Twin Cities–Chicago line. The Federal Radio Commission (a precursor of the Federal Communications Commission) gave Northwest its own set of frequencies to use, including one reserved for emergency communications.

Despite its growth and increasing technological savvy, Northwest retained its small-company feel. During one of the staff Christmas parties of the 1920s, for instance, employees and their families assembled at 9:00 P.M. (after which the company's insurance policy prohibited it from flying) in the Minneapolis hangar, which had been emptied of planes. Brittin, who called the men "my boys," spoke briefly and gave everyone his personal gift of fur-lined leather gloves.

These personal touches could not hide the competition lurking in Northwest's garden. In 1928, without the safety net of an airmail contract, bus-transportation mogul Edgar F. Zelle began

Aircraft in the Northwest fleet in a company hangar, circa 1929.

The glory of flying Northwest in the 1920s: a Ford Tri-Motor in the air.

operating a forty-five-minute-long air route between Minneapolis and Rochester, Minnesota, using a Ford Tri-Motor. Using the name Jefferson Airways, the company charged a formidable $20 per round-trip fare. Few passengers bought tickets. Jefferson lasted six months before closing its doors. A year later came Yellow Cab Airways, headquartered in Des Moines. Its founder, Russell Reel, hoped to establish a line from Kansas City to Minneapolis, with stops in Des Moines and Mason City. Although Yellow Cab did begin flights to Minneapolis in May 1929, Reel's plan did not gel, and the airline was soon history.

Other upstarts followed: Canadian-American Airlines, which ran daily flights between St. Paul and Winnipeg during 1929 and died within months because of the Great Depression, and Northern Air Lines, a merger of three small Minneapolis aviation firms that pioneered in-flight movies between the Twin Cities and Chicago but simply could not stay afloat without the security of an airmail contract. These competitors never amassed any strength, but they presaged the fierce competition that would plague Northwest in the decades to come.

CHAPTER 2

NO RUNWAYS, NO PROBLEM

On May 17, 1931, twenty-thousand people at an air race in Omaha watched Charles "Speed" Holman, Northwest's founding pilot and operations manager, crash his Laird biplane into the ground with a loud popping sound, "as if a giant light bulb had been dropped onto concrete," as one spectator remembered. Holman died instantly.

When the news reached Northwest's operations center, it stunned and demoralized everyone. The walls of Holman's vacant office, covered with his flying honors, awards, and photographs—including one picture autographed by Eddie Rickenbacker with the inscription, "To my dear friend, Charles 'Speed' Holman, may all his landings be three-pointed"—told the story of the life now extinguished. To many, Holman *was* Northwest Airways, and they could not imagine how the company would get along without him.

Northwest struggled ahead. Brittin promoted chief pilot Chadwick W. Smith to succeed Holman as operations manager. One of the pallbearers at Holman's funeral, Smith had joined the company in 1927 at Holman's recommendation and had flown the first Ford Tri-Motor flight from Minneapolis to Chicago. Two of his brothers, Lee and Les, also became Northwest pilots, and his sister, Gladys Roy, reigned as one of the nation's premier wing walkers and daredevil parachutists until she was killed when she stepped into a spinning propeller while posing for a photo.

But another tragedy lay in wait for Northwest. Smith, just twenty-eight years old, died following an emergency appendectomy a few months after assuming Holman's job. An obituary in the *St. Paul Pioneer Press* mourned him as "an outstanding type of modern aviator, a professional pilot and executive as distinguished from the rough and ready flyer of the barnstorming era." Brittin needed another veteran of similar stature to fill the jinxed position.

On October 1 the job went to Walter Bullock, a longtime aviation enthusiast who had become America's youngest licensed pilot at the age of seventeen and had taught Holman

A Northwest Ford Tri-Motor goes aloft in Duluth, circa 1930.

Chadwick Smith, here reviewing a weather report in 1930, died suddenly after serving only a few months as Northwest's operations manager.

THE MYSTIQUE OF PILOTS

"I thought the pilot was God," observed passenger Bob Fliegel, who took Northwest flights during the 1940s and 1950s as a child. "Most of Northwest's pilots had been U.S. Navy or Army Air Corps aviators in World War II, and they were rakish fellows indeed. Though there was a door to the cockpit, it was left wide open for most of the flight. Any child who walked forward and peeked in was invited to chat with the captain and copilot. On a later occasion, the copilot arose and helped me into his seat!"

These uniformed figures always owned a commanding mystique, one that the airline propagated for decades. "Take the captain of a liner," recommended a Northwest publication during the 1950s, "add a soldier, meteorologist, radio technician, navigator, mechanic and a bit of an aeronautical engineer, and you'll have the makings of a Northwest Airlines pilot. It has been calculated that not more than 4 percent of the country's population would be physically and mentally qualified to become airline pilots. Whatever the figure may be, the typical Northwest Airlines pilot is the product of a highly selective training."

That training was not always formalized. The airline's first pilots, among them some of America's most famous early flyers, picked up most of their skills on their own for use in varied and unpredictable situations. Mal Freeburg, a law school dropout and former barnstormer who joined the airline in 1928, was flying to Chicago in 1930, using the train tracks as a visual guide. At Trevenia, Wisconsin, where a railroad bridge crossed the Chippewa River, he noticed that the trestle was in flames—and a Burlington Northern train was on its way to cross it. Blinking his plane's lights, he dove toward the train, trying to draw the attention of the engineer. When that failed, Freeburg grabbed several emergency flares and showered them on the tracks. That worked, and the train came to a halt just short of the damaged bridge. Freeburg's efforts saved the lives of everyone aboard the train, including golf legend Bobby Jones. (This was not the only time a Northwest pilot saved people from a fire's destruction. Captain Melvin Fried, flying the same route, once noticed a farmhouse aflame in the darkness below, and he buzzed it until the occupants awoke and fled to safety.)

Two years later, Freeburg committed an act of heroism so dra-

Captain Cassius Chamberlain at the controls, 1935.

After ditching a malfunctioning motor over the Mississippi River and possibly saving lives, pilot Mal Freeburg received the Congressional Air Mail Medal of Honor from President Franklin Roosevelt in 1932.

matic that President Franklin Roosevelt awarded him the first Congressional Air Mail Medal of Honor. While passing over Winona, Minnesota, in a Ford Tri-Motor flying to Chicago with eight passengers, Freeburg discovered that his five-hundred-pound left wing motor had nearly detached. As it lodged under the plane, Freeburg feared the outcome if it fell off, possibly hit someone on the ground, and set the Tri-Motor wildly off balance in its absence. "With the utmost delicacy and precision," Northwest historian Kenneth Ruble wrote, "Freeburg gently turned his stricken plane toward the nearby Mississippi River, holding his breath until he was well out over the water. Then he banked left, whipped his controls back and forth, and shook the motor loose. It

Famed Northwest pilot Leon "Deke" DeLong, 1931.

dropped harmlessly into the Father of Waters." Freeburg, who nursed his aircraft to an emergency landing twenty-five miles away, later served as Northwest's operations manager, chief pilot, and operations executive before retiring in 1952. His son James Freeburg also flew as a captain for Northwest.

One of Freeburg's colleagues, Leon "Deke" DeLong, pioneered Northwest's nighttime airmail flights and became expert at flying at low altitudes. "Many times we had to fly through storms with nothing more than a 500-foot ceiling. That meant we had to stay down low—just clearing the trees," he said. He learned to fly with the U.S. Air Force in World War I and earned his chops as a barnstormer. He joined Northwest in 1928 after briefly piloting for Universal Airlines, a predecessor of American Airlines. After a forty-year flying career (thirty of them with Northwest), he retired in 1959 at the age of sixty-five as the airline's senior pilot. (The mandatory retirement age for pilots was lowered to sixty in 1961, which abruptly ended the Northwest flying career of Walter Bullock, one of the Upper Midwest's most celebrated captains. Congress reset the age at sixty-five in 2007.)

Another piloting legend, Frank C. Judd, bought his own plane and learned how to fly by the age of twenty-two. Northwest hired him as a copilot in 1931 but laid him off after a couple of years. Then Judd became one of the intrepid pilots hired by the U.S. Army to transport airmail after the cancellation of commercial airmail contracts in 1934. He survived that dangerous assignment, rejoined Northwest, and worked forty years for the airline as pilot, superintendent of Northwest's Northern Region operations during World War II, flyer and trainer for China "hump" flights during the war (as a member of the U.S. Army), general manager, vice president of maintenance and engineering, and special assistant to Donald Nyrop.

Northwest employed several unusual family combinations of pilots, including Joe and Richard Ohrbeck, who in 1943 became the first father-son team to fly together, and Dale and Anne Simpson Hagfors, who in 1981 earned distinction as the airline's first married captain–first officer couple. For many years Northwest permitted a tradition of allowing seven-year-old children to fly in the cockpit with their piloting parents. One happily privileged kid later recalled that he accompanied his pilot father on a 1956 Northwest flight in a DC-6

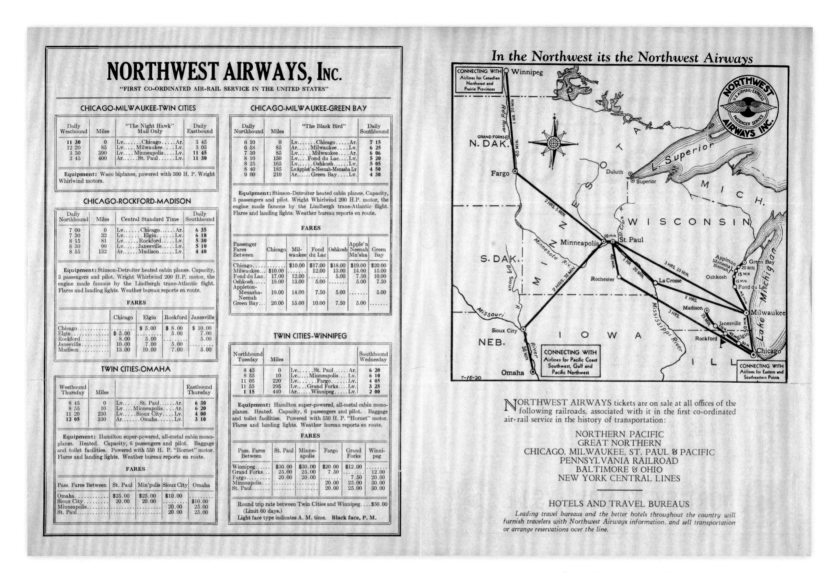

Northwest's route map, circa 1931.

begin serving Omaha from the Twin Cities. The Nebraska-bound planes carried little mail and few passengers, so Brown soon allowed Northwest to shut the route down. But Brittin often launched service to new destinations soon after the Omaha debacle, such as his opening of routes to Rochester, Minnesota, and its celebrated Mayo Clinic, to several cities in Wisconsin including Madison and Beloit, and to destinations in Illinois. The $1.50 one-way charge to fly between Janesville, Wisconsin, and Rockford, Illinois, surely ranked as one of the cheapest airfares in history. In 1931, Northwest announced a crucial

Northwest's facilities in Pembina, North Dakota, 1931. The airport complex included a hangar, radio station, weather station, passenger waiting rooms, and staff quarters.

A Sikorsky "Duck," perhaps the strangest aircraft Northwest ever sent into the air, lands on Lake Superior near Duluth in 1931.

coordination of its Twin Cities-to-Chicago timetable with the schedule of National Air Transport, an airline that had just been acquired by United Air Lines. Chicago passengers bound to and from New York City could easily board connecting NAT flights to New York, greatly easing the complexity of travel to the East Coast.

Brittin even began service to Duluth without waiting until the city's municipal airport, still under construction, could receive aircraft. No runways, no problem. The airline solved the difficulties of landing by buying some of the strangest aircraft it ever acquired. These two Sikorsky amphibian planes—which Northwest staff and passengers called "Ducks"—made use of the biggest open space around Duluth, Lake Superior. Featuring retractable landing gear that enabled taxiing in and out of water, they were designed mainly for use in tropical islands, but Brittin foresaw their unique value for airportless and water-blessed Duluth. Each Sikorsky seated eight passengers. When one landed, it trumpeted a loud horn, which added new dimensions to the craft's nickname. Then a rowed ferry met the plane and carried passengers and mail to Duluth Harbor. The route lasted two years before reduced airmail payments and its general unprofitability led to its end. Northwest never again flew the Sikorskys.

THE LONG REACH OF THE POST OFFICE

Postmaster Brown's preoccupation with the efficient movement of airmail inspired him to imagine an America in which two transcontinental air routes dominated: one over the central United States, and another across the southern part of the country. Northwest, whose domain in the northern tier of the nation lay outside these anticipated lanes of traffic, had little chance of reaping the benefits of the east–west expansion of air travel unless Brittin's resolve overcame Brown's dreams. Brittin often traveled to Washington to make the case for new routes that his airline wanted, and given the perceived unimportance of the frozen and lightly populated territory Brittin coveted,

The airline's elegant customer ticket office in the lobby of the Palmer House, Chicago, circa 1935.

Over several decades, Camille "Rosie" Stein guided many aspects of Northwest's operations. She retired in 1946 as the airline's manager of passenger services.

BRITTIN'S "RIGHT-HAND MAN"

Among Colonel Lewis Brittin's first acts after founding Northwest Airways was to bring Camille "Rosie" Stein into the enterprise. Having worked with her at the St. Paul Association, Brittin knew all about her abilities, but even he could not envision that Stein would become one of Northwest's most essential executives during the airline's first two decades. Over the years she filled a multitude of positions, rising from assistant secretary to member of the board of directors. But her most important contributions came in her roles as an interpreter of Northwest's public face and company culture, when she served as public relations manager, manager of passenger services, and overseer and trainer of the company's early flight attendants.

As Brittin's "right-hand man" at the St. Paul Association, Stein was accustomed to juggling many roles. This background well prepared her for the expectations she faced on the staff of a start-up airline. Stein's initial duties with Northwest would have made for a dizzying job description, had such a thing existed during the mid-1920s. "Rosie did anything and everything that needed doing," wrote company historian Kenneth Ruble, "with a smile and without being asked. She tended a coal fire in the pot-bellied little stove that kept the operations shack warm on chilly days, she answered the phone, sold tickets, took deposits (when there were any) to the bank, bought engine parts, chased an occasional stray cow off the landing field and—if a passenger got 'weathered in'—she'd whip up a lunch over the coal stove, clean off the Colonel's desk and invite the passenger to sit down." In a pinch, she also helped mechanics and maintenance workers.

Years later, Stein even kept warm memories of the role she played when Northwest was forced to operate amusement flights to stay in the black. "On Sundays," she recalled, "we used to come over to the airport, chase the cats away and haul sightseers at five dollars a ride. Sometimes we made as much as $500 in a day, and I took the tickets myself from dawn to dusk. The money helped plenty in those early days, but there was something more important. We showed people flying could be fun—and safe."

Stein handled public affairs in Northwest's formative years, and the airline never enjoyed better media relations. Newsmen loved her cheery disposition. According to company legend, she picked up her nickname when she repeatedly responded to reporters' questions about the health of the airline by responding, "Everything's rosy!"

Although it is not clear exactly when during the 1920s Stein achieved managerial status, she often wins credit as the airline industry's first woman executive. (Another contender for that honor was Amelia Earhart, who joined the board of directors of Dennison Aircraft in 1928.) Stein became assistant traffic manager in 1931, and five years later earned a seat on Northwest's board of directors. "Miss Stein worked unceasingly— time meant nothing to her," remembered another early Northwest staffer, Bill Kidder, "for she was doing everything that had to be done when no one else happened to be around to do it. . . . In those days she lived with her mother up on Capitol Hill [in St. Paul], and many times late at night I've taken her home from the office or flying field where she was working without any thought of overtime."

Northwest's health and welfare grew into Stein's all-consuming concern, especially after 1939 when, as manager of passenger services, she took over the training and management of the airline's stewardesses, soon after the acquisition of large DC-3 airliners made comfortable cabin service a possibility. She was the boss of Northwest's earliest one thousand stewardesses, whom she called "my girls." The stewardesses responded in kind by starting a baby boom of girls named Rosie. At the same time, she left her mark on Northwest's food menus and the interior decoration of its aircraft. Eventually Stein made more use of her customer service expertise as chairman of the passenger service committee of the Air Transport Association, an airline trade group.

She showed the depth of her concern for passenger comfort in her work to give customers better naps aboard Northwest flights. Stein noticed that she fell asleep during her own Sunday afternoon snoozes more quickly when she placed black fabric over her eyes. From that observation evolved the first blackout mask for air travelers, an onboard accessory that Stein perfected during the late 1930s. Northwest introduced the sleep masks on flights between the Twin Cities and Rochester and soon passed them out to passengers along all of its routes. Though commonplace today, they struck Stein's contemporaries as somewhat strange; one commentator marveled how the masks fit "over the eyes like those worn to masquerade parties, except there are no openings."

Stein retired from Northwest in 1946, by which time she had weathered the airline's hard times and earned substantial financial rewards for her devotion to the company. Living in the Commodore Hotel in St. Paul, a plush home that had once been the residence of literary stars F. Scott Fitzgerald and Sinclair Lewis, she kept in close touch with the stewardesses who idolized her. She died in 1954.

"God bless you, Rosie," Bill Kidder wrote in memoriam. "I know that St. Peter is going to say: 'Come on in, you have honestly earned your wings.'" •

A Ford Tri-Motor's cabin with passengers listening to radio, early 1930s.

Brown sometimes gave in, especially when members of the Northwest board of directors helped in generating support for the route requests.

Thus in 1930, when Minnesota and North Dakota politicians, business owners, and even officials of the Canadian postal system piled on Brown to give Northwest a new route serving the Twin Cities, Fargo, Grand Forks, and Winnipeg, the U.S. Post Office acceded—with the proviso that Northwest could fly only as far north as Pembina, on the North Dakota–Canada border, with Western Canada Airways flying the remaining sixty-seven miles to Winnipeg. When service began in 1931, Northwest's route mileage instantly doubled.

Brittin next set his sights on Bismarck, where the new airport had already been named Brittin Field to honor the airline's assistance in planning it. More support, lobbying, and letter writing targeted Postmaster Brown, and Northwest won the route in 1931. Northwest was getting good practice in the art of line extension. At the same time, Brittin liked glad-handing in Washington. He worked alone in the nation's capital, countering (and occasionally cooperating with) the efforts of teams of lobbyists serving the interests of the larger airlines. Growing comfortable in this role, Brittin would ultimately see his career unravel through this work in D.C.

How could the founder and spark plug of Northwest abandon the airline's headquarters in Minnesota for Washington? Only the hiring of a bold new executive made Brittin's move possible. In 1928, company president Richard Lilly had heard about a young Fargo native, Croil Hunter, through a mutual friend. Hunter, Lilly learned, was "the kind of young go-getter we ought to put on the payroll." After evaluating him for a few years in his own banking company, Lilly brought Hunter to Northwest as traffic manager in 1932. Funny and easygoing, Hunter could summon formidable determination and energy, and his administrative skills helped him rise to vice president and general manager.

Brown still held to his rule that northern regions like Northwest's should be allowed only north–south routes that branched from the main east–west lines of travel farther south. When Brittin proposed the route extension that he most wanted for Northwest, a Pacific expansion all the way to Seattle, the Post Office and its supporters resisted. "Our proposed Northern Transcontinental is much more practical [than more southerly routes] because it is far shorter," Brittin told a House committee considering the route. "The natural flow of traffic is east–west across the northern states." But a congressman threw up objections. "Your northern route will provide too many flying hazards. You could not maintain a decent flying schedule on a Northern Transcontinental with all those mountains, not to mention the weather problems."

Northwest's longtime president and general manager Croil Hunter.

A FLIGHT TO PROVE A POINT

Brittin could not stand the implication that natural barriers, especially bad weather, could hinder his ambitions. He had overcome such obstacles in the past, and he determined to prove the congressman wrong. West of the cities of North Dakota that Northwest already served, the next sizable metropolitan area was Billings, Montana. In the fall of 1932, Brittin tapped Walter Bullock to pilot a flight intended to show that Northwest could fly over mountains and through the severe weather of the northern Plains. Setting off in a Hamilton Metalplane on September 14, 1932, Bullock and Brittin covered the 1,025 miles from Minneapolis to Helena—far west of Billings—without problems in just over nine hours. Along the way they also stopped in Glendive, Miles City, and Billings to inflame support for the east–west route. In one town, ranchers gave Brittin a lamb as a gift. Northwest carried this animal home on the return trip, dressing it in a diaper for the hours in the air. The animal became the property of Bullock's nine-year-old daughter, at least until it grew too big to keep.

Brittin believed that the success of this demonstration flight—which crossed the two mountain ranges and the Badlands—proved that his airline could conquer the geography of the northern states. The following year, in the dead of winter, he would show Northwest's skills in handling cold weather during a demonstration flight to Spokane.

An imminent change of presidential administration in Washington brought a loosening of attitudes, and the federal government approved Northwest's application to extend a 392-mile route to Billings in 1933. Still in office, Postmaster Brown attached strings to the deal, demonstrating the exasperating complexity of the airline's relationship with postal authorities. Northwest had to give up its routes to various small cities in Wisconsin to balance out the added route mileage to Montana, and it had to awkwardly assume ownership of a mail route from Milwaukee to Grand Rapids, Michigan, and then lease it out to a third party, which had formerly owned the contract. Yet Brittin had achieved an important step toward reaching his goal of expanding Northwest's routes to the Pacific.

Brittin had little time to bask in satisfaction. Franklin Roosevelt's new postmaster general, James A. Farley, immediately slashed the budget of the Post Office, reduced airmail payments to Northwest and other airlines, forbade the approval of new airmail routes, and intimated that Northwest's Montana route might soon be history. (Airline executives understandably grew to dislike Farley, but the public soon found cause to lampoon him after he authorized the Post Office to release a series of postage stamps that FDR, a philatelist, had designed and exclusively received in special printings. Press coverage forced the Post Office to offer the stamps, derided as "Farley's Follies," to the public.)

Again Hunter and Brittin rallied their supporters, sparking business owners, mayors, and prominent people in Montana to voice their approval of the route along with

THE TRAGEDY OF SPEED

The death of Charles "Speed" Holman in an air crash in 1931 deprived Northwest Airlines of one of its most gifted and popular executives. As the company's first operations manager, he brought sense to the increasingly complex workings of the young airline. His public image—one of daring, determination, great piloting talent, and down-to-earth friendliness—rubbed off on Northwest and helped keep the airline in the news and in the black. Holman, who stood six feet five inches tall, was larger than life. "He was a giant of a man whose eager eyes flashed bright, and his smile was quick and broad and his laughter rolled like a storm of summer thunder," an enthusiastic magazine writer recorded in the 1950s.

That good humor soured at the mention of his nickname, Speed. His friends and family knew better than to address him by the tag that the public used. He much preferred being called Charlie.

Well before arriving at Northwest among its first pilots, Holman had proven himself one of the nation's most skilled flyers. Born in 1898, he grew up on a livestock farm a dozen miles south of the Twin Cities, in what is now the city of Shakopee. Enamored with everything mechanical and electrical, he left school early for a job with the telephone company, stringing wires. He quickly switched to running wires for the power company. Holman began racing motorcycles, and he won

so many races that somebody stuck him with that disliked nickname. Soon, though, airplanes seized his interest. The U.S. Army rejected him as a pilot for health reasons during World War I, but Holman struck up a lifelong friendship with Walter Bullock, an exhibition flyer who had once been America's youngest licensed pilot. Bullock gave him early instruction before Holman caught on with the stunting Larrabee Brothers Flying Circus. "He was a wing walker under the alias of 'Jack Speed,'" his wife recalled. "That's the first time his father found out about his antics. There was a Jack Speed performing locally, and his father walked over to the airport to see this guy walk on wings. It was his son!" Appalled at the dangerous feats his son was undertaking, the senior Holman offered to pay for a plane and proper pilot training. By 1920, Holman was soloing as a pilot.

Within a few years, Holman was stunt flying and participating in aerial shows every possible chance. He won his first stunt flying competition in 1923 at the National Pulitzer Races in St. Louis. In 1927, during the highly publicized National Air Derby, an early transcontinental race that went from New York to Spokane, Holman took a shortcut on an uncharted route over the Rocky Mountains to win in less than twenty hours. He was suddenly one of America's best-known flyers, a pilot as famous as his contemporaries Al Williams and Jimmy Doolittle. Both Minneapolis and St. Paul vied to hold a parade in his honor, and his Northwest boss, Lewis Brittin, wisely compounded the reflected glory for the airline by allowing both cities the privilege.

Holman understood that aviation's future was in commercial transport and not stunt flying, but his exploits continued after he began working for Northwest. In 1928, flying on one hour of sleep after a night spent bringing in booze from Canada, he set a world record by performing 1,433 loop-the-loops in five hours over the St. Paul Airport and won an air race from Los Angeles to Cincinnati the same year. He won the prestigious Gardner Trophy in 1929 by coming in first in a race from St. Louis to Indianapolis and back with an average speed of 157 miles per hour. His greatest triumph came in 1930, when he won the Thompson Trophy and a prize of $10,000 at the National Air Races in Chicago. The race covered twenty laps on a triangular course. He registered as a competitor at the last minute, and his victory came in an unusual biplane, less than eighteen feet long, that aircraft builder

Charles "Speed" Holman as thousands of people saw him—seated in the cockpit of his Laird biplane, 1930.

As a stunt flier, Holman often performed daring acts, including this event with motorcyclist Arthur Peterson at the Minnesota State Fairgrounds, 1925.

Matty Laird had designed. Holman could barely fit into it. "The continual turning around the pylons made him dizzy. Twice he nearly passed out from exhaust fumes," one account says. "The first time he came out in time to dodge a tree; the second time he nearly skewered himself on a railroad block signal." He won with a record average speed of 202 miles per hour.

Not all of Holman's races ended in victory, or even with his plane intact. Flying with his mechanic in a race in 1928, he crash-landed near Washington, Pennsylvania, after his fuel tank ran dry. "Sweeping

down through the fog over the side of a mountain, Holman glimpsed a small clearing, and slipped his ship into it to make what seemed like an impossible dead stick landing," a reporter wrote. The mechanic, Ralph Geror, went on to work for Northwest.

Holman lived for airplanes. One of his favorite leisure activities was talking about aviation with Brittin as they lounged about Brittin's apartment. "He would fly anywhere, talk to anyone, if he thought it would advance aviation," his wife said two decades after his death. "He was crazy about kids. I couldn't count the times I waited dinner for him because he would call up and say a troop of Boy Scouts or some other group was at the airport and he wanted to show them around. He always said the kids were the future of aviation." Children could also give him grief, however. He once flew on a trip from the Twin Cities to Lake Mille Lacs in Minnesota. Bad weather prevented a return by air,

Holman after landing the Laird, 1930.

and he drove back, temporarily leaving the plane behind. "When he returned [to Mille Lacs], kids had taken the tires off the plane, ripped up the fuselage and broken a wing spar," a Northwest old-timer related. "Speed found a fence post and wired it to the broken spar and took off without any tires and flew back to the Twin Cities."

Although well known for his kindness, Holman could sometimes show a quick temper. One day in the late 1920s or early 1930s, he was working in Northwest's hangar while standing next to a canvas curtain that served as a windbreak in the drafty space. "Suddenly he felt a kick," a friend remembered, "by someone on the other side of the curtain. . . . In this instance he really blew, and without investigating he heaved against the curtain with a mighty shove and then ran around the other side in time to see two little kids picking themselves up, more surprised than hurt." Holman's anger instantly vaporized. "The next moment found him brushing the kids off and reaching into his change pocket at the same time. While the kids were elated and getting all this attention from the great Speed Holman, he was heard muttering as he shooed the kids away, 'These damn airports aren't safe for anyone.'"

Airports had been safe for Holman for years, but one time only Holman lost his luck. In the spring of 1931, he took part in an opening-day race at the Omaha Air Show, which he won. With no appearances scheduled for the remainder of the show, Holman planned to spend time with friends. "I just want to see Jimmy Doolittle and some of the boys," he said to his wife.

On the second day, Holman telegrammed home that he would be back for dinner. But "during an unplanned delay in the program," Northwest historian Kenneth Ruble wrote, "the spectators began clapping their hands and yelling for action. Holman walked up to the committee in charge of the show and suggested: 'Why don't I keep them occupied by going up and doing a few tricks?' The delighted committee agreed, and the public address

system announced sonorously: 'Ladeez and gentlemen, presenting Charles "Speed" Holman, one of the greatest American pilots, in a daredevil exhibition of stunt flying.'"

Before twenty thousand fans, Holman took his Laird biplane up to two thousand feet over the airfield, then let it wilt into a dive toward the ground. "The spectators gasp as the plane dives steeply toward the center of the earth," the *Minneapolis Tribune* recounted. "Then a hundred feet from the ground the ship 'levels off' and Holman skims across the field—a black flash moving 300 miles an hour. Fifty feet from the ground, it straightens out, not more than a hundred yards from the stands." An

Holman maneuvers his Laird biplane into a flip, 1930.

Omaha reporter named Lawrence Youngman looked up from a phone in the airfield's press box and saw what Holman was up to. "I've got to hang up," he said into the phone. "Speed Holman is doing his stuff, and he's either drunk or he's crazy!" (Another *Omaha News-Herald* newsman in the crowd, Edward R. Murrow, took some photos of Holman's exhibition.)

Holman initiated one of his best-known stunts: he pulled the ship up to two thousand feet and let the engine stall. The plane turned onto its side, maneuvered into a wingover and barrel loop, and plummeted down toward the hard ground. Holman flipped it onto its back, angling it parallel to the ground just fifty feet up. "Then," the newspaper continued, "as Holman starts to climb with the plane upside down, it happens." Pilots in the crowd thought they saw Holman gripping the side of the aircraft to remain inside the cockpit and beating at the controls with his feet. The plane turned toward the grandstand. "There is a jerk. The plane points downward again. The ship hits the ground, Holman beneath it. There is a tearing crash. The plane folds up as if it were cardboard. Dust fills the air while pieces of wreckage are still flying. A sheet of metal goes bouncing to one side as the wreckage settles down. A thin stream of smoke rises from the motor where it lies apart from the other wreckage."

Pandemonium erupted in the crowd: screams, people running, people crying. Holman was dead. Investigators found his safety belt corroded and broken. Jimmy Haizlip, a pilot in the crowd, speculated that Holman had decided to add extra danger to his show for the benefit of the many pilots in attendance. Flying upside down with the engine at full throttle, Holman could not get the plane's nose up. "I looked away. For me the picture was complete. I could see the crash coming," Haizlip said. A call arrived from Omaha for Holman's wife, Dee. "[When] they didn't want to talk to me, I knew it had happened," she later said. "I knew he was dead."

The four-mile-long funeral procession and Holman's burial ceremony at the Acacia Cemetery, on a geographical feature called Pilot's Knob near Mendota, drew a hundred thousand mourners—more than any previous funeral in Minnesota history. Six pilots served as pall bearers. After Holman's death, the St. Paul Airport was renamed after him. •

The explosive crash that ended Holman's life in 1931.

St. Paul's municipal airport memorialized Holman and honored his achievements by adopting his name after his death.

its future extension to Seattle. The line remained. Meanwhile, Brittin began preliminary negotiations with Alfred Frank, whose National Parks Airways was available for purchase. National Parks operated 509 miles of routes connecting Montana cities with Salt Lake City. Any airline that bought them could circumvent Farley's ban on route extensions. But Brittin made his overtures to Frank without consulting Hunter, and Hunter blew up when he found out. "This matter of working for our Billings extension, and all other policies of the Northwest Airways, is not a one-man show. . . . I have repeated that you keep me fully informed as to what you are doing and to discuss with me any activities you contemplated, so we could all be working to the same end with the best advice that all of us may have," Hunter wrote in a memo to Brittin. He added, "You have repeatedly given me the run-around."

A Northwest mechanic recovers the wing of a Hamilton aircraft, 1933.

A Northwest Ford Tri-Motor follows the Mississippi River at St. Anthony Falls in downtown Minneapolis, 1934.

Aviator Amelia Earhart, who helped the airline survey the Pacific Northwest, with Northwest pilot Mal Freeburg, 1933.

DETERMINATION TO EMBRACE THE NORTHWEST

This spat illustrated changes in the workings of Northwest and the airline industry. In the early years, a dominant personality, the founder, could dictate the direction of the company and even its personality and culture. Who was qualified or brave enough to dispute him? During the 1930s, though, the business grew too complex, with too much money at stake, for one person's opinion to set Northwest's course. Many of the airline's staff now knew more than Brittin about various aspects of running the business. Brittin's role had altered; the company's board had made him an executive vice president focused on consulting and lobbying—limitations that have vexed many leaders of growing companies. To Hunter, now vice president and general manager, fell the responsibility of running the daily operations. "As General Manager, I am going to be held responsible for the success or failure [so] I want it distinctly understood that from now on all matters pertaining to the company are to be taken up with me," Hunter wrote to Brittin, and he meant it. The two men eventually reached an accord on strategies to press forward on Northwest's goal of clearing a route to the Pacific, which included lobbying to discourage any plan to leave northern cities with only north–south connections to other destinations on a transcontinental route.

Amelia Earhart confers with a group of businessmen in 1932, two years before her survey flight with Lewis Brittin helped open a route to the Pacific Northwest.

THE MARCO POLO OF AVIATION 🧭

Northwest's second chief executive, Croil Hunter, added a new ambition, international growth, to the airline. More forward thinking and explorative than his predecessor, Lewis Brittin, who had to focus on getting the company started and keeping it alive, Hunter won accolades as "the trailblazer of air routes, a modern Marco Polo of air transportation." On his watch, Northwest transformed from start-up to industry leader.

Hunter often speculated about the future of commercial aviation. Long before such a prediction seemed rational, he foresaw the development of Minneapolis–St. Paul into an important global transportation hub. "As our transports roar out of terminals and streak off at three miles a minute to destinations halfway across the continent," he said during the observance of Northwest's tenth anniversary in 1936, "I realize that tomorrow these ships will be supplanted with new marvels of speed, comfort, and luxury." Hunter wanted his airline to be among the earliest operators of those fanciful airships of the future.

People liked Hunter for his informality and easy manner. *Newsweek* magazine called him "as casual as the snapbrim hat he wears." He knew how to attract media attention to the airline, bringing his friend Amelia Earhart into a crew surveying a route to the Pacific Northwest as a stimulus to newspaper coverage. A man of energetic movements and wiry physique, he enjoyed playing tennis and golf, and he loved to hunt. (For many years, the mounted head of an antelope he had shot in Wyoming faced visitors to his office.) Most of all, however, Hunter relished flying, and he annually traveled a hundred thousand miles or more on Northwest ships. "Croil was easy to know, easy to like, had a sense of humor that could rescue a lost cause, yet he could take the hide off a rhinoceros when riled," said Frank Judd, a pilot and manager who joined Northwest at the same time as Hunter.

Born in 1893 in Casselton, North Dakota (where the nearby town of Hunter was named after his father, a prominent merchant and banker), raised in Fargo, and holder of a diploma from Yale, Hunter served as an artillery captain in the U.S. Army during World War I and saw action on the western front. He worked in his late father's department store for several years and then spent three years as a bank manager in New York City. In 1932 he came to Northwest with Brittin's encouragement. Hunter lacked aviation experience but had excellent business sense.

When Northwest brought him into the company, it had only two routes, totaling seven hundred miles: Chicago to Minneapolis–St. Paul and Twin Cities to Winnipeg. His task was to expand the route map. Hunter advanced rapidly, becoming general manager and vice president in 1933 when Brittin began focusing his time on lobbying on behalf of the airline in Washington, D.C. Strongly supported by Brittin, he first set his sights on breaking through the Rocky Mountains to establish a Northwest route to Seattle.

After the Northwest board made Hunter president in 1937, the airline's routes and destinations continued to multiply, soon extending to Alaska, Japan, China, and the Philippines. His exploitation of the "top-of-the-world" path to Asia, the polar circle route, began with survey flights to Alaska and Tokyo in 1939. This inventive approach to flying to the Far East would bring Northwest healthy earnings for decades to come. Yet he did not boast or exaggerate Northwest's accomplishments and claims on the future. In 1941, when a reporter asked him what the airline had in mind for the rapid expansion of commercial aviation that everyone expected after World War II, he simply replied, "Northwest Airlines is making its plans accordingly."

The early 1950s saw Northwest go through shaky times. Several notorious crashes of Northwest's Martin aircraft damaged the airline's reputation and took many lives. Hunter considered these tragedies the most discouraging events of his career. Hunter worked hard to fashion a merger with Capital Airlines, a combination that he believed would open Chicago as a busy gateway to the eastern United States. The merger also would have made him chairman of the transformed company. The effort fell through, however, and a group of dissatisfied shareholders wanted new leadership. To Hunter fell the new title of chairman of the board. By the end of his tenure as president, Northwest's network of routes ran twenty thousand miles, a thirtyfold increase from the meager pair of routes Brittin had handed him. His other innovations include the rollout of coach fares and reduced services for lower-paying passengers to fill seats.

Hunter served as board chairman until 1965. He died at seventy-five in 1970 in St. Paul. "There is a romance to this business of pushing new routes into faraway places," Hunter had said at the end of his tenure as Northwest president. He was the last of the airline's chief executives who could declare such a thing with conviction and a straight face. As Northwest evolved into a large corporation with international operations, romance flickered out as a guiding light. •

They pointed out that a northern transcontinental route was 250 miles shorter than United Air Lines' route that carried passengers from Chicago to Seattle, that the northern crossing of the Rocky Mountains was lower in altitude and safer than the crossing required farther south, and that travelers more urgently needed an east–west route through the northern states than any additional north–south connections. And Northwest proved the safety and speed of the northern route in 1934 by sending Brittin and famed aviator Amelia Earhart on a successful survey flight all the way to Seattle. Northwest's efforts gained momentum despite the steady discouragement of the Post Office.

Northwest battered down its objectors by seeding the northern tier with the emergency landing fields that the Department of Commerce required every fifty miles along commercial routes. For just $5,000, a community could build a functional airfield, and many cities between the Dakotas and Washington State took advantage of Northwest's offer to kick in the funds. The Post Office unexpectedly upped the ante, though, by taking a public position against any possible Northwest purchase of National Parks Airlines and an extension of Northwest's routes beyond Billings. In a letter to one of Northwest's supporters, Farley wrote that his department considered it "impractical at this time to consider any extension involving service to any territory at present without service, nor can it properly take any action with a view to urging one carrier to enter into negotiations for purchase of another."

Still Brittin and Hunter would not give up. Recalling the scheme that enabled them to reach for Billings, they offered to abandon Duluth, Green Bay, and Madison as destinations to make up for the route mileage they would gain by serving Spokane from Billings. They were willing to sacrifice other routes in order to focus on their transcontinental goal. Farley went along with this strange reasoning of allowing no net gain of mileage to Northwest while extending its westward tendrils in October 1933 when he approved the extension to Spokane, through Helena and Missoula. The next month, the Department of Commerce announced that it would spend more than half a million dollars to create a lighted airway between the Twin Cities and Seattle. All that was good news to Northwest, but other airlines coveted the possibility of controlling the 230-mile connection between Spokane and Seattle on this northern transcontinental route as well.

At the end of 1933, Brittin learned in Washington, D.C., that competitor United Air Lines was undertaking some very sneaky maneuvering. Although Postmaster Farley's ban on awarding new airmail routes applied to United as well as to Northwest, United was planning on locking onto the Spokane-to-Seattle route by applying directly to the Department of Commerce for a new passenger line between the two cities. Apparently nobody had ever tried that before, and the attempt harshly stung Northwest when it was so close to achieving its breakthrough to the Pacific and when United had previously shown little interest in serving these cities in Washington State. Brittin asserted that Northwest had a "moral priority" in the awarding of this route link, a business concept that must have perplexed the bureaucrats of the Commerce Department.

Morals aside, Brittin and Hunter decided to beat United at its own game. They rushed through Northwest's own application for the same passenger service between Spokane and Seattle, to begin just one day before United's proposed service. Brittin hand-delivered this application to the Commerce Department on a Saturday afternoon. Government officials approved the application almost immediately, and on the next day, December 3, 1933, Northwest inaugurated its most hastily arranged line. A just-hired Northwest captain flew early in the morning from Spokane to Seattle in a Waco biplane containing no passengers or mail. He did the same thing on his return afternoon flight to Spokane. The next day, a Monday, saw a repeat performance, except that the pilot continued on from Seattle to Tacoma before turning around.

Few potential passengers knew about the flights, but a reporter for the *St. Paul Pioneer Press* was aware of them. "When a plane of Northwest Airways roared over the route from Spokane to Seattle last Sunday morning," ran his account, "its throbbing motor heralded the finish of one of the most dramatic fights for an air route in the history of commercial aviation. It marked the end of a contest, reminiscent of the early days of the railroad when competing lines fought tooth and nail for first entry into regions unreached by the iron horse."

Many others predicted that this routing coup would rocket Northwest to a new level of prosperity and dominance. But such prognosticators failed to foresee that the stubborn dysfunction of the Post Office Department would again bestir. In 1934, government authorities would first bring Northwest, as well as other airlines, to the brink of financial ruin and then cause founder Brittin's descent into ignominy and shame.

AN AIRMAIL TRAGEDY

By 1934, the executive and legislative branches of the federal government had heard many complaints of irregularities in the Post Office's awarding of routes and airmail contracts. The very largest carriers, including United and American, were disproportionately rewarded and seemed to benefit from favoritism. Some politicians feared that the Post Office was paying way too much for airmail service. In a sweeping act, perhaps an overreaction, President Roosevelt invalidated all existing airmail contracts and charged the flyers of the U.S. Army Air Corps with the job of carrying the mail. The nation was stunned when the inexperienced pilots of the Air Corps crashed much too frequently.

With the sudden loss of its airmail business—which still brought in 80 percent of the airline's earnings—Northwest's future looked bleak. Before the president's action, Northwest had announced that a government takeover of airmail delivery would require the airline to liquidate its assets and go out of business. In comments tinged with sarcasm, Northwest's new president, Shreve Archer, questioned the legality of the cancellation of airmail contracts and reminded reporters that his airline had not seen any of the money— "those millions we have heard are floating around"—that whistleblowers said the Post Office was wasting and funneling to favorites. He added, "In the event of cancellation of these [airmail] contracts, we simply cannot go on. We will have to close and will do so. That is a foregone conclusion. We will pay our employees up to the first of [the] month, after which it will be goodbye." The Upper Midwest would lose the rippling benefits of Northwest's annual payroll of $375,000.

With these forebodings of doom, Northwest offered to sell its assets "on a basis of actual cost less depreciation," Hunter said, to two competitors: the Great Northern Railroad and the Northern Pacific Railroad. The railroads turned down the proposal with little discussion. How altered America's transportation history would be had they decided differently.

The actual nationalization of airmail service, however, led Northwest to greatly moderate its response. It dropped routes dependent on airmail business and laid off about a third of the 150 people in its workforce. The rest of the staff continued working on partial wages. Soon, though, cries of distress reached Northwest from communities along its new northern tier route. Brittin and Hunter could not bear to give up the line and leave those towns without their air connections. "This splendid service—without mail—can only be operated at a great financial loss," Hunter declared, "but this territory must be served. . . . We trust that very soon we will again be flying the air mail over this route under the direction of the government."

Meanwhile, the U.S. Senate began its own investigation of the airmail fiascos. Colonel Brittin, who was caught red-handed destroying letters and memos that the investigating Senate committee had subpoenaed, was hit with the Senate's wrath. Found guilty of contempt of that legislative body, he was sentenced to ten days in prison and suffered much public embarrassment. Northwest accepted his resignation and had to face the future without its founder.

Brittin's fall was just one way in which the "airmail follies" of the mid-1930s affected Northwest. Instead of taking advantage of the Post Office's embarrassing series of faux pas to press for highly favorable airmail contracts, Northwest and its competitors so badly hungered for airmail payments that they settled for far less than they might have received with a more aggressive response. A badly weakened Northwest now faced devastating losses. The visionary Brittin was gone. Airmail rates had plunged to six cents per ounce.

The airline emerged from the reorganization of airmail routes having lost its contract to carry mail between the Twin Cities and Chicago—which forced it to soon abandon the passenger service, too—as well as its mail-carrying business between the home base and Fargo and Pembina. As consolation, it won the airmail contract for Fargo-to-Seattle deliveries. Strangely, Northwest's closest airmail terminal was now more than two hundred miles from its home airport. Just as painful, new airmail legislation required the airline to reorganize its company structure and give up its very identity as Northwest Airways, emerging as Northwest Airlines, the corporate name it would retain faithfully for the next seven decades. Other airlines were forced to make similar changes: Eastern Air Transport morphed into Eastern Airlines, and American Airways became American Airlines.

As it turned out, the new operator of the Twin Cities–Chicago airmail route, Hanford Tri-State Airlines, quickly discovered that it was going broke carrying the letters. By the end of 1934, Northwest bought the contract from Hanford for $46,000 and was able to resume its profitable passenger line between the two cities. With that one gap on the map finally filled—with routes covering nearly two thousand miles—Northwest had evolved from a regional carrier to a foremost American airline. Carrying passengers between Chicago and Seattle was possible, the realization of Brittin's and Hunter's dream. Northwest still lagged far behind the route strength of such competitors as American Airlines (about ten thousand miles) and United (about five thousand miles), but the upstart was knocking at the door.

BIGGER AND FASTER

New routes demanded new airships. For several years, Northwest had depended on the reliable service of its Fords, Hamiltons, and other planes, which increasingly seemed too small and too slow. If Northwest wanted to successfully compete against United's flights to Seattle (via Salt Lake City), its only choice was to upgrade its fleet. The plane it chose to blaze the trail of the new route was the Lockheed 10-A Electra, which could comfortably carry ten passengers at a cruising speed of 180 miles per hour. In thirteen hours, the metal, twin-engine planes could fly from the Twin Cities to Seattle. Northwest placed a half-million-dollar order for thirteen of the Electras—and waited. Lockheed was behind schedule in constructing the aircraft. The airline needed a substitute to fill the gap.

Here Northwest bought from Lockheed a set of three Orions. The five-passenger Orions had 200-miles-per-hour speed but were only a temporary fix until the arrival of the Electras. With their wooden construction and manually retracted landing gear, they appeared more a relic of the pioneering phase of commercial aviation than the dawning transcontinental era. (Pilots found that the manual operation of the landing gear helped

Passengers board a Lockheed Electra. The aircraft's 180 miles-per-hour cruising speed put Seattle within thirteen hours of the Twin Cities.

bulk up the muscles of their right arms.) These were the last Orions that Lockheed ever sold for airline use, and the Civil Aeronautics Administration soon banned them from commercial routes because of the inherent dangers of single-engine planes. By that time, however, Northwest no longer needed them. It sold off the three aircraft, and one ended its days as a Spanish Civil War fighter plane for the Spanish Republican Air Force when it was shot out of the sky in 1937.

At last, in May 1934, Northwest became the first airline to accept delivery of the long-awaited Electra, which served the company ably during the remainder of the decade. Two engines were safer than one, and pilots loved the way the planes handled. Passenger Vivian Grace Gibson, probably flying one of the Electras between the Twin Cities and Chicago in 1935, memorialized the trip with a description of its conclusion. "It is 10:45 P.M. and we have completed our return trip," she wrote. "We leave the plane at the St. Paul airport; but life is just a little different. I have flown in the clouds like a bird and have been to Chicago just for the ride!"

Despite such magic, competition from the railroads was increasing, and Northwest soon sought an airplane that would trounce the best efforts of high-speed trains. Together with Lockheed, it planned and designed the 14-H, nicknamed the Super Electra or Sky Zephyr, an $80,000 aircraft that moved up to twelve passengers, cruised at 223 miles per hour, and knocked more than an hour off the Electra's flying time to Seattle. Private pilots liked them, too, at least at first; Howard Hughes flew one around the world in less than four days.

The Sky Zephyr joined the Northwest fleet in 1937 and worked the Twin Cities–Chicago and Chicago–Seattle lines. Less than two weeks after the model's introduction, Nick Marner, the Northwest pilot who had made the company's first (empty) passenger flight into Seattle, crashed a Sky Zephyr near Bozeman, Montana. Other perplexing accidents afflicted the aircraft: Fred Whittemore, Northwest's vice president for operations, died with eight others when a Lockheed test pilot smashed a Sky Zephyr into a canyon wall while ferrying the plane from Lockheed's plant in California to Minneapolis, and another crashed near Miles City, Montana. These accidents wiped out all the airline's profits for the year. Investigators found a flaw in the Sky Zephyr's rudder, and the planes were grounded until the defect had been fixed.

This modification came too late to prevent the airline's pilots and customers from forming a bad opinion of the airplane. Northwest's new operations manager, George Gardner, faced the unenviable task of figuring out what to do with ten new Sky Zephyrs that Northwest had recently received from Lockheed. (The airline kept the original Electras in the fleet for several more years.) He found a brilliant way to dispose of them, selling them back to Lockheed at the full purchase price as a partial payment on a half dozen revolutionary planes that would carry Northwest into a new era of flying.

A GIANT WITH WINGS

Several other airlines had already paid $125,000 for each of these legendary craft, the Douglas DC-3, whose twenty-one-passenger seat capacity and overall size made it seem enormous. As early as 1930, Lewis Brittin had predicted the evolution of much bigger aircraft that could transport passengers at tremendous cost savings, and the DC-3 seemed a big advance toward this dream. It had many of the features we now consider essential in a modern airliner: autopilot, feathered propellers that could be rotated to parallel the path of airflow to reduce drag in case of an engine failure, comfortable seating for passengers, and advanced instrumentation and radio gear. Compared with the rest of Northwest's fleet, the DC-3 flew quietly and efficiently, carrying passengers above the clouds at ten thousand feet at a low cost—if Northwest could consistently fill it. In March 1939 Northwest leased a DC-3 from American Airlines to train crews in its operation. With a loan from the Reconstruction Finance Corporation, a federal agency founded during the New Deal Era to spark business activity, Northwest paid for its first fully owned DC-3 the next month—with nine more to arrive in the next few years. Dozens more would arrive after World War II.

With a complete galley and a center aisle that struck passengers as being as long as a bowling lane, the DC-3 required Northwest to hire its first flight attendants, or stewardesses

The legendary Douglas DC-3 joined the Northwest fleet in 1939.

BALANCING A TRAY ON A TURBULENT FLIGHT

When Northwest brought the Douglas DC-3 into its fleet in 1939, it acquired an aircraft with more cabin room, more passenger seating, and better galley equipment than any plane the airline had previously owned. But even more important to the company's culture, these improvements inspired Northwest to introduce cabin stewardesses to its customers.

In the earliest days, Northwest copilots—and occasionally pilots—had responsibility for cleaning the plane, loading mailbags, collecting tickets, stowing baggage, fueling the aircraft, and making passengers comfortable. A team of male stewards later assumed those duties on some flights, "all for 78 bucks [a month]," former steward Joe Kimm noted. "I realized I had the wrong job, so I figured I'd better learn to fly." Kimm became a long-tenured Northwest pilot.

The twenty-one-passenger capacity of the DC-3 gave maneuvering space for a new category of Northwest employee. Mal Freeburg, Northwest's director of passenger services in 1939, hired the first stewardesses. (Although the "steward" job name now sounds off to our ears, "stewardess" rang strangely in those pioneering years.) First to join the staff were Dorothy Stumph, a veteran of flight attendant service with United Air Lines, and Virginia Johnson. Helen Jacobson, Olga Loken, Frances Macagno, Marie Wanda, and Louise Rudquist soon followed.

Rosie Stein, Northwest's master of all administrative functions, soon succeeded Freeburg, and she promoted Helen Jacobson, a native of Winthrop, Minnesota, to become her primary assistant. Their hiring criteria were inviolable. All the early recruits had to be female, unmarried, attractive, morally irreproachable, between twenty-one and twenty-five years old, five feet two to five feet five in height,

(Top): Stewardess Burnece Sorby personified the optimism, charm, and professional skill that Northwest sought to instill in the first flight attendants it hired in 1939.

(Bottom): Burnece Sorby with another stewardess in 1939.

under 120 pounds in weight, and able to see well without correction and pass a personality test.

The final requirement was certification as a registered nurse. (Phyllis Curry remembers that she first applied to Stein in the mid-1940s at the age of nineteen; by that time the RN requirement was gone, but the flight services manager told Curry to go home, get some education and business experience, and return when she was twenty-one.) Although there were occasional medical emergencies and the presence of an employee with some medical training certainly reassured passengers, Jacobson wrote that "nurses were hired because of their intelligence, poise, friendliness and ability to deal tactfully and graciously with people." Stewardesses also had to pass a physical exam, which the airline repeated every six months.

Stein declared that "the stewardess is one of the airline's best advertisements," but in those years, once stewardesses aged, gained weight, or got married, Northwest dismissed them. (Jacobson, who wrote Northwest's stewardess manual with Stein and taught training classes, lost her job when she became a bride in 1942.) They worked up to forty hours a week and one hundred hours a month for $110 per month after training, which went up to $120 after six months. "Due to the fact that Northwest Airlines has gone to considerable expense for my training as stewardess," their employment contract stated, "I agree to remain in their employ for a period of at least one year; I further agree that there is no responsibility on the part of Northwest airlines to retain me in their employ past the age of thirty." Stewardesses based in Minneapolis were eligible to receive chauffeured rides to the airport, and those who chose to commute on the streetcar had escorts waiting to meet them at their stops.

"Stewardesses were charged with the care of passengers from the time they boarded the plane until they deplaned" (that strange verb *deplane* began appearing in newspapers and magazines during the 1940s and spiked in usage during the 1980s), Jacobson wrote. "They anticipated the wants and wishes of the passengers as much as possible. Conversation with the passengers was encouraged."

Among the myriad duties of stewardesses were checking in passengers, fastening the unfamiliar seatbelts, distributing reading material, lighting cigarettes, and caring for airsick passengers by dis-

tributing medicine and oxygen. Sometimes airsickness afflicted the entire flight, and stewardesses made sure each seat had an empty ice cream bucket stowed beneath. For nausea, the stewardess manual recommended dispensing Seconal along with ammonia inhalant; in addition, it told stewardesses to place passengers in a "semi-recumbent position, open individual vent, [apply] cold cloth to head, pull curtain, . . . dry crackers may help prevent airsickness." One passenger wrote to Jacobson after a flight: "If my stomach was found on the plane (Flight 6 to Chicago, January 4) I would appreciate its return. . . . P.S. Sorry I was such a nuisance."

Stewardesses sometimes had to act as law enforcers. Although alcoholic beverages were banned aboard flights until 1949 and stewardesses were empowered to take them away from passengers, Curry recalled dealing with intoxicated customers during the late 1940s. "Once two drunks got on and I wouldn't let them board," she said. "But they insisted, and we had to call the police. The cops threw them off." In 1940, stewardess Eunice Otsea found a young man huddled in the rear blanket storage area of an aloft DC-3, and it turned out that he had sneaked into the baggage compartment while the plane was on the ground in Renton, Washington, and eventually crawled to warmer quarters in flight. Otsea and the crew turned the stowaway over to police when the plane landed in Fargo.

"Kids got special treatment," remembered Bob Fliegel, who flew Northwest as a child during the 1940s and 1950s. "The stewardesses gave us little kits of goodies—crayons, coloring books, and the like. Adults received folders of Northwest stationery, post cards, pens, and decals. And remember the gum? It was always peppermint Chicklets. The stewardesses distributed little packs of it during the frequent periods of turbulence and just before landing to help passengers cope with airsickness."

An on-plane birth was always possible. On September 14, 1953, during an approach to Anchorage, stewardess Connie Walker coached out a passenger's infant as the purser read instructions from a manual titled *How to Deliver a Baby*. The parents named Walker the little girl's godmother. (Thirty-six years later, when Walker worked her final flight at age seventy after more than four decades as a stewardess, both the mother and the godchild helped her celebrate retirement.)

A Northwest stewardess serves passengers in the late 1940s.

Hollywood Beckons Northwest Sky Beauty

PI 11-7-41

Stewardess Taking Screen Test With M.-G.-M.

Mary Harriet Shepherd, Northwest Airlines stewardess, made her regular flight from Billings here yesterday and then raced home to pack her things.

Today glamorous Mary Harriet will report at Metro-Goldwyn-Mayer studios for a film test.

After that—well, there may be

MOVIE-BOUND—Lovely Stewardess Mary Harriet Shepherd, who reports in Hollywood today for screen tests on request of director who spotted her at work.

no more trips from Billings here, at least for a while. If she qualifies, Mary will be cast in a forthcoming picture.

She is a graduate of the Virginia Mason Hospital school of

nursing and is the niece of Mrs. Maude Williams, 803 W. Howe St. Her chance for what every young girl dreams of, a screen test, came recently when an M-G-M director spotted her during a routine flight.

Newspapers reported Mary Shepherd's theatrical "discovery" while working as a stewardess aboard a Northwest flight in 1941.

Marketing duties claimed stewardesses' time as well. "We were required to present talks and appear at public functions, be interviewed on radio and serve on 'Tea Flights,'" Jacobson noted. "These were important in the public relations at that time. The Tea Flights encouraged women to travel by air. Tea, coffee and cookies were served, and places of interest were identified as we flew over the city."

The early stewardesses had to walk a difficult line between friendliness and maintaining professional reserve with male passengers. Stein inserted into the stewardess handbook several bits of advice from Ruth Millett, a World War II–era syndicated newspaper columnist:

Pilar Apostol, Monsie Aguado, and Carmen Guitieres joined Northwest's stewardess corps in 1947 after the airline added routes to Asia.

she can't think up a good retort she just smiles and moves on. She is exactly as attentive to the men who don't angle for her attention as to those who do. She manages to be sparing enough with her attention to keep the men wishing she had more time for them. She does her job so efficiently and quickly that she gains the respect of even the men who would like to date her, if they could manage it.

She usually remembers not to antagonize women by giving them any less attention than she gives to the men, so she doesn't run into that old criticism that women never get any service from women. She is nice-looking, agreeable, conscious—but not too conscious—of her sex, and that's an unbeatable combination for women whose job depends on her being able to get along with men.

Within nineteen months of Northwest's use of the first DC-3s, the airline had twenty-four stewardesses divided between bases in Minneapolis and Seattle. In a year, there were sixteen more. Initially, stewardess training included Northwest-led classes held at the Commodore Hotel in St. Paul and the Curtis Hotel in Minneapolis, in which they learned about Northwest's history, airline terms and codes, routes, aviation equipment, parts of the plane, rules and regulations, and even a little meteorology. Then came a stint at the Zel McConnell Modeling School in Minneapolis for comportment instruction in "makeup, gait, posture and social graces," Jacobson wrote. The curriculum taught the stewardess "how to recondition her body if it had noticeable faults; to stand at ease with perfect balance; to walk lightly; to sit without scrawling. . . . 'Make yourself believe that your living depends upon perfect grooming,' they are told," according to a 1945 account, which added, "Each student must write a thesis before graduation, a booklet in which she sets down her aims and records her daily accomplishments."

One stewardess stood out among the early recruits: Mary Joyce, a seaplane pilot who lived in a hunting and fishing lodge near Juneau, Alaska. Several years before her hiring, Joyce had led a champion dog-sled team on a thousand-mile trek to Fairbanks and had gained media attention for her rescue of a marooned boatman from a swift-running

A stewardess chats with passengers on a Northwest flight to Taiwan in 1950.

The girls who have made the airline passengers comfortable have perfected the "you're attractive—but keep your distance" technique. And that is something every woman who works has to develop. . . . She looks straight into the eyes of the person who speaks to her and really listens to what they have to say. She smiles when she answers, and if

Alaskan river. She reserved her winter time for her favorite outdoor activities, but she spent several summers in Northwest flight cabins. (Another early stewardess, Lucille Fisher, was also a licensed pilot.) But all stewardesses enjoyed celebrity status in the early days. "I was often asked to sign autograph books after flight," Jacobson remembered.

The DC-3 occasionally transformed into a kind of airborne Schwab's Pharmacy for motion picture recruiters on the lookout for new talent. One movie producer focused his attention on stewardess Mary Shepherd—who had previously appeared without credit as a dancer in the film *Artists and Models*—during a 1941 flight and sent her a telegram from Hollywood to audition for a part. She landed a role in the MGM comedy short *What about Daddy?*, but there her cinematic career ended.

Stein opened the gate to taller stewardesses after World War II, when Northwest began flying DC-4s, which had bigger cabins. The postwar years and the anticipated start of Northwest's service to the Far East brought an emphasis on giving stewardesses greater familiarity with international cultures, which could include them "chatting with Chinese customers and greeting a Russian in his own language as he steps on board, serving tea to Britishers on a flight out of Calcutta—even discussing the latest fashion trends with a girl from the Philippines," observed one reporter in a profile of Stein. Ten Filipino and Chinese stewardesses joined the staff in 1947 for work on Asian flights.

Stein left her job and retired from Northwest in 1946. Dorothy Stumph, Northwest's first stewardess, outlasted Stein and ended her career by marrying in 1951; she had tallied more than three million miles in the air. At the end, she complained that nothing exciting had happened to her on the job. "I've never had any trouble in flight, not even a missing engine," she said.

Stewardessing long remained an adventurous occupation in the public mind, however. Marjorie Burns, a reporter for the *Minneapolis Star Journal* who shadowed Northwest flight attendants aboard flights for two days in the 1940s, concluded that "it's heaven to do your daily stint of work up in the clouds. . . . [The experience turned] my very ordinary shoulder blades into wing sprouts. And from now on I'm going to give those sprouts every opportunity to grow into full-fledged wings by spending all the time I can in the air."

African Americans did not have the opportunity to sprout wings until 1962, when Lenora Bolden of Washington, D.C., became Northwest's first black stewardess. For years before Bolden's hiring, however, the airline had mismanaged the employment of Marlene White of Detroit, who had applied to be a stewardess in 1957. (That same year, Mohawk Airlines had hired the first African American stewardess, Ruth Carol Taylor, and TWA followed by employing Carol Grant in 1958.) Northwest turned White down and instead gave her a job as a reservations clerk. Then in 1962 the Michigan Fair Employment Practices Commission, which asserted that White met all the requirements for a stewardess, began hearings on her case. Ultimately the commission ruled that Northwest must accept her into its next stewardess training class and ordered the airline to free its hiring of discriminatory practices.

"I knew there was discrimination," White said after the commission's decision. "I am very happy about the ruling. I still want the job and will confer with my attorney immediately to learn what I should do next." But her saga was far from over. After she enrolled in the stewardess training course in St. Paul—graduating in the top third of her class—and flew as a probationary trainee in 1963, Northwest fired her. The reason, the airline said, was White's inability to master emergency aircraft evacuation procedures, a charge she called "utterly ridiculous" and the result of harassment and pressure to resign. "I would say it's a campaign of retribution, since I filed the suit [with the Michigan commission] and won the case." The Air Line Stewards and Stewardesses Association again appealed her case to the Michigan commission and to federal authorities, and Northwest rehired her at the end of 1963. Several years later she left the airline to earn her Ph.D. and work as a financial consultant in Chicago.

Soon to come were relaxations of Northwest's employment policies so that stewardesses could keep their jobs past their thirty-second birthdays, through marriage, and beyond parental leaves of absence. A lawsuit brought by Mary Pat Laffey and forty other flight attendants and twice argued before the U.S. Supreme Court produced these changes; Northwest fought it for fifteen years. The plaintiffs also won the right to work as pursers at the same salaries as male employees, refuse mandatory weight checks, and wear glasses. Meanwhile,

Stewardess glamour: two flight attendants look perfectly dressed and coiffed after a Stratocruiser flight, circa 1952.

Three Northwest stewardesses of the late 1950s, Nora Neal, Laverne Richter, and Margaret Olson, pose for a publicity shot.

Identical twins Gloria and Gladys Thorvaldson of Winnipeg graduated together in a stewardess class of 1964.

while Northwest had hired men to work as in-flight stewards for decades—often to face down inebriated passengers—they did not generally perform the same duties as their female counterparts or win acceptance for doing so until the 1970s. With more than sixty years of seniority at the age of eighty-seven, Robert Reardon ranked as North-west's (and later Delta's) longest-tenured flight attendant in 2012.

During the 1980s and the acquisition of Republic Airlines, North-west's legions of flight attendants grew from 4,000 to 7,300. Twenty years later, another merger—the Northwest-ending combination with Delta—led to another momentous event: the end of their sixty-three-year-long union representation. The Association of Flight Attendants barely lost a vote of its Northwest members with only 49 percent choosing to continue the collective bargaining agreement. As a result, the Northwest employees joined their Delta peers in working without a union.

Members of the profession have undergone startling changes— from stewardesses to flight attendants and from aviation celebrities to less-than-glamorous aviation laborers. More than forty years after her hiring, Helen Jacobson Richardson began to hanker for a gathering of the stewardesses who had served between 1939 and 1941. She wrote to Northwest's president Steven Rothmeier suggesting that the com-pany host a reunion, but he did not reply. The company also declined to sponsor a luncheon for the pioneering flight attendants. So the women got together on their own. "Not a small percentage still wore high heels, dressed sharply and looked as if they'd have no problem balancing a tray on a turbulent flight," wrote *Minneapolis Star Tribune* reporter Peg Meier, who attended one such event. Many expressed sorrow over the transformation of the job, which was already evident when they gathered in the 1980s. Someday, they may have hoped, the stewardess would rise again. •

A Northwest flight attendant doll, complete with snack cart, circa 1985.

A Northwest DC-3 in action in 1939.

as they were then called—all of them at first registered nurses. Previously pilots or copilots had tended to passengers' needs, with occasional dire results due to the distractions of the crew's other responsibilities. Bert Ritchie, a Northwest copilot during the airline's Ford Tri-Motor runs, remembered one time when he dealt with a passenger carrying aboard a cat. Ritchie stored the pet in a baggage compartment at the tail of the plane, became distracted, and forgot about it. Near the flight's conclusion he suddenly remembered the cat and rushed back to retrieve it. The frozen feline was "stiff as a board," and he prayed that setting the cat on a heater would revive it. "She thawed out and was as good as ever when the plane reached the Twin Cities," a company account of the incident concludes.

Passengers initially saw the DC-3s on the airline's route connecting Chicago with the Twin Cities, and the planes were soon flying between Minneapolis and Seattle as well. The reliable but now diminutive Electras flew most of Northwest's other routes.

In time, Northwest showed it could fill the DC-3s, and the aircraft helped generate a remarkable increase in Northwest's passenger traffic throughout the 1930s. Its passengers carried climbed from twelve thousand in 1934 to thirty-eight thousand in 1936 and to seventy-five thousand in 1939. Unlike the early years, when the annual tally of passengers could fit inside a movie theater, Northwest was now flying the equivalent of the population of a pretty-good-size city every year. The decade that had passed since the start of the airline's passenger service had made Northwest, in Hunter's words, "a hoary old pioneer." Gone were the symbols of Northwest's rough start: Ford Tri-Motors, a dusty car-racing track in the middle of the airport, navigation by eye. In their place came speed, power, and more people.

BREATHING ROOM

With Northwest's airliners now routinely flying at an altitude of two miles, and even higher when climbing the Rocky Mountains, the company had to give attention to the breathing needs of the crew members in unpressurized cabins. The airline had kept it secret from the press and public, but pilots sometimes complained of sleepiness and sluggish thinking at the highest altitudes. Just before the arrival of the DC-3s, Croil Hunter sought advice on high-altitude respiration from a frequent passenger and member of the board of directors, the surgeon Charles William Mayo. Mayo's father was a founder of the Mayo Clinic, and Mayo famously practiced there as well. He listened to Hunter's stories of the pilots' wooziness and knew the cause. "Sounds like oxygen deficiency to me," Mayo said.

Working with a team that included another surgeon, a physiologist, and a dental surgeon, Mayo grappled with the complexities of providing air crews with oxygen in ways that enabled them to also eat and talk using radio equipment. The group tested various oxygen-supplying equipment in a pressure chamber at the Mayo Clinic that could mimic high-altitude conditions. One of the team members, Arthur Bulbulian, M.D., had previously devised a technique of creating latex noses for reconstructive surgery, and he applied these skills to fabricating a small mask, adaptable to nearly any adult face, that could deliver an oxygen-air mixture through the nose only. Mayo technicians then had to conquer the problems of properly mixing the oxygen and air blend. In the end, the Mayo team was spectacularly successful. Trials in the pressure chamber suggested that the Mayo-

With higher altitude flights came the danger of oxygen deprivation in unpressurized cabins. In 1938 Northwest was the first airline to offer breathing masks to passengers.

designed equipment would safely deliver oxygen to crews flying up to forty thousand feet up, and Northwest's test flights confirmed the effectiveness of the masks in July 1938 during a test run in a Sky Zephyr flying from the Twin Cities to Los Angeles.

That flight caused a media sensation. Many reporters wrote that the masks made pilots look like men from Mars, and a radio journalist who hopped aboard the return flight to Minneapolis convinced pilot Mel Swanson to briefly remove his mask at high altitude. "Without his mask," he told listeners, "Swanson's lips and fingertips have started turning blue!" Northwest soon installed the masks in its own planes, licensed the technology to other airlines, and became the only airline to provide oxygen equipment to passengers as well as crew. The Mayo team went on to develop the A-14 oxygen mask—a commonly used piece of wartime aviation equipment with the added improvement of including a radio microphone within its workings—for the U.S. Army Air Corps.

Other important route expansions were in the offing. In 1935, Northwest gained approval to fly mail across the border to Winnipeg, ending the awkward termination of its route at Pembina. Suddenly the airline was an international carrier. In one of the last route decisions that the government made before the creation of the Civil Aeronautics Administration, Northwest won an extension of its Seattle route to Portland, via Yakima.

In 1938, the board promoted Hunter to president and general manager. With the Pacific Northwest conquered, he now envisioned the airline trailblazing a "Northwest passage" to the Far East.

CHAPTER 3

PULLED INTO
THE MODERN AGE

In the late fall of 1944, Mrs. Mary Berens of Minneapolis climbed off a Northwest plane in Rochester, Minnesota, on a visit to her son. A few days later, she boarded another Northwest aircraft en route to Chicago to spend time with her daughter. Both trips attracted the attention of newsmen because Berens was considered one of the oldest people yet to have braved the experience of commercial air travel.

One article referred to her as "spry Mrs. Berens, whose alert mind and twinkling eye belie her 88 years." Born in Whitewater, Wisconsin, she had relocated with her family by oxcart to the western part of that state when she was six years old. "She recalls that it took them a month to travel around 150 miles, and that they had to depend upon shooting prairie chickens, wild pigeons and deer for their food," the newspaper account noted.

So by the 1940s, with its fleet of new airliners and routes that reached to the Pacific Ocean, Northwest was transporting passengers who had once traveled by oxcart, probably also by stagecoach and covered wagon. In other respects, as well, the fifteen-year-old airline still had a foot in olden times. It began the decade by reporting that its fleet of twenty-one planes still generated more revenue from airmail fees than from passenger fares. As late as 1941, that fleet included at least one of the old Hamilton metal biplanes, which had flown every route on Northwest's map. The company, controlled by a small group of private investors, had never made a public stock offering. And despite its petitions to the Civil Aeronautics Board to serve New York City, which the federal agency denied in 1938, 1940, and 1943, Northwest was still without a foothold on the eastern seaboard of North America.

Whatever other echoes of quaint business practices remained in the organization, they would all fall silent as the decade wore on. The 1940s inexorably and forever pulled

The Northwest ticket office in the Davenport Hotel, Spokane, Washington, 1944.

Northwest's city ticket office in Portland, Oregon, 1940s.

Brochures market the airline's connections, schedules, and fares between the Upper Midwest and the Pacific Northwest, 1940s.

Northwest into the modern age. Within a few years, the airline's home base grew into one of the nation's leading air terminals—a center of cargo transport, aircraft construction, aviation research, and air logistics for the military. War made it happen.

Japan's attack on Pearl Harbor, Oahu, on December 7, 1941, drew America into a conflict that had been raging for more than two years in Europe, Asia, and Africa. World War II's fields of battle—the Philippines, the small islands of the mid-Pacific, the western and eastern fronts of Europe, the deserts of North Africa—were far from the industry, military bases, and population centers of the United States. America needed planes and trained crews to bomb distant targets, transport supplies, ferry troops, patrol, and defend. It needed lots of them.

An early hint of the war's sweeping changes came four days after Pearl Harbor, when Northwest received a sabotage warning from the government. The cautionary directive mandated that "no baggage was checked through or carried on the airplane unless the passengers to whom the baggage belonged traveled on the same flight," remembered early stewardess Helen Jacobson Richardson. Two weeks later arrived a new security bulletin: Without written authorization from the U.S. attorney general or the secretary of war, enemy aliens, including nationals of Japan, Germany, Italy, and Manchuria, could not fly. "Japanese dressed in uniforms of United States armed forces were investigated as to [their] identification or travel orders," Richardson recalled. "Civilians had to produce positive proof of their American citizenship."

When it fully shifted into war mode, the federal government began regulating all sorts of aspects of Americans' lives. It rationed food, gasoline, and other essentials. At the same time it seized control of the nation's skies, securing airports, requisitioning planes from airlines, and dictating where and how often commercial routes could operate. The U.S. military transformed passenger airliners into cargo planes, including six of the thirteen DC-3s that Northwest owned, and took charge of half the planes in commercial hands. All nineteen airlines operating in the United States during the war shifted to military control.

The government told Northwest that it must temporarily halt its "nonessential" Minneapolis–Duluth, Fargo–Winnipeg, and Seattle–Portland connections, and it had to curtail the frequency of its Minneapolis–Chicago and Seattle–Tacoma flights. "Service on Northwest Airlines, Inc., will be cut less than half," the *Minneapolis Tribune* told readers. Around the country, airlines carried 25 percent fewer passengers than before the war, but flights previously half-empty now flew full. Meanwhile, the importance and variety of its assignments from the military were astounding. Many of Northwest's most experienced employees—some 2,000 by the middle of the war—had joined every branch of the military. But the airline hired many more than that to work on war-related government projects. From 881 employees before the war, Northwest's staffing soared to more than 10,000 during

SECURITY BEFORE TERRORISM ✈

Northwest's first security chief was a man born in 1889, whose career began first as a Seattle dockyard blacksmith and next as a dance hall bouncer long before the advent of international terrorism—or, for that matter, the invention of commercial air travel. Formerly the chief of detectives for the Seattle Police Department, Ernest Washington Yoris had earned a reputation as a detective skilled at apprehending killers and kidnappers. He arrived at the airline in 1942 to run security at Northwest's new bomber modification plants.

Soon Yoris was directing one of the largest security forces in the Midwest, a collection of a thousand guards, investigators, police officers, and firefighters. His team had to look out for saboteurs, spies, thieves, blabbermouths, trespassers, and others who could threaten the confidential operations at these top-secret plants.

From that high-stakes vigilance, Yoris greatly reduced his forces and focused on more mundane activities after World War II: pilfering, vandalism, and the passing of rubber checks. "Passengers give us about sixty bad checks a month," he said in 1955, when his Northwest title was director of internal security. "Mostly it's just a case of bad bookkeeping on their part. Occasionally we get a 'no account' check or a forged job. Then we have a real problem." His territory encompassed the entire Northwest route map, from New York City to Manila, and his collection of distinctive footwear (three pairs of crepe-soled shoes with canvas tops in green, blue, and maroon) became internationally known. He insisted that he preferred crepe-bottomed shoes because they were comfortable, not because they allowed him to sneak up on people.

It is not known how long Yoris headed Northwest's security, but he died in 1967, just as the industry saw a rise in airplane hijackings and the arrival of a new era in aviation security. •

a wartime peak. This increase convinced the airline, at last, to create its first personnel department.

Despite their loss of routes, civilian capacity, and independence, Northwest and its competitors did not financially suffer during World War II. "One the whole, both military and commercial war activities have been profitable to the airlines, several of which had been operating at a loss before Pearl Harbor," observed a midwar report by the Office of War Information. In the first six months of the war, Northwest flew a million pounds of cargo through Minneapolis alone, a huge increase over peacetime figures. During the same period, two thousand Northwest employees were at work on war-related projects and assignments.

NORTH TO ALASKA

Perhaps Northwest's biggest contribution to the war effort happened in a place few Americans knew or even thought about. Early in the war, with Japan's navy ranging far across the Pacific, U.S. military leaders grew concerned over the vulnerability of Alaska's Aleutian Islands. As possible stepping stones to the North American mainland, especially the Pacific Coast, the islands were crucial to the defense of the United States and Canada. Military leaders decided that only the construction of a lifeline between Alaska and the provision centers of the United States could stop the Japanese from gaining a potentially disastrous foothold on the continent. The armed forces looked for help from Northwest, with its hard-earned experience trailblazing formidably cold destinations. Nobody had ever before established an air route from the continental United States to Alaska through Canada—a reach from the Twin Cities of nearly four thousand miles—and the region lacked even the most rudimentary landing strips, radio navigation facilities, living quarters, and hangars.

The airline's massive Alaska partnership with the military, in essence an attempt to instantly set up a completely new airline, began in February 1942. Supervisory responsibilities for this new Northern Region of activity initially went to Frank C. Judd, a Northwest pilot since 1931 who had once managed to launch a crippled plane by replacing the propellers, attaching skis to the damaged landing gear, and taking off while gliding down a hill. Just as when it opened new routes to Montana and the Pacific Coast, Northwest launched its Northern Region service with a survey flight from the Twin Cities to Alaska, with a stop in Edmonton, Alberta. "We were all gung ho to tackle the challenge of creating an aerial lifeline, so the moment the contract became official, we rushed out to buy cold weather gear and took off in a Douglas DC-3 on the 1,092-mile leg to Edmonton," remembered George Gardner, then the airline's vice president of operations.

Things went wrong the instant the survey crew landed in Edmonton. "The Canadian

ISLAND OF QUONSET HUTS

During and after the Japanese occupation of some of the Alaskan Aleutians, Northwest carried thousands of U.S. service members to a military base on Shemya, a distant outpost in the island chain. Set between the Pacific Ocean and the Bering Sea, the eight-square-mile speck of land suffered from fog, strong wind, and desolation.

Few people would then have guessed that Shemya would remain an important part of the airline's commercial operations long after the war's end. In the early years of Northwest's Asian operations, Shemya served as a fueling stop in the long stretch over the polar route between Tokyo and Anchorage. With astonishment, international passengers took in this rocky isle that must rank as the most remote and unlikely way station in the history of American aviation.

Northwest employees expressed their irreverence for the place through their nickname for the island, "Schmoe." When the military abandoned its base, Northwest president Croil Hunter persuaded authorities not to destroy what it left behind. The company had plans to reuse the godforsaken facilities. Shemya's Quonset huts became living quarters, mess halls, maintenance shops, and offices for fifty-five airline employees working yearlong shifts and for the flight crews that overnighted there. One staffer who signed on for three straight hitches on Shemya justified the decision by declaring the island "a great place to save money—no place to spend it." Stewardess Phyllis Curry remembers being told by coworkers that Shemya was notable because "they said it snowed horizontally there."

During stops to and from the Far East, Curry shared with other stewardesses one of the converted Quonset huts, which for a time bore a sign that read, "Home for Wayward Girls." "We had one-third of the hut, and the manager of the airport had two-thirds," she said. "For

stewardesses there was a two-bedroom living unit and bath. It was very comfortable. Because of all the snow, we couldn't walk around, so they would pick us up and drive us to meals which were given in another Quonset hut." In their idle hours employees played marathon poker games, hunted the army dump for souvenirs, and occasionally found stone tools from an old native culture. They also kept track of a dog that had escaped from a passenger during a refueling stop and ran loose on the island for about ten years. "Whalebone sometimes washed up on the island. . . . I thought, 'If only my mother could see me now,'" Curry said.

Later the U.S. military again used Shemya as a wartime fueling point during the Korean Conflict, when Northwest and other airlines airlifted personnel and supplies to the war zone. Finally the army deactivated Shemya as a base in 1954, dismantling ground approach and weather equipment. Northwest left the island and moved its refueling facilities nine hundred miles away to Cold Bay, Alaska. But after two years of suffering greater fueling needs, the airline leased back Shemya from the government and set up its own ground approach equipment. Shemya's military facilities, now called Eareckson Air Station, currently house early warning radar equipment and run under the management of a caretaker contractor. •

gendarmes met us, marched the entire group to the McDonald Hotel and put us under house arrest, while one soldier with a rifle and long bayonet stood guard over our plane," Gardner said. Unfortunately, nobody had notified the Canadian government that the flight was arriving. The survey crew had to turn around and return to Minnesota, but "just as soon as proper clearances had reached Edmonton, they welcomed us back with open arms," Gardner remembered. The second survey flight, piloted by Judd, examined the route all the way to Alaska.

Edmonton quickly became the hospitable headquarters for Northwest's Alaska operation, the start of a long route to the Aleutian Islands that included such remote settlements as Fort John and Fort Nelson, British Columbia; Watson Lake and Dawson, Yukon Territory; Fairbanks; and Anchorage. All equipment earmarked for new landing strips, hangars, living quarters, other buildings, and radio towers had to be disassembled and flown in, including a thousand-gallon gasoline truck and a few ten thousand–gallon storage tanks that traveled with their own welding crews ready to complete the assembly. "Load 'em heavy, gas 'em light. Send 'em out in the Yukon night," went one ditty credited to a Northwest dispatcher in Edmonton.

Sometimes unsure who actually owned the land they were using, Northwest crews began working and asked questions later. (Once asked to produce a lease for a Far North property, a manager spooled off yards of toilet paper and said, "Here's your lease.") It was wintertime during one of the coldest years in memory with temperatures of minus seventy degrees Fahrenheit and below.

Because overexposure of the skin or lungs to arctic air could cause severe injury, mechanics and construction staff avoided working outside. "Bare hands doing delicate work could stand the icy winds and the silent cold for no more than a few seconds at a time on the coldest days," wrote a reporter for *Air Transportation* magazine. "Rubber hose shattered into pieces like glass. Fingers quivering with cold tried to fix a nut to a bolt and succeeded after possibly an entire hour of trying. Three men had to work in shifts to change one spark plug. Workers wore scarves over their mouths to keep their lungs from freezing and engines had to be kept running for fear that once shut off they could not be started again." For longer stays, mechanics drained the engines of oil and stored the lubricant indoors. The cold affected more than the ground workers. "On one hop with a planeload of military personnel," detailed a report of the Office of War Information, "the pilots were alarmed by strange vibrations that shook the ship periodically. They finally discovered the source—the passengers were stamping their feet to keep warm."

High winds forced maintenance workers to hold onto lifelines as they refueled planes, and mechanics had to crawl across ramps slicked with windblown ice. Ultimately, though, "six great airports, capable of handling the largest military aircraft, have been carved out

A Morse code telegraph transmitter went into service at the airline's station at Watson Lake, Yukon Territory, Canada, in 1942.

Portable warming houses offer a refuge from the Canadian cold for Northwest workers Robert Mehlin and Joseph Bordreaux in 1943.

in the Canadian wilderness in what Canadians call 'the greatest feat of bush engineering of all time,'" the *Minneapolis Star Journal* observed.

Many of the heroics were cloaked in secrecy, and the American and Canadian public was in the dark about Northwest's activities in the Northern Region. In one secret construction project that the army asked Northwest to complete in typically harsh conditions, the airline flew into Alaska an electricity generating plant for a communications center, assembled it in place, and got the plant going—all in daylong darkness and what an observing reporter called "frightful weather conditions" of minus seventy-three degrees Fahrenheit with sixty-miles-an-hour winds blowing. The departure of frigid weather in the spring did not provide much relief, because fields turned to mud, flies descended en masse, and mosquitos arrived in swarms.

The shimmering of the region's fabled northern lights disrupted radio communications, which Northwest technicians overcame by using signals at rarely used ends of the radio spectrum. Flying crews faced other dangers. Many crews crashed after getting lost or hitting bad weather, including one that went down in February 1943 in icy conditions two miles short of the runway at Watson Lake, Yukon Territory. It took two months for searchers to find the remains.

Northwest employees were not prepared for what awaited them up north. Upon his arrival at the still uncompleted airfield in 1942 at Watson Lake, pilot John "Red" Kennedy approached "the only large building I could see. It was made of logs. A very large man came out to meet me. I introduced myself . . . and told him I'd like to get to town or to the hotel," Kennedy later recalled. His welcomer laughed and "told me to forget about a town or hotel—that my new living quarters was a tent down by the lake. This would have been fine in the summer, but it was still cold and more than forty inches of ice was still on the lake. . . . It was tough to stay warm."

The Watson Lake work camp was so remote and its airfield so primitive that supply pilots sometimes flew past it, depriving workers of mail and parcels from home. Once radio communications were functional, the camp staffers would let Edmonton know of its plight. Soon afterward the flight from Edmonton would swoop low over the Watson Lake airfield and drop bags of mail onto the frozen ground. "The mail was wonderful," one Northwest employee remarked, "but mom's sugar cookies didn't stand the drop so well."

Despite these hardships at Watson Lake, Northwest employees considered the station at Fort Nelson, British Columbia, to be the worst stop on the route. "We lived in Army Stout houses made of fiberboard," remembered one unfortunate worker sent there. "They were 10-by-10 feet, or 10-by-12, and slept four. They were heated with kerosene stoves. The Army produced them by the millions. The 'town' of Fort Nelson was five miles away on the Nelson River, and the only thing going there was the Hudson Bay Trading Post. We worked 12 hours a day, seven days a week. There was no running water or inside toilets. And the Army took over the mess hall (need I say more?). I was there a year and a half."

Amid all the planned work, Northwest flight crews frequently had to jump into action when other military workers unexpectedly needed help. On one occasion, the airline flew in a complete sawmill for use at a construction site. Another time, a military hospital in Nome burned down; within two days, Northwest flights originating in St. Louis had loaded and carried in the entire contents of a medical facility. The airline quickly responded to the grounding of a cargo ship off the Alaskan coast by hauling two tons of dynamite used to free the vessel. During December 1942, the airline delivered a planeload of ice cream, candy, turkeys, and the makings of holiday dinners to workers along the line from Edmonton into the heart of Alaska. Nobody panicked when the ice cream, frozen rock hard, was inedible. Northwest staffers heated the ice cream on a stove before serving.

Within weeks after Northwest agreed to be the military's "flying boxcars" to Alaska, the airline began regular service to the Far North on March 15, 1942. An enormous stream of personnel, supplies, fuel, mail, equipment, and building materials traveled the route, much of it to airfields Northwest had built alongside the new Alaska Highway. And the effort had begun none too soon, because, as feared, the Japanese invaded Alaska in June 1942. The Aleutian Islands of Kiska, Attu, and Agattu were in the enemy's possession. Northwest pilots ferried bombers and bombs in preparation for the ouster of the invaders. In one instance, a pilot made seven two-thousand-mile round-trips from Anchorage to Umnak Island, one of the Aleutians still in U.S. hands, in a single shift before sleeping. In a land long traversed by dogsleds, a few trains, and a small fleet of ships along the coasts and up rivers, Northwest had battered open a new entry by air.

As an important part of Northwest's Northern Region responsibilities, pilots ferried planes and supplies through Alaska to the Soviet Union, whose pilots picked up these essential materials in Fairbanks or Nome and flew them across Siberia to the war's eastern

A Northwest crew manning a tractor and sleigh work at Fort Nelson, British Columbia, circa 1943.

The cramped fuselage of an Air Transport Command U.S. Army Air Force plane carrying cargo and passengers between the Lower 48 and Alaska, 1943.

front. Most of the Russian pilots were women, and the Americans were not allowed to fraternize with them. The Soviets arrived on transport planes that, bizarrely, had stovepipes protruding from the fuselage to vent a woodstove in the main cabin. Fighter planes that arrived by this long route changed the course of the Battle of Stalingrad, thus handing the German military a devastating setback. (A crew of Northwest workers in Missoula, Montana, had painted the distinctive Communist red stars on the fighter planes.)

The winter of 1942–43 was even colder than the previous one. For long stretches temperatures lingered at minus forty degrees Fahrenheit. Aircraft mechanics did their work only with the help of canvas tarps that made instant enclosures and massively powerful heaters that ran on aviation fuel and blew warmth through flexible hoses. So much snow fell that plowing became impractical. Instead, workers drove corrugated rollers over the runways to compress the snow, which worked fine until the alternating thaws and freezing of spring. Then the rolled runways "got awfully rough," one worker observed.

In the spring of 1943, Allied soldiers dislodged the Japanese occupiers of Attu—killing 2,350 of the enemy—and within months Kiska and Agattu were similarly liberated. It happened with Northwest's help. "According to navy officials, retaking of the Aleutians would have been postponed for months if air transport had not been able to fly in men and cargo quickly, and in great quantity," the Office of War Information reported. With all North America back in U.S. and Canadian possession, Northwest's role in Alaska gradually diminished to supplying the remaining military bases in the Aleutians and on the mainland, including flying three daily round-trips to the westernmost island of Attu. By the end of the war, mostly piloting converted DC-3s, Northwest captains had flown more than twenty-one million miles along the route to Alaska, and this experience served the airline well when peace returned.

Several Northwest employees won Army Air Medals—rarely awarded to civilians—for their work on the Alaska campaign. Frank Christian and Raymond Dyjak were honored after they died while flying supplies, and Roman Justiss and Lloyd Milner earned the medals for training military aircrews in the use of navigational equipment. Northwest's Northern Region staff was not officially part of the military and received no military benefits at the war's end. Not until decades later, and by an act of Congress, did they become eligible for some benefits.

MODIFYING BOMBERS

Just days after the company committed its help to the Alaskan airlift, a group of British War Mission and U.S. Army officers arrived in St. Paul to ask Northwest to seal another military-related pact. "This was the problem they outlined," wrote airline historian Kenneth Ruble. "America's industrial might had roared into high gear, turning out critically needed bombers on an assembly line basis that the Axis Powers could not match. But it was not practical to slow down these fast-moving assembly lines in order to incorporate sophisticated new scientific improvements being created almost continuously. Nor was it practical to slow down production by pausing to customize a portion of the output for special missions or for service in different climates."

Northwest could help by planning, constructing, and operating in St. Paul a gigantic plant to modify aircraft in need of specialized equipment for combat. The bomber manufacturing facilities elsewhere could keep cranking out planes at top speed, while Northwest employees could put customized finishing touches on the aircraft that needed them. The plant would focus on the modification of B-24 Liberator bombers and B-25 Mitchell bombers. This would be no small task, requiring the hiring of nearly six thousand new employees and a massive undertaking to build and equip the modification plant.

Northwest agreed and began work within a half-week with the appearance in the Twin Cities of a group of B-25 bombers requiring retrofitting for desert warfare; these aircraft needed camouflage painting and the installation of equipment suitable for use in the African heat. The British planned to use them as soon as possible in the Sahara against the forces of Nazi general Erwin Rommel. Scraping together a few dozen workers and space in its own Holman Field facilities as well as a borrowed Air National Guard hangar, Northwest got the facility (nicknamed the "Mod") going and found a way to give the

A poster glorifies the labors of Northwest wartime workers in the Far North.

British bombers what they needed. These early modification jobs spilled out of the buildings and onto nearby fields and runways, protected from the elements by tarps, wooden planking, and hastily constructed sheds. Clearly, however, the airline had to accomplish much more planning and training in the techniques of plane modification before it could significantly shorten the list of aircraft awaiting changes.

The airline began by launching an enormous effort to train hundreds of workers. Many people already skilled in aviation mechanics had joined the U.S. military, leaving behind homemakers, retirees, autoworkers, office workers, salespeople, and students not engaged in essential war work. The Office of War Information colorfully characterized them as "beauty shop operators, barbers, soda fountain workers, school teachers, [and] milkmen." Northwest quickly taught these people how to install radar equipment (a new technology obliquely coded "H2-X" because of its secrecy) and autopilot gear, replace carburetors, equip planes with state-of-the-art cameras, and position machine guns, among many other duties. Meanwhile, construction began on a new modification hangar, one-third of a mile long, that was completed in December 1942 as work began on the erection of a similar building nearby. The second hangar would be ready for partial occupancy within six weeks. Together, the hangars enclosed 13.4 million cubic feet and could accommodate twenty-six bombers and swarms of workers.

A self-sufficient town of sorts arose alongside the Mod. The complex included a cavernous cafeteria that could feed twenty-five hundred, employee lounges, and a post office dedicated to the modification plant. The plant's employees could read their own newspaper, call their own fire department to extinguish blazes, and travel between facilities on their own bus service. The plant boasted a security force of four hundred directed by Ernest Yoris, a former detective for the Seattle Police Department.

Working around the clock on military planes—each valued at about $300,000 ($4.2 million in today's dollars)—Northwest employees installed weapons, heated suits,

Northwest produced posters to honor its wartime efforts and boost morale.

One of the hundreds of women who joined Northwest's workforce as St. Paul Bomber Modification Center employees, circa 1943.

windows, and oxygen outlets for new gunner stations; fitted reconnaissance planes with three-lensed cameras that spotted Japan's main base in the South Pacific on the island of Chuuk; and painted camouflage markings on bombers bound for desert and jungle regions. After six months in operation, the plant began modification work on planes slated for action in the Northern Region of Alaska and Canada. Northwest engineers devised the first winterization design for these aircraft, which included supplying the cabins with additional heat and window defrosting, installing carburetor and propeller deicing systems, and fashioning engine oil and hydraulic delivery systems that could function in temperatures far below zero. "Husband-and-wife teams, I was told, working together, often achieve the best production score. . . . Unusual labor-saving devices have been perfected," wrote St. Paul reporter Paul Light after touring the plant. "I can't discuss them very fully."

During the course of the war the St. Paul bomber modifiers tweaked more than thirty-two hundred aircraft. These accomplishments, among many others, were "scarcely less glorious than those of battle," said a U.S. Army official. And the press often covered and praised the work going on at Holman Field. "Each time America's huge Liberator bombers dropped their eggs on Hitler's European fortress and the [Japanese Pacific] bases, the skill and spirit of 4,500 men and women of the Twin Cities ride along," observed the *Minneapolis Times* in 1943.

Around that same time, a "celebrity aircraft" returned for additional work at the plant. It was a Liberator bomber previously modified some months earlier, which had then seen action in Allied attacks of the German naval base at Keel. It arrived in St. Paul "with a hole in the tail and another in one wing, each large enough for a man to walk through, with one tire shot off, all twelve of the propeller blades hit at least once, and with 300 major holes and . . . 2,000 minor holes," the Office of War Information noted. Before repair work on it started, modification plant staffers designated it "the most shot up plane in the European theater" to date.

The workforce was far more diverse than any that had previously walked through Northwest's doors. Bob Bailey, a mechanic measured at four feet one inch, often posed in photos next to the plant's tallest employees. More than fifteen hundred women worked as crew chiefs, mechanics, welders, and guards. Twelve blind workers performed an unusual assortment of specialized tasks for which their sensitivity to touch, the company believed, uniquely qualified them. For months, plant workers had been throwing out metal pieces and shavings that accumulated on the floor. These piles, however, included valuable dropped parts. A team of the blind employees went through the waste before disposal and was able to sort the recoverable items by type. They could distinguish the two dozen different sizes of bolts to within one-sixteenth of an inch—not to mention between a wide variety of screws, washers, and rivets—and the parts they rescued saved the plant thousands of dollars each month.

The secrecy surrounding radar—a technology not yet in the enemy's possession and credited with enabling Allied bombers to target hard-to-see industrial sites and even submarines—added awkwardness to the fast installations demanded of Northwest employees. Security guards followed the radar units from their arrival by train

St. Paul Bomber Modification employees gather for a celebration of the plant's Army–Navy "E" Award on November 24, 1944.

through their setup aboard the bombers and their shipment to Europe. Northwest's installers complained that they could not meet their installation quotas due to the guards' intrusive presence. Northwest sought advice from the manufacturer of the equipment, which assured the airline that security breaches were unimportant because of the rapid evolution of the technology. "After that," noted the supervisor of the modification plant, "we just took with a grain of salt any regulations that stood in the way of fast production, and kept on meeting our quotas." The security and regulations were well worth the trouble; radar allowed bombing to proceed during the poor weather of the D-Day invasion at Normandy and let aircrews pinpoint countless concrete-protected German submarine pens along Europe's Atlantic Coast.

The successes of the St. Paul modification plant led the army to contract Northwest at the end of 1942 to set up a similar facility in Vandalia, Ohio, near Dayton, which employed fifteen hundred people when it opened the following year. Called the Accelerated Service Testing Center, the plant examined, tested, and test-flew the first three planes of all new

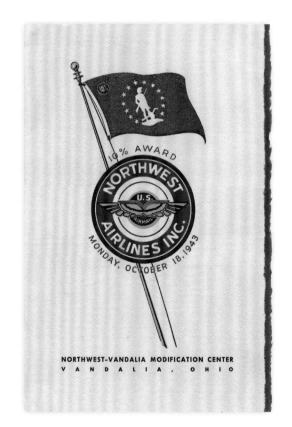

A printed program for an award celebration in 1943 from Northwest's test flight center in Vandalia, Ohio.

Vandalia mechanics Alvin Smith and William Kuntz outfit a transport plane with wing deicers, circa 1943.

A crowd of Northwest workers surrounds the St. Paul modification center's final aircraft, 1945.

aircraft models that American manufacturers produced for the military, including fighter planes, bombers, and even gliders that delivered anti-tank guns in the Normandy invasion. Debugging reports and recommendations from Northwest's employees in Vandalia went to the aircraft production factories to ensure that new planes coming off the assembly lines would fly as perfectly as possible.

The bombers modified by Northwest changed the course of the war. During the summer of 1944, for instance, nearly two hundred b-24s used equipment installed at Northwest's facilities to stage the important destruction of Romania's Ploiesti oil refineries, depriving the Germans of much-needed fuel. The government recognized Northwest's extraordinary contributions to aircraft modification in the fall of 1944, when thousands of people gathered at the St. Paul plant to receive the Army and Navy "E" Award for production excellence. Within a half hour of the ceremony's end, though, workers cleared away the seating, platform for dignitaries, and decorations and once again started up the modification lines. Northwest was "back at the grim task of making planes ready to deal death and destruction in foreign skies," a reporter for the *St. Paul Pioneer Press* wrote.

After the war's end, the St. Paul bomber modification plant—now nearly deserted—was useless. Peace had created a huge "white elephant." Northwest razed the facility in the fall of 1945 to clear space for the Metropolitan Airports Commission's planned expansion of Wold–Chamberlain Field, and the government struggled to find a home for eighty bombers, many bearing the insignia of the Australian Air Force, in the process of modification when Japan surrendered. "The planes are being readied to be flown away and eventually will be stored in the Utah desert, near Ogden, where some may be used for practice but most of them are likely to rot away through the years," the *St. Paul Dispatch* reported. Some fifteen thousand items worth millions of dollars went out the door as surplus property.

MILITARY RESEARCH AND TRAINING

Northwest's final major wartime undertaking for the military gathered together scientists, engineers, and army officers to train military personnel and conduct research on a variety of obscure but important topics. One group studied what happens when airborne water droplets strike the wings of planes. The goal was to reduce the hazards of icing, which under the wrong circumstances could afflict any aircraft, regardless of the latitude at which it flew, and change the aerodynamic contour of the craft or burden the plane with debilitating weight. "We tested everything—propeller icing, wing and tail icing, cabin heating, even several different types of propellers, including some that were hollow, and our missions went as far as Alaska," remembered Northwest's Walter Bullock, who piloted many of the experimental flights. "It was on a flight to Edmonton that we made the final tests before heat exchangers were put into assembly manufacture for the B-24." The team's newly developed technologies to remove ice left wings "almost as clean as a dentist's fingernails," according to *Time* magazine. As a result, American bombers were soon fitted with heated wings and propellers, which prevented crashes.

In 1943 the Naval Research Laboratories asked Northwest to help determine how dust and moisture in the air produced static that disrupted aviation radio communications. The airline built a hangar at Wold–Chamberlain Field that housed a lightning generator to create storm replicas, and it conducted test flights in snow, dust, and rain storms. It eventually developed an aircraft antenna that reduced static in tumultuous weather and built other devices to overcome the radio disturbances of bad weather.

In another research project, Northwest teamed up with engineers from Honeywell to test the effectiveness of an autopilot system, which for security reasons was code-named "George," and the famed Norden bombsight. The autopilot held the course of the plane during bombing runs, thus improving accuracy, and the bombsight gave bombardiers ways to more accurately direct the bombs upon release. Northwest also tested Honeywell's B-3 Turbo Supercharger Regulator System, which so greatly boosted the power of aircraft engines that bombers could climb higher than their opposing antiaircraft fire could reach.

In other wartime programs, Northwest trained more than seven hundred military pilots to fly cargo planes over long-distance routes to bases in the Pacific, taught instrument training at centers throughout the Midwest and West, led the instruction of complete military flight crews bound for action overseas, and taught navy personnel how to maintain plane engines and propellers aboard aircraft carriers.

OVER THE HUMP

In addition to these formalized programs, the U.S. military assigned Northwest a few hard-to-classify yet undeniably important wartime missions. One sent the company's flight crews on a notably hazardous route deep into Asia.

In April 1943, Chinese fighters were in great need of provisions and war supplies as they battled the advances of Japanese forces. The military's air transport command wanted to ferry ninety tons of materiel to India and then to the city of Kunming to support the Chinese, and it asked Northwest and Trans World Airlines to provide pilots and crews to get it all there, with assistance from army personnel, aboard a fleet of Curtiss Commando transport planes. Flying the route was no easy matter because of Japan's dangerous military presence, however, so the crews—which included fifteen Northwest pilots, one of them only twenty years old, and famed Northwest captain Frank C. Judd—had to follow a long and perilous route nicknamed "The Hump."

Flying "The Hump" required crossing the Himalayas at altitudes as high as twenty thousand feet, far higher than the unpressurized transport planes' safe altitude limit. The airline crews began their overseas journey—the longest mission of transport planes then ever attempted—in Miami, Florida, before making the ocean crossing to Asia. Once in India, the squadron could look ahead to a mountain crossing already littered with the aluminum hulls of crashed and shot-down transport planes. The squadron made it over, but at much risk and some emotional cost. Captain Judd, for instance, never discussed the mission after the war. "He didn't talk about these things," said a relative after Judd's death in 1984. "Like most people of that era, after the war, he just got on with life. We only wish we had known about his adventures when he was alive."

Two years later, the U.S. military made one last request of Northwest. Although the Allies had achieved victory in Europe, the effort against Japan was still underway. Large numbers of America's European fighters had to find a way to the Pacific Coast. Military authorities asked the airline to create yet another cross-continental air route, as it already had done from the Midwest into Alaska. "For this impromptu transcontinental line," historian Kenneth Ruble wrote, "the Air Force provided a fleet of 15 transports while Northwest supplied flight crews, maintenance and all operational services on a regular schedule of four round trips per day from Newark to Seattle via Buffalo, the Twin Cities, Fargo, Billings and Spokane. This temporary airline continued to operate for six months, because after Japan's surrender, it helped speed returning GIs to separation centers in the East. More than 30,000 military passengers were carried in all."

And with that quickly assembled effort, Northwest's military duties ended. The company's civilian passenger business had sunk to a wartime low in 1943, with only ninety-three thousand passengers carried. But ahead lay an exciting period in which the airline's traditional civilian business regained focus in the midst of the new technologies and tactical skills that Northwest had developed during the war.

RAPID GROWTH

Prognosticators gave a glorious forecast of the good times ahead for the airline. "Picture, for instance, a luxury airliner plunging through the overcast at 300 miles an hour, piloted by a man who is not even on board!" declared Carl Swanson, Northwest's supervisor of communications. "He sits at a table in the airport control room, perhaps 50 miles away, with only a light on the screen before him showing the position of the plane. And back in the bar-lounge of the big ship, you, one of 100 passengers, watch the progress of the Minnesota-Iowa football game by television."

Even earlier, one of Northwest's plant engineers had foreseen a postwar airport that would dazzle passengers accustomed to rather small and simple facilities. Exotic grocery stores, he believed, would soon populate the commercial centers he envisioned for airports. "In the early future," he said, "Minneapolis will undoubtedly be no more than 60 hours away from any spot on earth, so delicacies, which otherwise would spoil in the long shipment from India, for instance, could easily be shipped by plane and sold fresh at these markets." Northwest architect Francis Meisch predicted that factories manufacturing airplane parts and other goods requiring quick shipment would also fill these airport cities.

Although these advancements did not materialize as expected, other genuine hints of the future appeared. During the war, thousands of people in military and government service traveled by airplane for the first time in their lives, and the experience made enthusiastic air travelers out of many of them. They appreciated the comfort and time savings of going aloft. New military routes like Northwest's Northern Region flights to Alaska had blazed trails, as well. "The interest in air travel created by the war has been tremendous," observed Bert Kinsman, Northwest's general traffic manager. "Aviation is one industry that is going forward after the war."

Northwest had to prepare for this postwar business boom by acquiring the Douglas DC-4, a four-engine plane ideal for longer routes and capable of carrying sixty-two passengers; it already had performed well in wartime duty. Many other airlines also waited in line. Northwest rented a surplus military version of the DC-4 to learn its flight characteristics and maintenance requirements as a head start. And when the new aircraft arrived—eighteen by the fall of 1946— Northwest had trouble running its schedules on time. Too many new planes were joining the fleet, too many passengers crowded the cabins, and the high demand for flights forced the airline to hire inexperienced maintenance crews. Quick growth was painful.

All airlines felt the imminent explosive growth of their industry. As a sign of things to come and in a strange reversal of wartime modification work, military transport planes, including many DC-3s, began undergoing conversion

Passengers aboard a Northwest flight during the 1940s.

The Douglas DC-4, adapted from a troop and cargo carrier of World War II.

for use as civilian airliners. Northwest crews repainted the company's colors over camouflage designs and installed standard passenger seating in cabins that had been stripped to hold troops and cargo. In the summer of 1945, one of these DC-3s hosted a highly unusual event. A team of astronomers from the University of Minnesota, Princeton University, and General Electric Corporation boarded a regularly scheduled flight on a scientific mission to take in an extended view of a total eclipse of the sun; it was the nation's only commercial flight that intersected with the twenty-five-mile-wide "belt of totality" over Montana and Idaho. While stewardesses handed out smoked glasses to all the passengers, the scientific team made its observations above bad weather that foiled the efforts of other scientists on the ground. The Northwest crew helped in the gathering of data.

In other respects, too, Northwest's fleet changed after the war. The modern Martin 303 attracted the airline as a replacement for the hard-worked DC-3s, but Martin could not deliver the 303 quickly and recommended that Northwest accept the fast-flying but smaller 202 instead, which was designed for midrange flights and one of the first commercial planes to come with its own loading ramp. Northwest agreed, making the worst plane acquisition decision in its history. The airline received twenty-five of the 202s but eventually canceled its order for fifteen more. Unfortunately, a defect in their wing spar produced instability and made them dangerous rides. One Northwest Martin 202 crashed in 1948, and three more accidents followed in 1950. Within a few years, even after safety modifications of the aircraft, these disasters caused most airlines to pull every Martin plane off their routes. The Boeing 377, the legendary eighty-three-seat Stratocruiser, arrived in 1947.

In 1945, the passenger tally had climbed nearly fourfold from the wartime low. That

The ill-fated Martin 202 joined Northwest's fleet in 1947.

Northwest's Midway Ticket Office in the Twin Cities, circa 1948.

New York mayor Fiorello La Guardia accepts flowers from Northwest stewardess Rose Oedbauer on the occasion of the airline's route expansion to America's largest city, 1945.

Packets of gum distributed to flight-discomfited passengers during the 1940s and 1950s.

Stewardess Joanne Larpenteur (center) helps a Yakima chamber of commerce official and the local Apple Blossom Princess load fruit for the opening of Washington National Airport in 1948.

year's addition of a route extension to New York City, making Northwest a true coast-to-coast airline, helped boost the passenger totals. (Once settled in New York, Northwest was subject to the sometimes unusual scrutiny of its local media. In June 1949, for instance, the *New Yorker* included in its "Talk of the Town" section a brief item about one of its reporters who witnessed a bird carrying twigs into the tail section of a Northwest plane parked at LaGuardia Field. The item concluded: "He is of the opinion that the simplehearted bird was not laying a fire but building a nest.") By the start of 1946, Northwest had 388 pilots and within a few months could claim a net worth of $9.9 million, fifth largest of U.S. airlines.

Nine months before the war's end, on the Alaskan island of Adak, employee Ben Blenner became one of the first people at Northwest to hear the news that the Civil Aeronautics Board had finally approved the airline's application to extend passenger service to New York City. His source? A broadcast of Tokyo Rose, a Japanese radio propagandist who targeted U.S. service members.

The elected officials of the newly linked regions completed the formalities of this route by exchanging presents the following year. Minnesota governor Edward J. Thye sent his New York counterpart, Thomas E. Dewey, a frozen great northern pike, and the mayor of Seattle, William Devin, offered New York City mayor Fiorello La Guardia a totem pole. Northwest launched its first transcontinental flight from Seattle on June 1, 1945, making five stops before reaching New York.

The Civil Aeronautics Board awarded Northwest many other new (or previously discontinued)

Northwest's western routes greatly increased in number after World War II.

routes during and immediately after the war: to Spokane in 1944; Duluth in 1945; Newark in 1945; Anchorage in 1946 (a reward for the airline's stellar service in Alaska during wartime; Northwest flew twenty-nine-ton prefabricated homes from Wisconsin to Anchorage to shelter employees during an acute housing shortage); Washington, D.C., in 1947; La Crosse, Wisconsin, in 1947; and Hawaii in 1947. Two thousand islanders met the first Northwest flight to Honolulu in 1948, and the plane was in good shape for the journey after four native Hawaiians gave it a ritual splashing with the waters of the Mississippi River, Puget Sound, and Pearl Harbor before taking off. The airline's operation of a "shadow" service several years before, completely on paper, greatly aided the logistical planning required to serve Hawaii.

HEADING WEST TO THE EAST

Northwest's commercial expansion to Alaska was but a step toward a much larger prize: the Far East. For years, Croil Hunter had coveted Asia as the airline's first overseas destination. Northwest had undertaken each step westward—to Montana, to Seattle, to Anchorage—with the idea of extending its reach across the Pacific. In 1931, Charles and Anne Morrow Lindbergh had shown that following a polar air path to Asia saved significant time and distance over routes that paralleled the mapmakers' lines of latitude. Five years later, a team of Soviet aviators had further established the practicality of the route by successfully undertaking the world's longest nonstop flight from Moscow and over the pole to Vancouver, Washington.

Traveling over the North Pole from New York to Japan cut two thousand miles off the distance that mid-Pacific routes required. Northwest, with its success and experience flying in cold climates, was the first U.S. airline to seriously consider a polar route to Asia, and it presented its scheme in its route applications with the Civil Aeronautics Board. The airline called this course the Great Circle route.

The Civil Aeronautics Board showed its satisfaction with Northwest's planning in 1946 by certifying the airline for service to the Far East from New York and Chicago via Minneapolis–St. Paul, Edmonton, and Anchorage, with a second line originating in Seattle and stopping in Anchorage. When Senator Pat McCarran of Nevada tried to block Northwest's rollout of Asian service by introducing a bill that would instead subsidize a single air carrier—most likely Pan Am—in exercising a monopoly on the routes to avoid costly competition and repel foreign airlines, Hunter hastened to Washington to denounce the threat to business. With some exaggeration, he termed McCarran's bill "a serious threat to the American system of free enterprise that would lead to government ownership of all transportation." Hunter's testimony helped kill the bill.

ESCAPE FROM SHANGHAI 🧭

Northwest began service to Shanghai, China's largest city, in 1947, when a civil war between the Nationalist army of Chiang Kai-shek and Mao Tse-tung's Communist forces already was smoldering. Inflation raged out of control. "To meet our Shanghai payroll, an assistant and I used to take a truck to the bank once a week and load boxes, barrels and bags with $500,000 bundles of Chinese money," said Northwest employee Paul Benscoter. "Our Chinese employees would carry their pay home in gunny sacks."

The war overwhelmed Shanghai by the opening months of 1949, and the airline's final flight into the city carried a fresh supply of U.S. currency, the one stable medium of payment, for Northwest's Orient Region vice president Don King. Although it was clear that the city would soon fall to the Communists, King and district traffic manager J. P. Farrell did not evacuate with other businesspeople and their dependents. They remained behind to save as much airline property as possible.

Northwest's planes offered some of the few available means of escape, and the company scheduled extra flights out. Staffers removed the armrests to accommodate additional passengers, who could see the battle lines of the civil war from the air as soon as they lifted off. A heartbreaking scene surrounded the departure of the final flight from Shanghai. "We had four passengers loaded in every double seat, but that good old DC-4, a great airplane if there ever was one, strained off the Lunghwa Airport runway, all four engines at full throttle, out over the bay toward Tokyo," Benscoter recalled. "The plane was overloaded and I don't care who knows it. Thousands of persons, both Chinese and foreigners, were left behind. Some were crying. Some begged on their knees for a seat on the plane. They offered thousands of dollars for seats. One offered his life savings, another a fortune in jewels. It was the most difficult thing our personnel ever did to say no to these people. Machine-gun fire was hitting the airport as the plane door was shut in their faces."

Northwest's red tails would not again offer commercial service to China for another thirty-four years. •

As in the past, Northwest used a set of survey flights to scout the route to Japan, Korea, China, and the Philippines. The survey planes were DC-3s stripped down to create space in the cabin for six 100-gallon fuel drums. The extra fuel more than doubled the flying range of the DC-3s. "We spent three or four days setting things up," remembered Paul Benscoter, Northwest's Orient Region vice president, of the events immediately following the first survey flight. "All of us were horrified by conditions. The Japanese had no food, and block after block of homes were in irreparable condition. One of the first commercial places to be reestablished in the postwar period was the Takashimya department store, the Marshall Field of Tokyo. They had practically nothing, a few fish in the basement, postcards and carved wooden dolls and strangely, shelf after shelf of Kiwi shoe polish." Charcoal powered the taxicabs. Northwest employees found Shanghai considerably more prosperous and cheerful. Benscoter noted that

Members of Northwest's crew survey the route to Asia, February 1947.

Northwest heavily promoted its new service to Asia in 1947.

"our early operation in the Orient was pretty much 'played by ear,' and we subsisted largely because of our ability to scrounge."

Northwest staffers began the enormous task of setting up maintenance and fueling bases along the route, building radio towers, arranging housing, and hiring workers in preparation for the inauguration of Far East service. The company established an office in Tokyo two blocks from General Douglas MacArthur's U.S. occupation headquarters, and it built a subdivision of twenty homes for staff in the suburb of Shibuya. Some staff, however, overnighted in a home that formerly belonged to a member of the Japanese royal family. A grand circular staircase led from the reception hall to the upstairs rooms. "The pilots and stewardesses stayed there," recalled retired flight attendant Phyllis Curry. "The stewardesses had a room that was cute, and it was just as the Japanese had left it. It had straw mats and straw sliding doors, although they furnished it with beds to replace the sleeping mats." The house also included dining facilities, "where we were encouraged to eat so we wouldn't get sick from the Japanese food," Curry said.

The airline hauled two million pounds of equipment, fleets of buses, trucks, and automobiles, entire electric generating plants, and nearly 250 employees to sites in Asia. It built Tokyo's first long-range air-to-ground radio-telephone station, which it later gave to the Japanese government. Just as important, Northwest started its staff on a path of understanding the customs and business traditions of the East. Northwest managers overcame language barriers in unexpected ways; during one meeting with Chinese partners in Shanghai, they established rapport with the Chinese by teaching them the game of Rock, Paper, Scissors.

Using its new DC-4 airliners, Northwest began three-times-weekly service to Asia on July 15, 1947, which established the first scheduled commercial flights between the United States and Japan. A chain of celebrations followed the

The housing complex for Northwest crew in Tokyo, formerly the home of a Japanese royal family.

The crew (and Chinese soldiers) after Northwest's first flight to Shanghai, 1947.

The ceremonies began in New York for Northwest's first flight to Asia in 1947.

Girls in ceremonial dress offer gifts to Northwest crew members after one of the airline's first commercial flights to Japan in 1947.

The crew members of Northwest's inaugural commercial flight to Tokyo, Seoul, Shanghai, and Manila, July 15, 1947.

inaugural flight eastward across the United States. Northwest employee Jack Hinkley recalled that although the inaugural airliner was supposed to receive in New York a ritual bathing of Okinawa seawater, "the water actually came from a faucet in NWA's LaGuardia 'facilities.'" An order of Minnesota-made artificial limbs was among the first cargo shipments to Japan that the airline carried.

For the next five years, until Northwest introduced Stratocruiser aircraft to the route, passengers spent thirty-six hours, thirty-five minutes en route from the Twin Cities to Tokyo aboard the unpressurized planes, allowing customers to "eat breakfast one day in Minneapolis and breakfast the next day in Shanghai," calculated the *Minneapolis Star Journal*. The spectacular scenery included the rugged terrain of western Canada, the snowy peaks and frozen tundra of Alaska, the western part of the Bering Strait, and the endless breakers of the Pacific Ocean.

A promotional poster for flights to China, 1950.

Northwest's ticket office in Taipei, Taiwan, late 1940s.

The initial flights were limited to twenty-four passengers (a seating capacity later enlarged) because tanks of extra fuel occupied much of the cabin space. Military service members and their families often filled the passenger lists. "On one DC-4 that I flew out of Tokyo, there were forty-four passengers in seats—a full load—and twenty-two babies," recalled Phyllis Curry. Flight crews could bring into Japan up to ten cartons of cigarettes on each trip, which were worth a small fortune on the black market. Relief crews boarded the flights at Anchorage, at a refueling stop on the Aleutian island of Shemya, and in Tokyo. "Looking back, I consider that I was flying in the days of the dinosaurs," retired radio operator Jerome Koerner later said. Northwest's Far East service later enlarged to include flights to Okinawa and Taipei, Taiwan.

Five years after opening its route to Asia, Northwest played a surprising role in the launch of Japan Airlines. U.S. occupation regulations did not allow a homegrown airline to purchase its own planes, so Northwest provided a start-up fleet of four aircraft for JAL's initial operations in 1951. It helped more, however, by loaning crew members to the new airline, training personnel, and coaching JAL in maintenance techniques. Northwest supervised the new airline's first flights connecting Tokyo, Nagoya, Osaka, and other cities. (Rumors persist that Northwest trainers had to dissuade the new Japanese ticket agents from overbooking flights by selling standing space to "strap-hangers.") Northwest gave similar assistance to aviation authorities in China, helping set up a government regulatory agency modeled after America's and guiding the construction of airports and radio systems.

The first DC-4 with "Northwest Orient" painted on its tail, circa 1947.

The spacious and uncrowded western terminal at Wold–Chamberlain field, 1947.

CLOTHING THAT WEARS LIKE IRON

Aside from branches of the military, youth scouting groups, athletic teams, and police departments, few organizations depend on uniforms as much as airlines to imprint an image upon the public. Airlines make uniforms stand for professionalism, sobriety, worldliness, hipness, and a host of other qualities that they want their employees to embody.

Northwest introduced its first uniforms for crew members in 1929. Pilots were fitted with six-button coats, later adorned with wings on the left breast and stripes—two for captains and one for first officers—on the sleeve. When stewardesses first joined the company in 1939, they opened up a new world of tailoring possibilities. "Our uniforms were dark brown worsted wool, with a pointed cap to match," remembered Dorothy Stumph, Northwest's first stewardess. Beneath the jacket was a blue blouse. The outfit had a Northwest Airlines logo embroidered on the blouse and jacket, and stewardesses were required to wear the hat every working hour. Some described the hat as "a giant-sized beret." Brown shoes, a brown purse, and gloves accessorized the uniform. ("General Dwight Eisenhower might have gotten his pattern for the famed 'Ike' jacket from this early uniform," the *St. Paul Pioneer Press* speculated years later.) "Rosie Stein bought [the uniforms] at Field & Schlick in St. Paul, and they wore like iron. In fact, we kept hoping they'd wear out a little sooner than they did," Stumph said.

During the summer, Northwest's early stewardesses donned sharkskin shirts with matching small hats. "The tan sharkskin uniform wrinkled badly and was soon replaced in 1941 by a summer uniform from Harold's store in Minneapolis," wrote Helen Jacobson Richardson, the third hired stewardess. "The uniform was a light blue, one-button suit with two skirts, a matching hat, with the Northwest Airlines emblem embroidered in navy blue on the left breast pocket and on the matching hat. The first hat was a flat tam which did not stay on." With that

Northwest captain Walter Bullock models a flight coat in use during the late 1920s and early 1930s.

A graduating class of flight attendants in 1968 shows their olive colors.

A flight attendant wears the stylish red uniform of the early 1970s.

A flight attendant's uniform of the 1970s.

flaw soon corrected, stewardesses could comfortably meet the public in warm weather.

The winter stewardesses' uniform had already changed, as well. The new suit was navy blue gabardine with an eight-button jacket adorned with the Northwest insignia on the left breast. "A conventional white blouse, navy blue shoes, purse and pigskin gloves finished the uniform," Richardson recalled.

Stewardesses of the 1950s wore powder-blue uniforms and white blouses; outdoors they could add a full-cut coat with hood. During the fashion-conscious 1960s, new pieces—Oriental jackets, Hawaiian muumuus, and lounge jackets—made up the uniform, and hip miniskirts with knee-high boots soon joined the mix. Northwest's embrace of psychedelic-era trends, however, never attained the heights of such airlines as Pacific Southwest and Southern, where leg-baring stewardesses were a main selling point.

These uniforms underwent continual evolution. To replace a stale line of conservative red outfits in the late 1980s, Northwest asked several fashion designers to take part in a competition. The winner, creator of a set of maroon uniforms that cost the airline $4 million, was Chicago-based Hart Schaffner Marx. (The firm later tailored many of President Barack Obama's suits.) Northwest's supervisor of flight attendants captured the symbolic weight of the uniforms when he called them "a fantasy of what air transportation used to be, reviving Northwest's 60-year legacy of dedication to the best in air travel." The airline introduced the uniforms to their wearers in a series of musical fashion shows presented at Northwest bases around the world. In the difficult days after the Northwest-Republic merger, the uniforms bore the burden of representing the airline's pride, spirit, and renewed dedication to customers.

Twenty years later, uniforms strategically announced to passengers the finality of Northwest's acquisition by Delta Airlines. Flight attendants, pilots, and gate and ticketing agents began wearing Delta's trademark red and blue uniforms nine months in advance of the merger's conclusion. •

A tailor helps fit flight attendant Mick Barens with a new uniform in 1986.

Flight officers, flight attendants, ground crew, and service agents in uniform in 1976.

FLYING IN THE 1940S

Many of the cramped domestic airports that Northwest flew from, poorly equipped for growth or the accommodation of larger aircraft, needed expansion. One passenger remembered the Twin Cities' Wold–Chamberlain Field of the 1940s for "the smallness of the terminal, the absence of chaos, and the well-dressed waiting passengers. We might all have been preparing to board the *Queen Mary*." Wold–Chamberlain underwent a transformation to become Minneapolis–St. Paul International Airport in 1948. Similarly, a new airport succeeded Seattle's Boeing Field, built in 1929. At an initial cost of $1.35 million, Bow Lake Airport (later called Sea-Tac) arose starting in 1947 halfway between Seattle and Tacoma to become the home of Northwest's Western Region, with many later expansions to come.

A hint of what technology would offer in more sophisticated form in the future: Northwest in 1947 announced its use of an early computerized information-retrieval system that was speeding up flight reservations. The airline's reservations director called it an "electric brain" capable of providing agents with seating information within a fifth of a second. "Essentially the electronic brain consists of a magnetized metal drum which would accept electronic impulses flashed from other cities along [Northwest's] system, requesting seats," a newspaper article reported. "This drum is capable . . . of storing complete information on seats available on every NWA flight for 30 days."

Passengers and Northwest employees could only dream of what the 1950s would bring. Most, at first, would feel disappointed.

CHAPTER 4

LITHE MAN WITH A BRIGHT SMILE

Northwest Airlines moved through the first part of the 1950s in disarray, and the state of the fleet reflected the company's internal disorder. Aside from its Boeing Stratocruisers, which customers loved but cost a fortune to keep in the air, the airline's remaining aircraft were an aging, ragtag bunch. The company had sold off many of its remaining DC-3s and DC-4s during the late 1940s, but the Martin 202s in which Northwest had invested so heavily as replacements were quickly gone, casualties of crashes and the resulting loss of confidence in their airworthiness. "The Martin 202 has become a bad risk. . . . Now, I know how much of an investment Northwest Airlines has in this particular ship. . . . It is time now to ground them. And not for a period of a few days," radio commentator Paul Harvey had declared on the air to millions of listeners after another fatal crash in 1951. Northwest president Croil Hunter lamented the unluckiness of his company's predicament: "You go fourteen years without scratching a passenger, and then the accidents hit you all at once," he said.

Now Northwest had to scrape together an assortment of leased Douglas aircraft, the same types it had just sold off, to meet its route commitments. Other airlines had larger and newer planes. While most of its competitors greatly enlarged the number of seats they could offer passengers per mile during the early 1950s, Northwest's seats had actually grown fewer. Profits shrank. (And to further frustrate Northwest, the hexed Martin aircraft it had flung away went on after modifications to fly long and safely in the service of other airlines.)

This elderly mix of remaining planes did worse than simply hold insufficient seating. They also produced piloting confusion and inefficiencies. "There were eight different types and configurations of the DC-4 alone," remembered general manager of flight operations

Northwest's city ticket office in downtown Minneapolis, 1950.

During the spring of 1952, the floodwaters of the Mississippi River inundated Northwest's operations facilities at Holman Field in St. Paul.

Northwest made strenuous efforts to help the public understand the advantages of flying the polar route.

Water rises in the engine shop at Holman Field during spring flooding in 1952.

Bill Hochbrunn, "different warning light systems, different switches, different locations for important controls, even different directions in which they were activated." Pilots who moved from the DC-4s to DC-3s and Stratocruisers suffered even more bewilderment.

The fatigued fleet dragged down the company. "Public confidence had been shaken, . . . employee morale sagged, financial lenders were frankly dubious about the company's future, and competitors could better any planes Northwest had to offer except the Stratocruiser," company historian Kenneth Ruble concluded. It looked like the airline was spiraling down. Rumors swirled of Northwest selling its most valuable routes to the Far East, and the company's common stock plunged in value.

To make matters worse, the flooding waters of the Mississippi River made Northwest's operations home at St. Paul's Holman Field a mess during the spring of 1952. At risk were aircraft, parts, equipment, and supplies worth millions of dollars. Seven hundred employees fought to save the company's hangars and maintenance buildings from this record inundation, using armies of trucks, mountains of sandbags, and whatever equipment lay at hand. They built a five-foot-high and twenty-five-hundred-foot-long wall to protect the base, but water still seeped through and entered one of the hangars. Workers jacked up a disabled and dismantled DC-4 high above the rippling waters, where it looked like a strange aquatic beast. Some employees had to pilot boats to work. The losses to Northwest totaled $550,000 in equipment costs and damage as well as in suspended operations.

STRUGGLING TO CHANGE COURSE

In this dismal time—the most difficult period in the company's history since the loss of its airmail contracts during the Great Depression—president Croil Hunter and Northwest's board of directors grasped at improvements. In 1952, Northwest began negotiations with Capital Airlines and ended with a preliminary agreement to merge the two carriers. The resulting airline would boast a nation-high combined 8,089 miles on its routes, outdistancing runners-up United and American. "The combination is a natural," Hunter said, "because Capital's routes fit so well into our pattern. Most important, it opens the Chicago gateway to the East." Capital, founded in 1927 as Pennsylvania Airlines, mainly served the industrial cities of the Northeast as well as destinations in the South. Since the end of World War II, it had experienced declining business and profits.

The proposed merger alarmed the Twin Cities community, which would undoubtedly lose employees and a corporate headquarters to the dominant partner, Capital. (The new entity would have Capital's chief, James H. Carmichael, as its president, and Croil Hunter as its board chairman.) In addition, people in the Upper Midwest feared that a

A NEW THEATER OF WAR

On July 25, 1950, Bill Hansen, Northwest's district sales manager in Seoul, Korea, burned his stock of unsold tickets, filled a briefcase with thousands of dollars of the company's cash, threw in a toothbrush and a shirt he had bought for his mother, and headed for the airport, which was under attack and would soon be captured by North Korean forces. Only a few minutes earlier, he had volunteered Northwest's help to the U.S. ambassador. Along with scores of other Americans, Hansen was soon on his way to safety in Japan. During the next three years, more than 1.8 million Koreans, Chinese, Americans, and people of other nationalities would suffer casualties in a terrible armed conflict.

Only five years after it wound down its support of the U.S. military during World War II, Northwest was about to provide valuable services in this new theater of war. When the United States led a United Nations force charged with protecting South Korea from invasion by North Korea, Northwest's experience in the region and its history with the Great Circle route inspired the military to ask it to serve as the primary commercial airlifter of soldiers and supplies in and out of the Korean peninsula. The airline flew one particularly famous aircraft, a venerable Tokyo-based DC-3 that a Northwest captain dubbed "UN-99" after the train that bucked Casey Jones in an old ballad; it transported UN observers to refugee camps and to investigate reports of atrocities around the fields of battle and drew much attention to Northwest's work for the military. "I don't think there was ever an airplane of its size that bounced on and off more dirt strips," remembered one of the crew. (UN-99 ultimately met its end when it lost power and crashed into a sandbar along the Han River while taking off from Seoul.)

For three years the airline's employees flew and serviced many other Korea-bound planes, however, including six DC-4s, and in total Northwest's airlift carried more than one hundred thousand U.S. and UN troops, families and dependents, hospital workers, and others during 1,380 flights across the Pacific that covered thirteen million miles. Some of the airlifted cargo included unexpected items. Northwest carried a load of chicken hatching eggs to Pusan and flew a DC-4 packed with Iowa porkers, along with transporting war materiel, medical supplies, and food. A Northwest press release noted that "whenever the news from Korea is favorable, Northwest crews feel a glow of satisfaction at the part they are playing. When it is not so good, they dig in grimly to step up their efforts further."

When the Korean War ended with a truce in 1953, Northwest went back to its strictly commercial activities in the Far East. •

combination with the eastern-leaning Capital would result in weakened service for the nation's central region.

When the time came to cast ballots, Northwest's shareholders rejected the merger proposal. (Although 716,835 approved of the merger and only 167,995 voted against, 300,000 Northwest shareholders registered no vote, denying the proposal the required two-thirds majority vote; meanwhile, Capital shareholders overwhelmingly voted in favor of the merger. A few years later, United absorbed Capital into its airline system, and this unrequited partner was gone.) Hunter was deeply disappointed; he believed that mergers offered the best way for airlines to bring efficiencies to the national route map and that this merger in particular could save the airline that he had headed for the previous sixteen years. "Now that it has not been approved, Northwest will go ahead in the future as we have in the past to make as great a success of this airline as we can," he said after the vote.

If Hunter's enthusiasm sounded weak, it was because Northwest's listlessness greatly troubled him. The airline's prospects were dim. Expenses climbed faster than revenues, the company had stopped paying dividends on its shares of common stock, and the board of directors could formulate no way to halt the airline's decline. Hunter, out of ideas and willing to relinquish some of his responsibilities, talked with an aviation up-and-comer, Civil Aeronautics Board chairman Donald Nyrop, about stepping in as Northwest's president. Nyrop, however, did not want to leave the federal agency.

After more discussions among members of the Northwest board, a committee formed to search for a new president. Starting with two hundred names thrown into consideration, the committee and a hired executive search firm gradually narrowed down the candidates to a single person: Harold R. Harris, vice president of Pan American Airways, who accepted the job and its salary of $50,000 (equal to $425,000 in today's dollars). In surrendering the presidency, Hunter became chairman of the board.

RESCUED FROM A DEBACLE

Like Colonel Lewis Brittin before him, Harris enjoyed being addressed by his former military rank, general. He boasted a seemingly impeccable background. During World War I he had flown bombing missions over Italy, and after the war's end he went on to serve with distinction as an army test pilot. He set several flying records and won fame as the first person in aviation history to make a successful emergency parachute evacuation when his plane broke apart over North Dayton, Ohio. When he left the military in 1926, he managed a crop-dusting firm and then served as general manager of Peruvian Airways (later organized as Pan American). As chief of the Air Transport Command during World War II he earned the rank of brigadier general and won numerous military decorations

Harold R. Harris spent just a year as Northwest's president and chief executive officer, then left the office mysteriously.

The Lockheed Super Constellation, an aircraft that was Harold Harris's undoing.

before taking the job of vice president of American Overseas Airlines. When Pan American bought American Overseas, Harris took over Pan Am's Atlantic operations.

Upon his assumption of Northwest's presidency on January 1, 1953, Harris surprised company directors by refusing to sink roots. Instead of buying a house or even a car, he took a temporary flat in the Minneapolis Club. The reason? He did not intend to spend much time at Northwest's headquarters. Instead, he planned to move the airline's top administrative offices to his idea of a more suitable home, which he had already leased, at 535 Fifth Avenue, near Grand Central Station in New York City. He explained the move as an attempt to improve productivity and efficiency. He also asked an executive committee to investigate the feasibility of relocating the company's maintenance base from Holman Field in St. Paul.

Harris's next decisive act as president—and also one of his last in office—was to enter into a multimillion-dollar agreement with Lockheed to buy six Super Constellation aircraft. This transaction required him to put up as loan collateral Northwest's Stratocruisers and DC-4s. Consequently, workers solemnly riveted to these aircraft metal plates announcing, "Mortgaged to Banker's Trust Co." The company's board members, reluctant for the airline to take on the financial burden of the Lockheed aircraft and upset over the expense of the Manhattan office rental, were under pressure to resume the payment of stock dividends. They wanted to economize when Harris wanted to spend.

Increasingly estranged from the board of directors and abhorred by the local business community, Harris lasted only a year as president before disappearing on what the company variously called a medical leave and an indefinite leave of absence. Reportedly suffering from dysentery and paroxysmal tachycardia (dangerously rapid heartbeat), he spent two weeks at Abbott Hospital in Minneapolis before returning to his permanent home in New Canaan, Connecticut. He denied any plan to resign, and when asked whether there was dissension on the Northwest board, he remarked, "I suppose there is. There is on every board." He claimed not to have seen or spoken with any board member since his hospitalization.

Board members would not confirm or deny rumors that Harris had been fired. Speculation on the true cause of Harris's vanishing act further eroded whatever confidence in Northwest remained among money lenders and business partners. The *St. Paul Pioneer Press* published its conviction that Harris was "on his way out."

A month after Harris decamped, news leaked that a Wall Street figure and retired geophysicist named William Salvatore had led a battle to remove Harris from office. Salvatore was reported to represent the estate and vote the shares of the lately deceased Maurice Wertheim, an eminent financier and patron of chess players (as well as father of the historian Barbara Tuchman). The Wertheim estate may have been Northwest's largest

THE PUDGY PLANE THAT COULD

It arrived in Northwest's fleet more than a year late, but in August 1949 customers got their first look at the Boeing B-377, nicknamed in moderne style the Stratocruiser, a wondrous double-decked airliner. Capable of carrying up to one hundred passengers and powered by four engines more than twice as powerful as those on Northwest's DC-4s, these pudgy planes cruised at more than three hundred miles per hour and cut eight hours off the flying time from the U.S. mainland to Tokyo.

Northwest was the only U.S. airline to introduce Stratocruisers, acquired at a cost of $20 million, to domestic service, and by the following year the planes were flying most of the airline's long domestic routes. The Stratocruiser figured prominently in a $35 million equipment improvement program that president Croil Hunter had pushed through three years earlier, funded by loans and special issues of preferred stock. Hunter pinned his hopes of attracting new business on the seductions of the aircraft, of which Boeing manufactured only fifty-six.

Passengers loved the planes for the unheard-of comfort they offered, and they quickly took a prominent place within the lore of luxury commercial flying of the late 1940s and early 1950s. The plane's popularity came at a great financial cost to Northwest, however. Employees joked that the Stratocruiser, a notorious fuel guzzler, could turn a profit only when carrying 110 percent of its passenger load.

Bob Fliegel was among the earliest Northwest passengers to board this airliner in its premier year. The flight burned into his memory. "Looking out the terminal window onto the tarmac, I saw the magnificent double-decker Stratocruiser. A stunningly gorgeous stewardess . . . dressed in a smartly tailored Northwest Airlines uniform and stiletto heels, greeted us at the base of the stairway," he wrote nearly fifty years later. Fliegel was nine years old when he began this momentous experience of his boyhood.

And this boy was hungry. "The [food] trays plugged into holes in the arms of the seats, as there was too much distance between the

Northwest Airlines Stratocruisers — Finest . . . Fastest

With its cigar shape and blunt nose, the Stratocruiser showed a unique profile in the world's skies.

Northwest Stratocruisers await boarding at Wold–Chamberlain Field, Minneapolis, circa 1955.

The Stratocruiser lounge offered room for children to play.

Adams also took note of the bathrooms. "The ladies' powder room has the elegance of the Waldorf," he wrote. "Fluorescent lighting, gold mirrors, plenty of space for primping. Even the men's room has been given a lot of attention. Ample room for shaving, for instance." After shaving, a gentleman could complete social plans after landing using commercial aviation's first air-to-ground telephone.

But Fliegel, the nine-year-old, focused his attention elsewhere. "During periods of relative calm," he wrote, "children enjoyed climbing [the stairs] between the two decks." These spiral stairs left a strong impression on passengers. "I've been trotting up and down stairs at a height of 15,000 feet, and my head is still in the clouds," wrote columnist Ed Creagh of the *Seattle Times* in the Stratocruiser's first month of operation in the Northwest fleet. "Trotting up and down? That's right. In a plane. Stairs in a plane. Maybe that leaves you several degrees under the boiling point, but you are younger. You're at peace with the 20th century. To me it's frightening." He concluded: "What's next? Escalators?"

rows to have allowed the seat-back tray-stowage system of today," Fliegel remembered. "Meals were served on real plates, placed on small white tablecloths—and passengers ate with real flatware, not plastic forks."

The main attractions of the plane, however, were not at the assigned seat. "The Stratocruiser's lower-deck lounge was accessible via a short stairway from the passenger compartment," Fliegel recalled. "Though the lounge did not run the full length of the aircraft, it featured seven seats available for sale in addition to the chairs and tables available to all." The lounge, which seated fourteen in "the intimate, comfortable atmosphere of a very luxurious cocktail lounge," wrote the *Minneapolis Tribune*'s Cedric Adams, boasted built-in glass racks, glass holders for each seat, and cushy furnishings "that would make an ideal addition to anybody's amusement room." (When flying Northwest's Far East service, the lounge offered chopsticks and became what was called "the Fujiyama Room.")

The world's most luxurious commercial passenger plane in flight, circa 1955.

The distinctive layout and size of the Stratocruiser inspired cutaway diagrams and front-nose shots in promotional brochures.

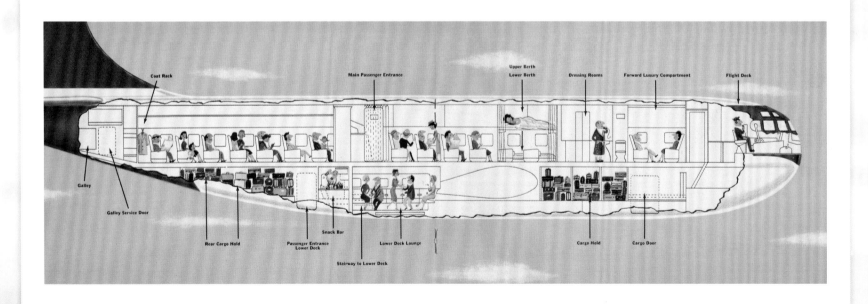

ten reasons why people fly.......

When roaming the stairs tired passengers, other comforts were available. "Passengers in the first few rows had access to overhead bunks that pulled down from the area of today's carry-on stowage compartments," Fliegel wrote. "I remember the mattresses as thick and comfy. For privacy you pulled a curtain across the bunks—it was quite a trick to get into one's pajamas in such a restricted space, but at age nine I was a skilled (and small) contortionist." Company lore tells of a flight in which the crew was having trouble maintaining pressurization in the cabin. "The entire plane was searched for air pressure leaks, until one man in a berth was found with the emergency exit open slightly," a Northwest press release reported. "'I always open the window when I go to bed,' he explained."

Did the Stratocruiser receive any low marks? "The ride was often bumpy, the cabin smoke-filled, and the cross-country flights longer than we care to remember," Fliegel recalled. While the Stratocruiser let passengers fly like royalty, it demanded queenly treatment to keep up in the air, which eventually led to its removal from the Northwest fleet. A maintenance supervisor remembered it as "a lovely plane, but you couldn't charge enough to pay for the mechanical and fuel bills for it. It sucked gas and it sucked maintenance." It was, according to one company executive, "a stockholder's nightmare but a passenger's dream." The last were retired in 1960.

Passengers prepare for a Stratocruiser slumber, circa 1956.

Stratocruisers in the fleet were an important selling point for Northwest Airlines.

Passengers harmonize in the air during Northwest's publicity stunt to install a Lowrey organ in a Strato-cruiser cabin.

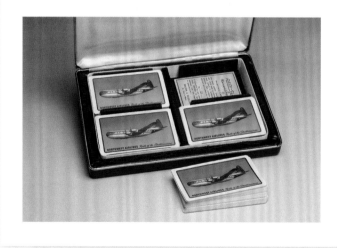

THE SATURDAY EVENING POST

Castle in the air !

NORTHWEST

Stroll around . . . saunter downstairs to the smart club lounge . . . on Northwest's double-deck Stratocruiser, world's finest airliner . . . *at no extra fare!*

Wide, soft berths . . . *another* luxury feature you'll enjoy. Only Northwest gives you Stratocruiser service coast to coast and to Hawaii!

NORTHWEST AIRLINES

FINEST COAST TO COAST . . . OVERNIGHT TO HAWAII . . . SHORTEST TO ALASKA AND THE ORIENT

NEW YORK, WASHINGTON, PITTSBURGH, CLEVELAND, DETROIT, CHICAGO, MILWAUKEE, MINNEAPOLIS - ST. PAUL, SEATTLE - TACOMA, SPOKANE, PORTLAND, HONOLULU . . . CANADA . . . ALASKA . . . JAPAN . . . KOREA . . . CHINA . . . FORMOSA . . . OKINAWA . . . THE PHILIPPINES

A year before the end, though, Northwest's vice president of sales, Gordon Bain, engineered one final publicity coup and advance in luxury for the airline's Stratocruisers. The Northwest Organ Company of Minneapolis installed a Lowrey organ in one Stratocruiser lounge, and notable organists of the Upper Midwest took turns playing such standards as "Autumn Leaves," "My Funny Valentine," and "Nearer My God to Thee" in flight. The Stratocruiser soon sang its swan song. •

The Stratocruiser had undeniable appeal, but Northwest soon discovered the high cost of sending castles into the air.

When the novelty of flying in a Stratocruiser wore off, passengers could play cards.

shareholder at the time, and Salvatore wielded great influence on the board; he had earlier helped block the merger with Capital Airlines. Harris's credibility as leader fell another few notches.

After shuttering its New York office, the airline finally announced in March 1953 that Harris had resigned because of "basic and irreconcilable differences of opinion with the company directors." Harris emerged from seclusion to hold his own news conference: in his defense he pointed out that the airline had tripled its earnings during his year in office, but that he could not find acceptance within the company for his spending plans to make Northwest even more profitable. (Harris, who never again held an executive position with an airline, moved on to head a company that helped new airlines find funding; he died in 1988.)

Meanwhile, Northwest began its search for Harris's successor. "Rumors in the trade . . . indicated two prominent officials of other airline firms who had been approached about taking the job laughed off the proposals," a reporter wrote—and that is how low Northwest's fortunes had sunk.

But Croil Hunter had not forgotten Donald Nyrop, the c.a.b. chief who had turned him down two years earlier. Since then, Nyrop had left the federal agency to go into the private practice of law. Hunter and two other Northwest board members arranged a meeting with Nyrop a few months after Harris's resignation. Nyrop later said he believed his visitors "wanted some legal work" done. Instead, they asked him to become Northwest's president. Nyrop made no commitment either way, but asked for two months to consider whether he should jump into a company so

Advertising poster, 1950s.

Croil Hunter *(left)* with Donald Nyrop, circa 1955.

notorious for its financial and organizational troubles. He also let the board know that he would decline the job if Northwest sold off its most important assets: its Far Eastern and Pacific routes and its Stratocruiser aircraft.

It was just like Nyrop to unhurriedly stroll through the process to make a careful and methodical decision. Unlike Harris, he was a taciturn and economy-minded mid-westerner, a native of Elgin, Nebraska. He had worked as a schoolteacher and account-ant before attending law school. During World War II he briefly spent time as an assistant to the C.A.B.'s head, then worked four years as Harris's subordinate in the Air Transport Command. He moved on to the Air Transport Association and C.A.B. before becoming chairman of the C.A.B. on the appointment of President Harry Truman at the age of thirty-nine. Many people thought he looked ten years younger, and they often underestimated him for it. His tenure at the C.A.B. brought him attention as a controller of wasted money and time.

After his two months of review, Nyrop grew convinced that if it were properly man-aged and run efficiently, Northwest could again attain reliable profitability and leadership in the airline industry. The company's board, desperate to bring in a real leader, voted unanimously to make the hire. In October 1954, at age forty-two, he became the nation's youngest chief executive of an airline. "A tall, lithe man with a bright smile, he walks fast, talks with ease and a quick, decisive quality and has facts at the tip of his tongue," noted a reporter covering Nyrop's first appearance at Northwest's St. Paul offices. The new presi-dent seemed handcuffed to his briefcase.

Some, employees and customers alike, could not understand his optimism. He began his Northwest tenure by working ten hours a day, including every other weekend, absorb-ing details of the company's operations, listening to the reports of employees, and touring the outposts along the airline's routes. In time, he claimed to know the first names of half the airline's five thousand employees. Avoiding meetings and the appointment of committees, he interrogated department heads on their budgets and their justification for every staff member they employed. He built a reputation as a financial wizard: a president who could scan columns of numbers and see Northwest's weaknesses, excesses, and future.

THE PRESIDENT'S DIAGNOSIS

Nyrop interpreted that financial information to prescribe treatments previously unseen at Northwest, or at any other airline. "Fluff," meaning unnecessary or overly costly services, practices, and traditions, had to go. (At the C.A.B., Nyrop had disposed of scores of automobiles that employees had driven less than eight thousand miles per year, reasoning that a car driven that little was not really necessary.) The president mandated rounds of psychological tests for scores of upper and middle managers to assess their strengths and weaknesses. "The company hired an accounting firm to make an efficiency study of its operations and use the results to identify attainable work goals," a reporter detailed. "It also began to rely heavily on a manpower planning system that listed employees needed during a 24-hour period. The company even took such economy measures as building its own baggage carts from inexpensive parts ordered from a farm equipment dealer." Nyrop's cost-cutting fervor struck many as overbearing, but few denied that his heavy-handedness kept Northwest from spinning into insolvency.

Results came quickly. Less than a year after Nyrop became president, the company resumed its payment of quarterly dividends to shareholders—a benefit it had abandoned nine years earlier. In 1955, he told members of the Minneapolis Chamber of Commerce, "Northwest Airlines is the only airline in the United States that doesn't owe a dime." His aim, he concluded, was "to run an excellent airline, an airline unsurpassed by any carrier in quality of service." It had been a long time since any Northwest executive had voiced such a lofty goal. Gradually, through his careful oversight of the company's finances, Nyrop—still putting off his first vacation since 1952—was restoring the confidence of moneylenders and investors.

Nyrop realized that the best way to boost passenger confidence, as well as the bottom line, was to judiciously upgrade Northwest's fleet to return it to efficiency and reliability. He hastened to undo Harris's rushed order of the six Lockheed Constellations because he believed another aircraft, the pressurized Douglas DC-6B, was a better fit for Northwest. By 1956, the DC-6B became the airline's most dependable and hard-worked ship. Northwest spent $52 million on that plane and its successor, the DC-7C, which it advertised as one of "America's fastest, finest long range airliners." So Nyrop happily sold to TWA two of the six Constellations, and he assigned the remaining Constellations to international

Northwest employees Helen Johnson and Ramona Weber reupholster airline seats in the 1950s.

Airliner undergoing overhaul, 1950s.

A Northwest maintenance worker jokes at inflating a Stratocruiser tire, circa 1954.

routes and later sold them at a profit. Relying on different models of Douglas aircraft, rather than the hodgepodge of makes of planes that Northwest previously flew, brought substantial economies of parts, training, and maintenance.

By early 1955, the company's financial standing had improved so much that Northwest voluntarily gave up the government mail-carrying subsidies it had been receiving to underwrite its routes to Alaska and the Far East. Nyrop believed that subsidies dampened the invention of new efficiencies, and he professed a desire for his airline to operate with as little government assistance

Testing a Stratocruiser propeller in the overhaul base, circa 1954.

THE TALE OF A SWORD

By 1956, James Stannard, a plumber in North Dorset, Vermont, had suffered as much guilt as he could stand. As a U.S. Army lieutenant in occupied Japan during the months after World War II, his job was to help disarm civilians. He seized a fifteenth-century sword, crafted by the famed weapon maker Kanemitsu, that had been passed from one generation to the next within a Japanese family. "They offered me a wad of yen, and that must have been a couple of thousand dollars, but I had my orders," Stannard said. "I took the sword. As I was leaving their house in Nagoya, they begged me to treat it well. They told me to use nothing but vegetable oil on the sharp gleaming blade. When we were allowed to bring back a souvenir, I chose the sword to remind me of Japan. But it always reminded me of the man who begged that it be returned someday."

Aware that Northwest had a large operation in Japan, Stannard asked the airline for help in finding the sword's true owner. And Northwest succeeded in tracking down fifty-nine-year-old Isao Okuda of Nagoya. With Stannard's consent, the company worked out a plan to return the sword, which was three and a half feet long and sheathed in sharkskin, to Okuda. Northwest employees took charge of the voluminous customs and police paperwork necessary to restore the sword to its nation of origin. "The sword, tempered and still gleaming, was delivered in New York to stewardess Carole Kilander of St. Paul on today's flight," Ed Wallace of the *New York World-Telegram and Sun* wrote on January 16, 1957. "Miss Kilander will take the sword to Seattle and give it to another stewardess who will carry it on to Anchorage, Alaska. There it will be given to a third Northwest Orient air stewardess who will take it to Tokyo."

Paul Benscoter, a Northwest staffer in Japan, met the plane and took part at the exit ramp in the reunion of the sword with its owner. "Captain Moore turned the sword over to myself, and I in turn handed it over to Mr. Fujiyama, representative of the Japanese government, who in turn turned it over to its original owner," Benscoter wrote. A few minutes later, in a press conference inside the airport, a swarm of reporters and cameramen watched the kimono-clad Okuda accept the sword a second time. "He then, with the sword in his hand, expressed his heartfelt appreciation to Northwest Airlines and finally shook hands with me for about five minutes, making a speech all the while, most of which I did not understand," Benscoter noted, "but I presume he was again thanking me for the part NWA had played in the return of his family's heirloom." •

as possible. "If the present trend is followed, we will be the first international carrier to be free of government subsidy," Nyrop said. "And that's the responsibility of all airlines." The financial results were startling: Northwest reported earnings of $2 million in subsidy-diminished 1955, just 10 percent under its profits from the previous year when it had taken in $3 million in government money. Competitors, many of them dependent on the subsidies to maintain profitability, viewed Northwest's move as a blasphemous horror; many continued receiving the subsidies for decades. For years industry insiders referred to the airline's rejection of the subsidies in 1955 as "the time Northwest shot Santa Claus."

Nevertheless, in the remaining years of the 1950s, Northwest's income soared, as did the number of passengers the airline carried. The company further benefited from prearranged trade-in deals with plane manufacturers that gave

A Northwest airliner at Washington National Airport, 1950s.

Northwest (and its bankers) a clearer idea of funds forthcoming in the future. For years, lenders regarded Northwest's predictions of its financial results to be the most reliable in the industry. By the end of the decade, the airline's profits hit $5.7 million.

Politicians paid attention to Northwest's effort to remove itself from the government yoke. "I only wish that some of the other airlines, which seem to enjoy great favors . . . could show a similar record," said Illinois senator Paul Douglas. Northwest had hoped that freeing the federal government from paying subsidies would pay off in political favors, and it even offered to forego its mail subsidies on flights from Portland and Seattle to Hawaii in exchange for a monopoly on those routes. President Dwight Eisenhower dimmed Northwest's moxie by not only overriding the C.A.B.'s approval of that proposal, but by giving Pan Am sole operation of those routes. After hearing cries of protest from every constituent that Northwest could inflame, Eisenhower reversed his decision, claiming he had based it on erroneous information from his advisors. He awarded routes to Hawaii to both Northwest and Pan Am, following a path of apparent fairness while greatly disappointing Nyrop.

Employees set up a Hawaii promotional display, circa 1956.

Well-dressed passengers enjoy the Northwest in-flight experience, 1950s.

Northwest's promotion of flights to Hawaii during the 1950s emphasized convenience, fun, relaxation, and romantic allure.

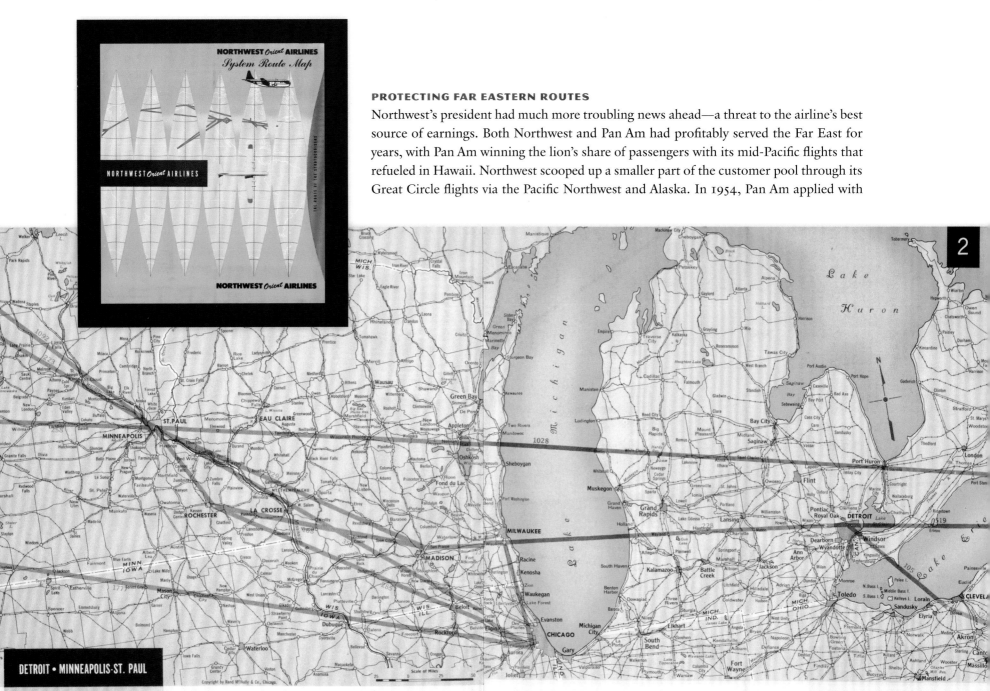

PROTECTING FAR EASTERN ROUTES

Northwest's president had much more troubling news ahead—a threat to the airline's best source of earnings. Both Northwest and Pan Am had profitably served the Far East for years, with Pan Am winning the lion's share of passengers with its mid-Pacific flights that refueled in Hawaii. Northwest scooped up a smaller part of the customer pool through its Great Circle flights via the Pacific Northwest and Alaska. In 1954, Pan Am applied with

DETROIT · MINNEAPOLIS-ST. PAUL

NORTHWEST *Orient* AIRLINES
THRU PLANE SERVICE
CONNECTING AIRLINES
916   AIR MILEAGE
RAILROADS
HIGHWAYS

✈ SAVE TIME ✈ FLY NORTHWEST

NONE of the irritations of land travel—the traffic, the circuitous routes—are your concern when you fly Northwest from Detroit to the Twin Cities. You fly high over land once populated only by wild life, scattered Indian tribes and a few brave pioneers. Tired eyes are soothed by the flow of green below. Forests and fields are tied with ribbons of roads, sparked here and there with gleaming rivers and streams. Mellow red barns, sheaf-scattered wheat fields, and livestock are spread out in miniature for your surveillance.

Your flight over Michigan is a flight over real vacation country, where fish-stocked streams and game-filled forests lure the sportsman and pollen-free air offers haven from hay fever. You'll catch a glimpse of Lansing, the state capital . . . of Grand Rapids, furniture store to the world.

Now you're flashing over Lake Michigan, an inland sea ringed by resorts—pointing like a signpost to Chicago, beloved city of Sandburg.

Look below—there's where you'll find the wonderful wienerschnitzel and a foam-flecked stein. That's right, Milwaukee is here—and gone!

Think for an instant of miles gliding by in minutes— you are traveling higher, faster, farther than man ever dreamed possible!

Now the view below is Minnesota—84,682 square miles of lakes and waterfalls; deep, enchanting forests; dynamic cities; and home of the most important iron ore producing district in the world—the Mesabi.

Soon you'll have your first glimpse of Minneapolis and St. Paul. Here you'll enjoy smorgasbord supper in the Scandinavian-settled community—spend a few sunny hours at the scene of Longfellow's Hiawatha, Minnehaha Falls, where water cascades over steep cliffs to join the headwaters of the Mississippi.

Though still anchored in the Upper Midwest, Northwest's route system was spreading around the globe.

the Civil Aeronautics Board for approval of its own Great Circle flights from the Pacific Northwest. The c.a.b. denied Pan Am's request, citing the lack of demand for two carriers to follow this route, and recommended that Northwest receive permanent certification for the northern flight path. President Eisenhower again overruled the c.a.b. decision in both parts and declared that Pan Am's application should receive more study.

Although Northwest had won temporary certification to continue its Far East service, it spent the next six years battling Pan Am for an advantage in Asia through refilings and new filings of applications. In the end, the airlines reached an exhausted truce in the aggravatingly slow and perplexing arena of the federal government, with President Eisenhower again flip-flopping ungracefully. Northwest got its permanent certification to fly passengers over the Great Circle to Asia from the Pacific Northwest but did not gain a mid-Pacific route via Hawaii; and Pan Am won rights to a completely new Great Circle route from Los Angeles and San Francisco to Japan, while failing to nab any route to the Far East from the Pacific Northwest.

One major route addition came to Northwest with fewer headaches. Nyrop set a goal to make Northwest's planes fuller during the normally slack winter months; the high number of empty seats between January and March accounted for the company's failure ever to earn a first-quarter profit. Eager to carry the many customers on its northern routes who wanted to reach warm destinations in the South, the airline had applied for the right to fly to Miami despite the apparent

The airline's ticket counter in the airport at Rochester, Minnesota, 1955.

The airport ticket counter in Atlanta, where Northwest began flying in the late 1950s.

Silent-movie star Buster Keaton lends a whimsical touch to promotion of Florida routes, circa 1958.

STORMY WEATHER 🧭

In the earliest days of commercial aviation, weather frequently blocked planes from their destinations, kept aircraft on the ground, and caused crashes. Fog and storms were not the only dangers; wind (often undetectable or unmeasurable from the ground) and airborne water that turned into ice when it hit wings or fuselage presented deadly perils. Information about weather was scarce and unreliable, dribbled to pilots through telegraphed messages and phone calls they picked up on refueling stops. During the 1930s, Northwest built a series of radio stations along its routes to put new wireless technology to use in communicating weather conditions. Directional radio signals directed pilots flying between Chicago and the Twin Cities through or around violent and soupy weather that could threaten safety and speed.

Decades later, Northwest became one of the first airlines to develop its own centralized radio network that could quickly relay up-to-the-minute weather information to its fleet. A main-base station transmitted counsel to thirty-seven unmanned stations around the country that ran without employees in attendance.

Sometimes flight crews aloft played a role in gathering weather information. On a clear day, pilots flying at ten thousand feet could take in the view for 150 miles around. "A few years ago, for instance, two Northwest Airlines pilots, flying in opposite directions on the company's commercial route through the northern tier of states, spotted a dark, cone shaped disturbance stirring up [dust] about 40 miles south of Dawson, North Dakota," a reporter wrote in 1946. "It had escaped the eagle eyes of on-the-ground observers. The pilots' messages were the first to reveal a tornado was on the way." Pilots often fed this kind of information to Northwest's flight control office meteorologists. Some captains intentionally approached significant storms for daredevil reasons—

among them, Northwest pilot Joseph McKeown, who during the 1940s as a U.S. Army flier skirted the edge of a hurricane to slingshot his plane to a transcontinental speed record.

And on occasion, crews met a bizarre but usually harmless weather phenomenon: St. Elmo's fire, which generated glowing flames on wingtips and other parts of the outside of the aircraft. Produced by a buildup of static electricity, St. Elmo's fire could sometimes surprise crews with its explosive intensity. "Just like a flashbulb in your face and a bang you couldn't believe, like a shotgun going off in your ear," a Northwest crew member recalled. "I couldn't see anything. I was blinded for a couple of minutes."

Starting in the 1950s, Northwest and its renowned

An assortment of weather instruments in Northwest's operations headquarters, Holman Field, St. Paul, 1933.

meteorological chief, Daniel Sowa, began research into the truly dangerous problem of air turbulence. At the time unpredictable and undetectable from the ground, turbulence could badly buck an aircraft, injuring passengers and crew. Sowa and his colleagues gathered an enormous amount of weather data from balloons and pilot reports and eventually could send to Northwest's fleet graphic representations of any turbulence that lay ahead. "Over a period of time, we developed the ability to forecast clear air turbulence precisely," Sowa said. "We learned what causes it, how to avoid dangerous turbulence, and when to advise the cockpit to put on the seat belt sign because moderate turbulence is ahead." Northwest's own predictions often arrived an hour ahead of those from the National Weather Service and the Federal Aviation Administration. As a result, Northwest could long boast no passenger injuries from air turbulence—the only airline that could make such a claim.

By the 1970s, the Federal Aviation Administration advised all airlines to develop turbulence forecasting systems similar to Northwest's, and the company shared its techniques with its competitors. Using the same sort of information gathering, Northwest also developed during the 1960s systems to predict the occurrence of low-altitude wind shear; these sudden changes in the velocity of headwinds and tailwinds formerly caused many accidents and injuries when planes made their approaches for landings.

Sowa received the Distinguished Service Award of the Federal Aviation Administration in 1988, among other awards from the National Weather Service and the National Flight Safety Foundation, for his forty years of important contributions to air safety. He appeared in an instructional film that Douglas Aircraft produced, costarring with Danny Kaye. Sowa stole the show by briefing an aircraft crew on the dangers of wind shear. He was once asked to describe the secret to practicing effective aviation meteorology. "You've got to have current data," he declared. "And if it doesn't seem to fit, you take it apart mentally and then you do it over again. Then, as you plot it, you analyze it. It's not very difficult."

By that time, the technological advances and scientific skills found in Northwest's eerily quiet meteorology center exposed Sowa's modesty. Weather information along Northwest's international routes filled "maps the size of small banquet tables," a reporter noted, and the display of Sowa's turbulence forecasts was the centerpiece of the office. •

The terminal and tower at Wold–Chamberlain Field, Minneapolis, 1957.

geographical contradiction to the company's name. (For the previous few years, Northwest passengers could get to Miami through a cooperative interairline transfer in Chicago and the Twin Cities to flights by Eastern Airlines.) Northwest won this route expansion after only a single initial refusal from the C.A.B., and flights began in 1958. (The first flight from the Twin Cities to Miami boasted an eighty-three-degree temperature differential between points of origin and arrival.) Soon Northwest added other southern destinations, including Atlanta and Fort Lauderdale. The mid-1950s also saw the airline finally gain a foothold in the high-traffic air corridor between Chicago and New York City.

THE START OF THE JET AGE

By the late 1950s, Northwest was readying itself for an entirely new era of air travel. The efficiency of piston-based propeller engines, which had powered commercial aircraft from the very beginning, lessened as planes neared speeds approaching the sound barrier. A new kind of engine, the gas turbine engine, promised to break that speed limitation by harnessing the power available from a stream of combusting gas. Rotating fans forced air into the engine's combustion chamber, where the air mixed with fuel to produce a heated gas that another turbine fan thrust out. The resulting jet of gas could propel a plane with great speed and efficiency. German and British fighter planes had first used these engines during World War II, and they became common in the fleets of many nations' air forces in the decade that followed. Starting in the late 1950s, commercial aircraft manufacturers offered jet-equipped planes to commercial airlines.

Nyrop and many others in the industry saw that jet-engine planes would replace propeller planes on the longest commercial routes, despite their greater initial cost. A portent of the future came in 1958, when Northwest sold off all of its remaining DC-3s, the last two-engine prop planes in its fleet. Although piston engines represented the technology of the past, Nyrop did not rush into the jet age, and the models of jet planes Northwest would buy came under the kind of deliberate study for which its president was famous. In short, Nyrop wanted to wait for the fastest ships in the business.

First into the Northwest fleet in 1959 came the Lockheed L-188 Electra, whose transitional "jet prop" technology—powering propellers with gas turbine engines—allowed for travel at 400 miles per hour and carried passengers with only one stop from New York to Tokyo. Next came the Douglas DC-8, a true jet airplane ideal for international flights because of its 139-passenger capacity, 550 miles per hour speed, and 4,400-mile cruising range. Northwest's orders for these two planes cost $66 million (spare parts included), the largest fleet payout in the airline's history. Beyond these costly purchases, however, Northwest spent $11 million to train employees and add new tools and equipment in preparation for its metamorphosis into a jet-equipped airline. In 1959, its pilots began training in a $300,000 flight simulator that mimicked the actions and responses of the newest commercial aircraft and did so more cheaply than did traditional in-flight training.

A NEW HOME

In this time of new aircraft and advanced technologies, Northwest's base and maintenance facilities had grown woefully inadequate. Chronic spring flooding at the Holman Field base confirmed the airline's need to move somewhere else. Several other cities, including Seattle and Chicago, courted Northwest. In the Twin Cities, the local economy depended

U.S. Senator Hubert H. Humphrey *(left)*, former Illinois governor and presidential candidate Adlai Stevenson *(center)*, and Minnesota governor Orville Freeman confer alongside a Northwest airliner in 1959.

on Northwest's $16.6 million payroll, millions more in local purchases, and three thousand employees remaining anchored in Minnesota. "After long and careful evaluation of the various alternatives," wrote company chronicler Kenneth Ruble, "NWA adopted a history-making plan that included far more than a new maintenance and overhaul base, and made Northwest the only major airline in the United States to centralize its total operation—General Office, maintenance and overhaul facilities, communications, flight operations and all related services—under one roof. The locale chosen was Wold–Chamberlain airport, where the airline had launched its career 30 years earlier." The decision hinged upon Northwest's conviction that Minneapolis–St. Paul would and should remain a key hub of air commerce for many decades to come.

Financed through a bonding deal reached with the Metropolitan Airports Commission (which also agreed to construct a costly new terminal), the new NWA base arose on seventy-six acres alongside the airport between 1958 and 1961. It was the Upper Midwest's largest building—a $17.5 million behemoth that enclosed 1.1 million square feet of floor space. The construction swallowed up one million bricks, seventy-two miles of pipes, and gigantic hangars that company literature said "could accommodate five football games at one time." The utility access that the base required—electricity, gas, water, and other essentials—equaled the needs of a city of ten thousand people. Northwest's offices occupied a windowless building in the complex that seemed drably institutional, but the no-frills administrative center matched Nyrop's "essentials-only" business approach and his desire to envelop as much space as possible at the lowest cost.

CHAPTER 5

ADVENTURES IN SCALE
AND EFFICIENCY

It is the early 1960s, and several mornings and afternoons per month, groups of all kinds—Girl Scouts, senior clubs, high school students, business associations, and foreign visitors, among many others—congregate at the main entrance of Northwest's new home at Minneapolis–St. Paul International Airport. (More than sixty-eight hundred people had appeared for the official opening of the main base in 1960.) "Welcome to Northwest Orient Airline's main base, the largest building in terms of ground area under [its] roof ever constructed in the Upper Midwest," begins an airline tour guide. "A total of eighteen acres under roof is included." With those words, the guide leads visitors through what the company clearly considers a showpiece: the most modern airline home anywhere in the country. It symbolizes not only how large Northwest has grown, but also the technological leadership the airline assumes in its industry and its prominent role in the world's transportation fabric.

After reminding visitors of Northwest's prominence in the region's economy, the guide shows the comptroller's and accounting offices before leading guests into the flight kitchen, "the most up-to-date and complete and one of the largest institutional kitchens in the Upper Midwest." Visitors next traipse by the airline's data center, a room containing a wall-sized Univac computer. "Through the use of the Univac," the guide says, "the reservations agent here at the airport can obtain confirmation on the sale of an airline seat on some particular flight in one second or less. From elsewhere on Northwest's domestic route system, average time required is five to seven seconds. A complete inventory for a month ahead of all seats sold on all domestic flights—more than 100 per day—is stored on six large magnetic drums, located in the four large cabinets at your left."

A short stroll brings the tour group to the airline's Twin Cities reservations office,

RUN OF THE MILL
JUST WOULDN'T DO...

[1961]

...THE TWIN CITIES DESERVE THE BEST....AND NORTHWEST BUILT THE BEST!

Northwest ushers in a new era in service to the Twin Cities . . . with completion of the giant new Main Base and General Office Buildings at the Minneapolis-St. Paul International Airport. There's a great future ahead for the Twin City area . . . and Northwest helps lead the way with the new $18,000,000 facility that has no equal anywhere . . . in size . . . in efficiency . . . in jet-era innovations in maintenance and service.

Northwest doesn't measure its Twin City service in the cold statistics of construction such as the million bricks used, the 72 miles of pipe, the huge hangars that could accommodate 5 football games at one time. Service is measured by people and in this case Northwest people . . . thousands of them . . . who will use the new "Home Base" to add new ease, comforts, conveniences and efficiency to Northwest's famed hospitality . . . creating the finest in jet-speed air travel for you.

Northwest was first to bring jet service to the Twin Cities . . . and is still first in jet service . . . with more flights in all directions than any other line. Fly Northwest . . . the Twin Cities own airline . . . serving you better, faster and more efficiently in the wonderful new world of jet travel. Northwest serves the business centers and vacationlands of the world. Call your Travel Agent or Northwest at Parkway 1-3511.

Promotional brochures extol the modernity of the company's new main base.

A VIP group tours Northwest's new main base in 1961.

a room filled with phone workers, "where your telephone call to Parkway 1-3511 is answered when you desire space on Northwest," the guide continues. "The large board against the far wall is used for a quicker reference on certain flights." The guide points out an illuminated panel up near the ceiling "called an annunciator board, indicating telephone activity and employee utilization. We have a new automatic call distributor to minimize if not eliminate the long waits normally encountered in getting to the reservation agent."

As the group advances through the complex, the guide explains that the entire building has been constructed without windows to create uniformity: "When offices eventually are built in the space, they will have the same appearance as those on the two floors above." How this is advantageous may elude some visitors, but they move ahead into an underground tunnel, past the heating boilers, and connect with Hangar No. 3, one of five in the base, where a captive jetliner may be under-

Off-limits to tour groups: Northwest's somber baggage lost and found office, 1960.

going a stripping at the hands of an army of workers, like Gulliver with the Lilliputians. The hangar is so big that "one hundred regulation-sized bowling alleys could be installed" inside, and above "the 320-foot spans across the width of the hangars are the longest clear steel spans in any building in the world. . . . Fifty potential designs of such spans were computed electronically on University of Minnesota equipment to determine the best one for these buildings."

Each Northwest plane visits a hangar like this after every three thousand hours of flying, about annually, for a complete inspection and overhaul. The teardown of each ship includes "re-soldering of all soldered connections whether the need shows or not . . . and after the third or fourth overhaul, paint is stripped completely and the aircraft is given a new paint job," the guide explains.

Past the sheet metal, propeller, machine, and engine disassembly shops, the visitors watch parts and engines travel between work areas by overhead monorail. (At the plating shop, which includes vats of dangerous chemicals, the tour script warns guides that "under no circumstances should tour groups of children—Cub Scouts, Indian Guides, etc.—be allowed to enter.") They see the main-base stores, which "stocks a total of 78,000 separate items, with inventory value of more than $11 million." After visiting the electric and instrument shops, the tour ends in the radio shop, which "overhauls 196 different kinds of radio, communications and navigation equipment, with an output of 154 units per week," as the guide points out. If a guest asks why a metal screen surrounds part of the radio shop, the guide responds, "The screened area is not to protect the radio mechanics from insects.

Rather, the metal screen isolates the room, radio-signal-wise, from the rest of the world." The radio signals originating in the shop remain within it; those from outside stay out.

With that positioning of the main base as its own world within a world, the tour ends. In 1962, a new addition arose next door at the airport itself: the $10 million Lindbergh Terminal, which was part of a much larger effort to upgrade the transportation hub. Within a few years, 4.1 million people would use this burgeoning airport.

ELIMINATING IRREGULARITY

If visitors learned anything from the tour (other than the guide script's affinity with business jargon), it was that scale and efficiency mattered to Northwest. Since his arrival in 1954, president Donald Nyrop had forced the airline into more streamlined operations that relied on new technology. The automated reservations process, computerized data retrieval system, and high-tech communications equipment were all the result of Nyrop's emphasis on lean productivity. Nyrop viewed irregularity as an evil deserving of quick elimination. Before his tenure, "we owned one of almost every ground radio device ever built," remembered Robert Gilschinski, vice president of communications and computer services. "Even when we had two alike, they were wired differently." Nyrop replaced them with uniform devices set up in nearly identical stations along Northwest's routes. The makeup of the airline's fleet reflected that same orderliness; a collection of similarly constructed Boeing planes with many interchangeable parts replaced the jumble of aircraft, no two alike, that Northwest flew during the early 1950s. Only two types of jet engines, for example, powered the Boeing fleet that Northwest acquired during the 1960s.

Nyrop and his managers had considered the differences among the various aircraft controls especially worrisome, not just because of the high cost of training mechanics and maintaining stores of so many different parts. When the dials and switches that activated safety systems worked differently and were located in unfamiliar locations of the cockpit, pilots who flew more than one type of plane could easily make mistakes. And mistakes in the air can lead to crashes. So Northwest developed an ambitious plan, initialed SOPA (for Standard Operating Procedures, Amplified) that aimed to standardize the piloting controls in all of Northwest's planes. "Even if they were blindfolded," observed Vince Doyle, a retired captain, "our pilots could reach out and touch the flap indicator, the air speed indicator, the de-icing switch or any other instrument. No matter what NWA cockpit you're in, you feel at home." At the same time, the airline standardized tasks—including the order of the crew's actions—during takeoffs, landings, and other flight procedures. This approach extended to the maintenance of planes; signed checklists of procedural instructions and X-ray and other new testing technologies replaced less thorough visual inspections of engines and other equipment.

HOT MEALS AND COLD MARTINIS

Northwest began refining its offering of food when it opened its new routes to Asia after World War II. With flying itineraries that could last nearly two days and a flood of new passengers whose palates did not match those of the customers who flew standard domestic routes, the airline had to think hard about how food could keep passengers coming back.

Northwest initially played it safe by shipping precooked frozen American-style meals to Anchorage and such Far Eastern stops as Tokyo and Manila. Made in the kitchens of Maxson, a commercial New York food preparer, the airline meals featured roast veal, turkey with trimmings, roast beef and gravy, Swiss steak, and country-style chicken. If these selections sound like they came from a TV dinner factory, they did. Though Maxson never sold its meals in supermarkets, it is often credited with inventing that frigid cuisine. "The meals are first cooked, then placed in a blast tunnel for fresh freezing, where hundreds of meals are handled at a time," the airline announced. The food could last frozen for up to three months and for as long as thirty hours in an aircraft's dry ice. "The food served on those early trips was really pretty lousy," first officer Warren Avenson remembered. One pilot resorted to bringing his own food to serve to passengers.

Even the frozen fare represented a step up from the eatables Northwest had previously offered on its planes. In the days before stewardesses in the 1930s, the short hops and lack of galley equipment allowed pilots and pursers to distribute to passengers only such snacks as chicken or peanut butter sandwiches and apples in cardboard boxes. Not until May 26, 1944, in a wondrous experiment, did the astonished passengers on a DC-3 flight from the Twin Cities to Chicago see a multicourse hot meal. This food had been cooked on the ground and packed in heat-preserving containers. Unfortunately, the meals eventually lost their warmth. "Often it meant that the last person served found his mashed potatoes and Swiss steak a little on the cool side," the company conceded.

Northwest worked on the preservation and presentation, and some food favorites emerged during the postwar years. On stops in Billings during the late 1940s, for instance, Northwest personnel loaded aboard

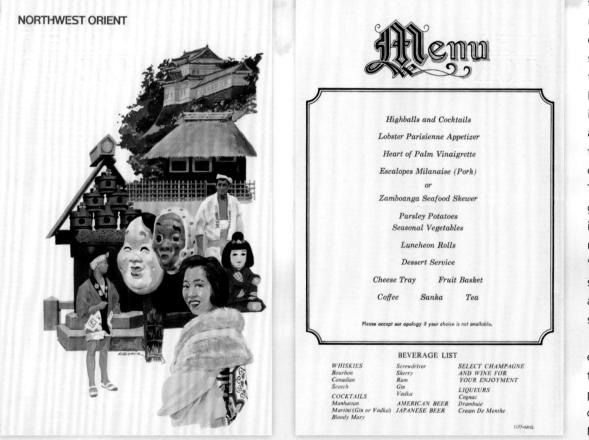

First-class passengers received this and similar menus on flights to Tokyo during the 1970s.

Northwest's master directory of recipes was compiled starting in the 1940s.

a selection of homemade pies that one reporter called "the pride of the line." Northwest kitchens went to work in Minneapolis, Billings, Anchorage, and Tokyo as the airline's routes expanded. A thick Northwest recipe book from this era contains cooking instructions for more than 450 dishes.

By the 1950s, the company was serving fifty thousand meals a month, and its home economists had developed a respectable menu that featured such dishes as Yankee pot roast, veal scallopine with marsala wine, crab meat alexander, Garden of Eden pie, Swedish cardamom bread, french fried shrimp, chicken with paprika, chocolate sundaes, and a dessert mysteriously titled Boston Brownies for University Men. For breakfast, passengers could request scrambled eggs, fluffy wheat cakes, and bacon. (One poultry farmer in Bloomington, lounges, which in 1955 the airline transformed through decor into what it called Fujiyama rooms, passengers could eat steaks and seafood in comfort. But the Stratocruiser had already ushered in an even more eagerly anticipated and momentous cultural shift: the serving of alcoholic beverages in the air. Among U.S. carriers, Northwest in 1949 became the first to start pouring liquor. (National Airlines then served drinks on some flights between New York and Miami, but only while the plane flew outside the territorial limits of the United States.)

The introduction of potent drinks gave the experience of flying a wholly new feeling, but it also opened thorny legal issues. Although Northwest maintained that the sky should remain free of the drinking limitations and regulations that ground-level state governments wanted to impose, legislators and attorneys general believed differently.

Beverage service, circa 1950.

Minnesota, was selling ninety dozen eggs daily to the airline in 1954.) The airline described most of its food preparers as "women past middle age who have cooked for their families for years."

The arrival of the Stratocruiser airliner and its large galley and dining spaces further improved Northwest's food. In the lower deck

The Story of **DISTILLED BEVERAGES** *prepared for* **CABIN ATTENDANTS** *of* **NORTHWEST** *Orient* **AIRLINES** THE AIRLINE OF SUPERIOR SERVICE

COMPLIMENTS OF HIRAM WALKER INCORPORATED

The introduction of alcoholic drinks required cabin attendants to learn the fine points of mixology.

A first-class meal, circa 1960.

A Northwest food assembler prepares meals in 1967.

Harold Lindbergh, director of food services, samples the kitchen's production in 1967, when it was producing up to six thousand meals each day.

Northwest eventually had to seek airborne liquor licenses from each state its routes passed over. Illinois and New York refused to grant any license, and other states imposed their own restrictions and requirements. So when taking off from New York City, Northwest crews had to delay the drink preparations until the Hudson River was behind them. Over Michigan and Washington State, they had to collect sales taxes. Many states were dry on Sundays and on Election Day. "Over South Dakota, it is illegal to serve a spendthrift, but Northwest hasn't yet challenged a passenger under this statute," observed a lengthy 1950 article in the *New Yorker*.

Because of space limitations, Northwest initially excluded beer and champagne from its beverage selections and stuck to martinis, scotch, manhattans, and whiskey. "For mixing purposes, you can have ginger ale, soda water, or, heaven forbid, Coca-Cola," the *New Yorker*'s writer noted. "During a descent, no one is allowed to hold the glass, lest he accidentally bite into or swallow it at touchdown."

Northwest's food, meanwhile, continued its evolution. When the airline introduced service between the Midwest and Florida in 1957, its chefs celebrated with a new menu that featured Scandinavian treats, curried shrimp, and lobster cocktail. In the late 1960s, it was serving seventy tons of tenderloin steak and sixty tons of New York strip steak yearly, along with a monthly offering of ten tons of coffee. The airline bought its silverware in Japan at a cost of twenty-five cents per set, and the covetousness of souvenir seekers forced it to replace twenty thousand sets each month. A 1990s innovation called A la Carte dining promised "the closest thing yet to a real restaurant at 40,000 [feet]," *USA Today* praised, but featuring recipes by famous chefs and offering a choice of side dishes did not pull any passengers back to memories of the savory experience of flying during the 1950s and 1960s.

In Northwest's final decade, food grew less and less ambitious—and subject to extra fees—except in the airline's first-class cabins. The days of curried shrimp had vanished forever. •

Employees prepare business-class salads in the Twin Cities production kitchen in 1999.

Flight attendants serve dessert in the first-class cabin, circa 1975.

INTERCONTINENTAL DC-8 JETLINER NORTHWEST ORIENT AIRLINES

Inside the cabin of one of Northwest's fleet of Lockheed 1049G Super Constellations, which for several years exclusively served passengers on routes between the mainland United States, Hawaii, and Asia.

The Douglas DC-8, a workhorse of the fleet during the early 1960s.

A Northwest crew flies a Boeing 707 over Honolulu, circa 1965.

Actor Buster Keaton helps promote fan-jet flights to Florida.

People queue up in Madison to tour one of Northwest's new 727s in 1964.

Less successfully, Northwest for a time focused its cost-cutting energies on discouraging passengers from expecting to see movies aboard its flights. In 1965 Nyrop told reporters that he would "greatly prefer not to incur the additional expense of providing in-flight entertainment, but if other airlines go forward we will meet the competition." He opposed turning planes into screening rooms, he said, because it "wouldn't mean any basic increase in traffic." Nyrop eventually lost that battle.

PROFITS GALORE

These efficiencies and controls on cost soon made a difference in ways that Northwest shareholders could truly appreciate. The decade of the 1960s ranks as the most financially successful in the company's history. Costs rose, but revenues greatly outpaced that increase. Despite employee work stoppages that periodically slowed or halted Northwest operations, the airline's profits multiplied by a factor of thirty-five between 1960 and 1969, soaring from $1.6 million to $51.5 million. By the end of the decade, Northwest ranked seventh in revenues but first in total profits, an achievement akin to a smaller chain of coffeehouses outgunning Starbucks in annual earnings. "In 1960 it took 96.4 percent of operating revenues to cover expenses, while in 1969 this figure had been reduced to 82.4 percent," wrote company historian Kenneth Ruble. The company's stock price and dividends took off. Nyrop's shrewd financial management allowed Northwest to hoard profits and issue lucrative stock offerings, allowing it to pay cash for new aircraft when its competitors had to lease planes or take on debt to buy them.

When the time came to buy airplanes, Nyrop made the decision himself, without the influence of committees and focus groups. Between 1961 and 1962 he yanked up Northwest's percentage of passengers flying jet aircraft from thirty to ninety. That latter year, the airline was operating seventy-two planes purchased during the previous seven years at a cost of more than $200 million. And by 1963, fan-jets powered nearly every member of the Northwest fleet. During the earliest years of the decade, the star of Northwest's air force had been the Douglas DC-8, a 120-seat ship whose speed allowed it to beat competitors' flights from New York to Japan by more than six hours.

Coach class inside a Northwest Boeing 727 in 1969.

THE RED TAIL

In its initial decades, Northwest did little to mold its public image. Potential customers already knew this much about the company's business: flying was a thrill, passengers were adventurers, and airliners—although marvels of engineering—sometimes crashed. Aside from straightforward ads, Northwest helped promote its business only with mesmerizing animated neon signs placed during the early 1940s

Northwest marketers tried odd advertising trinkets during the 1960s.

Northwest logos of the early 1960s.

outside ticket offices; they generated buzz by tricking the eye into thinking it was viewing a spinning propeller. (The signs, by one newspaper account, were "the talk of the nation.")

Northwest's advertisements of the 1930s and 1940s offered factual information on fares, departure times, and the new features of aircraft. As late as the 1950s, cost-conscious president Donald Nyrop boasted that Northwest spent only 1 percent of its revenues on advertising, the smallest sum in the business. In 1954 he dismissed the company's New York City–based ad firm in favor of the Twin Cities' Campbell Mithun agency to save money and because the local account executives "can get out here in thirty minutes," he said.

Meanwhile, the airline was evolving a graphic identity. After Northwest bought forty Martin 202 aircraft in 1946, president Croil Hunter decided to unveil the planes with a new painted design. The company engaged the firm of Charles Wilfred Butler—a New York industrial designer who went on to create the interior scheme for the

Red tails at rest, circa 1977.

Concorde supersonic aircraft—to give the Martins an engaging look. His staff first envisioned the marketing power of bestowing the aircraft with solid red tails—a feature that the company's craft would display for decades and grew into a Northwest trademark. (Butler's original color scheme also included red noses and wingtips, which the airline abandoned as too much of a good thing.)

At around the same time, during Northwest's thirtieth anniversary year, a newspaper strike in Detroit hampered the airline's efforts to publicize the landing in that city of the company's celebratory touring Ford Tri-Motor plane. Northwest's admen came up with a radio spot promoting the local ticketing office's phone number, which somebody realized spelled out "YODEL-00." So for days, hapless Detroit listeners heard a country singer yodeling out directions to dial the number while reminding them of Northwest's grand history and the pleasures of flying by Stratocruiser.

Another advertising promotion followed during the next decade, when the comedian Buster Keaton appeared in several of Northwest's earliest television commercials. In one spot, the unsteady Keaton attempts to hammer a suspended gong as a narrator describes the airline's route offerings, but the gong sounds on its own before Keaton can coordinate his motions. Nyrop initially rejected the gong campaign as the worst of several choices, but he changed his mind, and the ads went on to win several awards. The campaign reignited the career of Keaton, who had not done much acting since the days of silent films. "I guess a Gold Disc is still hanging on a wall at the Campbell Mithun agency as a reminder that I'm no ad genius," Nyrop said.

When Northwest introduced fan-jet service to Florida in 1963, it chose to leaven its biggest ad campaign ever focused on one market with some humor. Print and billboard ads showed an inverted map of the United States, with Florida occupying the northwest corner of the image. The headline read, "Flying South to Florida? Go Northwest!" When the ad went up on a billboard at the prominent intersection of Michigan and Randolph in Chicago's Loop, its ability to attract attention became clear. "I think you ought to know," declared a Chicago caller, who was one of many with similar complaints, "the painters are putting your map upside-down."

By the late 1960s Northwest had Boeing 747 jets on order and was putting its name on flights across the Atlantic, so it believed the time was right for a change in public image. Nyrop gave Bryan Moon, the airline's new assistant vice president of advertising, the assignment of redefining Northwest's identity for the decade to follow. "In my second meeting with Mr. Nyrop, he expressed concern with the image Northwest was projecting to the public and charged me with reviewing our position as an airline," Moon recalled. Moon and his staff eventually redesigned everything from travel brochures to ticket offices, adding new hues to the traditional red, white, and blue. At the same time, Clarence K. M. Lee created a new Northwest logo, while William Burke went over the logo typeface. Moon carefully rethought the painted exterior of the airliners and believed that Northwest's treatment of the solid red tail was dated. "It was the tail of the 707, our oldest plane, and just did not show Northwest as a big, aggressive, forward-thinking organization," he said. Instead, he placed the red tail within a design that included a shiny aluminum fuselage, a white stripe running around the plane, and a blue stripe over some of the white. The versatile Moon later headed an organization called MIA Hunters, which searches for the remains of missing U.S. military airmen around the world.

An equally ambitious refacing of Northwest came fifteen years later, when Northwest acquired a new corporate identity as a subsidiary of NWA, Inc. Away went such names of the airline as Northwest, NWA, NWO, and other variants, to be replaced exclusively by Northwest Orient. Again ticket counters, uniforms, and airliner paint schemes transformed. A new logo appeared—one that drew much admiration. It showed the letters *N* and *W*, along with the hand of a compass pointing northwest. Many graphic designers considered it a work of genius, but it disappeared during another corporate face-lift in 2003. •

A promotional photographer captures a Northwest 757 in flight, circa 1985.

Pilots train in the cockpit of an early flight simulator.

CAUTION
SEAT MUST BE OCCUPIED
FOR MANUAL VERTICAL OPERATION

Next into the fleet Nyrop brought the Boeing 720B (selling most of the DC-8s in the process), which could cruise at a searing 623 miles per hour. More Boeing aircraft arrived in the company's hangars, and the DC-8 was phased out, before the arrival of the 727 jet, ideal for use in airports with shorter runways, along with its long-body and cargo-carrying variants. This was the first three-engine plane in the fleet in decades.

Nyrop's acquiring vision had a long reach—in 1966 he expressed Northwest's first interest in the Boeing 747, a mammoth airliner that would not be available for four years. (Northwest prepared for the arrival of these jumbo planes by erecting an $18 million addition to its home base, a project more costly than the construction of the original base completed only seven years before.) Northwest finally removed the old DC-6B airliner from its routes in 1965, and two years later the airline's last piston-engine plane, a DC-7C freighter, left the fleet for donation to a vo-tech school.

EXTENDING NORTHWEST'S RANGE

Northwest used these new planes on an ever-increasing network of routes and route configurations, although the airline faced increasing competition on many of the new lines. Routes connecting such cities as Cleveland, Chicago, and Philadelphia sold many seats. The airline began nonstop flights between Seattle and Tokyo in 1964. Gone forever were the refueling stops in the Far North. In 1966, after years of delays and recalcitrance by the British government, Northwest won landing rights in Hong Kong—filling a big gap in its service to the Far East—and the company began daily service there from New York. The next year it added routes to Hilo, Hawaii, and Osaka, Japan. At the end of the decade, Northwest received government permission to add the mid-Pacific route to Japan that it had wanted for nearly fifteen years: a line running from San Francisco to Honolulu to Tokyo.

There were other oceans to cross, as well. In 1969 Northwest teamed with Pan American World Airways to offer its first trans-Atlantic flights between the Twin Cities and London, with Pan Am's planes handling the overseas part of the journey. Prized routes running north and south along the U.S. eastern seaboard and from Miami to Los Angeles still eluded Northwest, however. Echoing Croil Hunter's sentiments during the effort to merge with Capital Airlines nearly twenty years earlier, Nyrop believed the fastest way to acquire these lines was to buy an airline that already had them. At the end of 1969, Northwest agreed to merge with financially troubled Northeast Airlines. The Civil Aeronautics Board okayed the acquisition with one caveat—it denied Northwest the coveted southern transcontinental route from Miami to Los Angeles. Nyrop's lost his enthusiasm for Northeast after the C.A.B. removed this route from the package, and he gave up the deal. (Just as with Capital Airlines, United Air Lines soon scooped up Northwest's spurned partner.)

The complex computer-guided movement controls of a flight simulator.

The spirit of Northwest's jet age, circa 1965.

A graduating class of flight attendants and pursers, October 1969.

It was not long before another prospective merger partner appeared: National Airlines. Dudley Swim, National's board chairman, sought a financially strong airline for a combination that would wipe out his company's red ink. National flew routes along the U.S. eastern seaboard, through the southern corridor connecting the Southeast with California, and from Miami to London—perfectly complementing Northwest's northern and Asian focus. Swim died before the C.A.B. could approve the merger, however. National's officers lost interest in the proposal and pulled out.

DISASTERS REAL AND IMAGINED

The failure of these merger plans did not damage Northwest's reputation or the confidence of shareholders. At the start of the decade, the airline had matured in its public and media relations skills, largely as a result of a tragic crash. In 1960, a Northwest turboprop Electra flying from Minneapolis to Miami through Chicago went down in the countryside near Tell City, Indiana. The accident was horribly violent, killing all sixty-three passengers and crew members aboard. The totality of the destruction prevented investigators from identifying many of the bodily remains.

Northwest decided that its normal response to such a crash—trying to keep reporters from focusing on whatever blame the airline might bear, releasing a list of casualties but otherwise refraining from much comment on the accident, dealing privately with government investigators and surviving family members—was inadequate and possibly obsolete. For the first time in its history, it resolved to do more. The airline determined that this was the time to show the public that it was a corporation with a heart. In the weeks following the crash, Northwest organized a memorial service in Tell City for the victims, carried seventy-five family members to the memorial ceremony on specially chartered flights from Minneapolis and Chicago, and sent president Nyrop and board chairman Hunter as the airline's official representatives in attendance at the service. At the same time, Northwest bought land near the crash site for the burial of the remains and formulated plans for a large monument that would bear the names of those killed in the crash. Although these efforts undoubtedly brought small consolation to the grieving families, they characterized Northwest as an organization concerned with bringing solace to the mourners—a company with a soul.

PR Reporter, an industry trade publication, took notice of Northwest's unusual involvement in the mourning of the victims and the comfort of the family survivors—as, presumably, did the public to whom these conciliatory gestures were ultimately directed. The airline's response to the crash "demonstrated a salutary concern by the company for more than the physical loss of an airplane—a side of airline crashes which often steals

TAKE ME TO CUBA ✈ 🕐

Although terrorists, desperadoes, and political dissidents had occasionally hijacked commercial airplanes starting in the 1930s, a rash of air piracy spread in the late 1960s and early 1970s. While the stereotype of the new type of skyjacker had him seeking political refuge in Cuba, the destinations and motivations of the actual outlaws varied considerably. The most infamous of all U.S. hijackers, the mysterious and gentlemanly D. B. Cooper, who seized control of a Northwest flight in 1971, wanted only money. That year, nineteen U.S. airliners were seized.

Passengers and families are relieved at the end of a hijacked flight returning from Havana, Cuba, on July 2, 1968.

Northwest's first encounter with an air pirate came in 1968, when Mario Velasquez, a resident of Chicago in his thirties who had grown up in Cuba, stormed into the cockpit of a flight from Chicago to Miami, showed a gun, and shouted, "Go to Cuba! Go to Havana!" Velasquez forced flight attendant Barbara Schlosser to sit behind the pilot, Richard Simonson, and he kept his gun on them. Making conversation, the hijacker asked Schlosser if she had ever before visited Cuba. "I said no, and I really don't care to go this way . . . please don't hurt anyone," Schlosser later recalled.

When the 727 and its eighty-seven passengers made their unscheduled landing at the Havana airport, Cuban soldiers immediately surrounded the plane and awaited Velasquez's descent down the gangway. "They took him away," a passenger said. "I don't know where. . . . They appeared to be giving the hijacker a welcome. Soldiers patted him on the back and walked him inside." Schlosser observed that his reception "looked like a big homecoming party." Cuban authorities apparently allowed Velasquez to remain in their country, and after nine hours they finally let the Northwest plane return to Miami. "I feel twenty years older," Schlosser said when the trauma was over.

Three years passed until Northwest's next hijacking incident. This time the flight originated in Milwaukee and was carrying fifty-four passengers to Washington, D.C., with a scheduled stop in Detroit. The hijacker, Gerald Grant, produced a hatchet and a briefcase that he said contained a bomb as the 727 approached Detroit, and told the flight attendants he was taking control of the airliner. He sent a message to Captain Fred Walter to redirect the flight to Algeria. Informed that the 727 could not make the transatlantic crossing to Africa, Grant changed his destination to Cuba. "He gave no reason for the takeover," a passenger said. "He never went in the captain's cabin—he never even tried. He was cool and collected. But he was completely in command. And the rest of the passengers—no one seemed very worried. We just sat back and waited it out. Everyone was beautiful." The aircraft refueled in Detroit and continued to Havana uneventfully; nobody was harmed. Cuban soldiers took Grant into custody.

An Indianapolis man in his twenties, Everett Holt, did not get nearly as far several months later when he threatened to blow up a Northwest 707 en route from Minneapolis to Miami with a stopover in Chicago. Carrying a gun and seven sticks of dynamite, he fired two shots and demanded a $300,000 ransom. The gunfire harmed nobody, but Holt wanted pilot James Mancini to believe that a passenger had been killed. After receiving the money in Chicago, Holt allowed everyone off the plane except for the crew and two passengers. Meanwhile, police surrounded the 707 and refused to let it take off again. As Holt mulled over his next move, the hostages sneaked off. He soon surrendered, and the dynamite he carried was found to be fake.

The airline's later attempted hijackings were no less dramatic. In 1977, unemployed construction worker Bruce Trayer of Prairie du Chien, Wisconsin, declared he was "fed up with the United States" as well as with the use of food additives, and he tried to hijack a 747 that was flying from Tokyo to Honolulu. As he held a razor to a flight attendant's throat and demanded to be flown to Moscow, the crew's purser, Willem van Heuven, battered Trayer's head with the handle of a fire ax. The piracy attempt was over in ten minutes. Sent to a psychiatric hospital and released in 1983, Trayer later committed two armed robberies in Wisconsin.

Then, in 1980, seventeen-year-old Glen Tripp of Seattle boarded a Northwest 727 bound for Portland at SeaTac Airport and claimed to conceal a bomb in his briefcase. Holding fifty passengers for ransom, he spent ten hours negotiating with police on the runway. First demanding two parachutes, a light plane, and $100,000 in cash, he later amended his order to "a fast car, a head start, and three cheeseburgers." Tripp eventually surrendered without harming anyone. His briefcase turned out to contain only a jacket. Tripp was found to be developmentally disabled, but he served three years in prison. After his release, Tripp boarded the same flight at SeaTac and while airborne brandished a shoe box (later found to hold only paper) that he said contained explosives. He demanded to be taken to Afghanistan or San Diego but eventually agreed to fly to Portland. There he refused to enter negotiations with police and repeatedly threatened to blow up the plane. An FBI agent shot him to death. •

Yet another aeronautic crisis awaits Dean Martin and Jacqueline Bisset in *Airport,* a film made with the assistance of many Northwest employees.

the show," the publication observed. "Northwest's activities in this unusual PR situation attracted considerable favorable newspaper coverage [nationwide] and in the Indiana newspapers and in other cities having a direct interest in the crash."

Because of all the resulting publicity, Northwest received an unusually large number of letters about the accident in Tell City. One letter writer to the airline, incorrectly assuming that a bomb had downed the plane, drew up a detailed (and, given events of later decades, prescient) scheme for setting up X-ray equipment to screen passengers and luggage for weapons and explosives. "Hoping to hear from you about a comment on it," he closed his correspondence. Offering his speculation that an incendiary combination of fuel and phosphorus had caused the crash, a Maryland physician concluded that "no doubt all such possibilities have been thought of, but I thought it would do no harm to call it to your attention." Meanwhile, an eleven-year-old, promising Northwest that "I haven't sent this idea to anyone else," contributed his design for parachute rescue gear that "could be used to save lives in the future." (Nyrop's assistant wrote back in thanks and assured the boy that "this industry is growing rapidly, and will continue to offer interesting, challenging opportunities for enthusiastic young men.")

Although each idea was misguided or impractical, these letter writers looked benevolently upon Northwest's role in the accident and presumed that the airline had been emotionally shocked and wanted to prevent its recurrence—a view that the airline's PR response may well have helped shape. Few, if any, other airlines had previously taken this approach to the public management of an emergency.

At the end of the decade, several Northwest employees made the most of another aviation disaster—an entirely fictitious one. Much of the shooting for a movie based on Arthur Hailey's bestselling novel *Airport* took place at Minneapolis–St. Paul International Airport during the winter of 1969. The $10 million film, the first of a decade-long series of disaster movies, chronicled the plan of a desperate man to blow up an airliner in flight, set against the difficulties of a paralyzing blizzard. Playing bit parts were many Northwest stewardesses, baggage handlers, and mechanics, as well as a ticket agent, a mail room worker, and four secretaries, who all joined a cast that included Burt Lancaster, Jacqueline Bisset, and Dean Martin.

During production, the weather at the airport did not cooperate by providing snow, so the filmmakers hauled in bags of white plastic snowflake substitutes. The effort was worth the trouble, because *Airport* earned more than $100 million at the box office upon its release the following year, and it still ranks among the top seventy-five highest-grossing films of all time. (The aircraft featured in the film, a Boeing 707 rented from Flying Tiger, did not enjoy such a happy ending; it crashed in Brazil in 1989, killing twenty-five people and injuring more than a hundred.) Like the airline that provided so many of its faces, *Airport* amply rewarded its investors.

CHAPTER 6

PLANES LONGER THAN
THE FLIGHT AT KITTY HAWK

ON THE SECOND DAY OF SUMMER IN 1970, NORTHWEST LAUNCHED ITS BOEING 747
service with a flight from the Twin Cities to New York City. President Donald Nyrop was
on board the $21 million airliner, one of fifteen that Northwest had acquired in its initial
order placed four years earlier. He sat in a cabin that to some evoked the comfort of a
luxurious hotel lobby or living room. As in the earlier Stratocruiser, a spiral staircase led
passengers—this time up—to a spacious flight deck with room for a lounge and meeting areas, and customers reveled in the chance to leave the confines of their seats. When
seated, they could enjoy movie and audio programming.

The plane was easily the biggest in service (longer, in fact, than the Wright brothers'
first flight) and twice as wide as any other commercial aircraft, capable of carrying 362
passengers and 355 tons in weight at 625 miles per hour. In comparison with the Stinson
Detroiter with which Northwest began its passenger service more than forty years earlier,
the 747 was 230 times heavier and 3,000 times more expensive. Its mass and girth inspired
a host of imaginative nicknames, including "A Place in the Sky," "Fat Albert," "The Flying
Whale," and "Aluminum Overcast."

The public came to appreciate the vast size of the 747 in 1971, when news stories told
the exasperating tale of Garfunkel, a gray cat shipped via Northwest from Oshkosh, Wisconsin, to join its owner in Anchorage. An escape artist, Garfunkel slipped from his cage
in the 747 cargo hold and vanished by the time of his arrival in Alaska. For weeks, maintenance workers heard plaintive cries when they serviced the plane, and they determined
that the cat had wandered into an inaccessible and dark purgatory between the walls of the
cabin and the skin of the aircraft. No offering of cream, tuna, or catnip could lure him out.

A month passed after his disappearance, and everyone presumed the luckless feline

Donald Nyrop led Northwest through its most profitable years during the 1960s and 1970s.

dead. Then the 747 went to a Boeing facility for scheduled work, and crews discovered that Garfunkel was still alive, having traveled a million miles as an unwilling Northwest passenger. With the help of people from the Animal Humane Society, they extracted him from the plane. After Garfunkel recovered from serious dehydration and malnutrition, he once again boarded a Northwest plane—this time in the passenger cabin, on a velvet pillow on the lap of a flight attendant—to reunite with his owner in Anchorage.

Within months of their introduction, the jumbo jets were flying passengers only slightly less luxuriously on Northwest routes from the West Coast of the United States to Hawaii and the Far East. To cross the Pacific, the airline took advantage of Boeing's special version of the airliner, the 747B, with a range of 6,740 miles. But Nyrop did not bank his company's success entirely on the new Boeing. He soon added to the fleet another large intercontinental airliner, the 248-passenger Douglas DC-10, in a model especially configured for Northwest. Nyrop worked out a deal with Douglas to outfit the DC-10s with nonstandard Pratt & Whitney jet engines—the same engines that powered the 747s. This special order aligned with Nyrop's drive to bring standardization and its attendant cost savings to the airline. Although the substitution cost Northwest an additional $500,000 per plane, it saved the company tens of millions of dollars through the years. The airline industry averaged an investment of 20 percent of a fleet's cost in the purchase of spare parts. Because the 747s and DC-10s shared the same engine, however, Nyrop could hammer Northwest's parts investment down to just 9 percent. He reckoned the inventory savings at $120 million, not including additional savings in tools, training, and servicing equipment. Northwest's alterations to the Douglas aircraft also increased its range, which the airline proved in a 7,677-mile demonstration flight from Los Angeles to Hong Kong before the DC-10s went into service.

Only Nyrop's long-held faith in the future importance of supersonic transport (SST) aircraft—large passenger planes like the French Concorde that traveled faster than the speed of sound—proved errant. During the late 1960s, Northwest placed orders for four supersonic planes for expected delivery in 1975. Nyrop had called the SSTs "a giant step

The DC-10 airliners that Northwest bought from Douglas Aircraft had custom-equipped engines that saved money by standardizing maintenance procedures.

forward in the products that airlines have to sell: speed, convenience, and comfort," and he predicted that they would work in tandem with jumbo subsonic aircraft to revolutionize the transport of passengers and cargo. A single supersonic airliner, he believed, could make five daily trips between, say, Seattle and New York City, slashing the in-flight time and carrying five hundred thousand passengers a year. "Airport terminal and runway facilities in most cities must be completely rebuilt by 1976 to handle the coming new airplanes and traffic increases. . . . The next ten years in commercial aviation will be exciting," he added.

They were exciting, but not for the reasons Nyrop prophesied. ssts guzzled fuel, were expensive to maintain, and produced sonic booms that alarmed people on the ground, limiting most of their use to transoceanic flights. Nearly all airlines, including Northwest, ultimately avoided them. For Northwest, the excitement of the 1970s appeared in financial statements.

In 1973 Northwest teamed with technology firms Univac and Control Data to introduce some of the first computer-generated airline tickets. The new process allowed agents to produce 2.6 tickets per minute, a speed ten times faster than handwritten tickets.

WIZARDRY WITH MONEY

If anything, Nyrop's reputation for cost cutting and engineering savings had only increased over the years. A newspaper story credited him with monitoring all aspects of the company's finances, "from the cost of lightbulbs to the creation of a billion-dollar fleet." Stories, some legendary, circulated about his decisions, as shrewd and creative as a miser's, that saved Northwest millions. There was the airline's simple order to pilots to cut their speed on landing approaches by thirty knots, which saved more than six million gallons of fuel per year; the construction of an inelegant, $4,000 homemade air blaster to repair turbine blades, which saved $650,000 a year in engine reconditioning expenses; Nyrop's instruction to the company's engineers to create notches in main base hangar doors to accommodate the unusual height of the DC-10s, eliminating the need to spend an additional $3.5 million to raise new hangars; the adaptation of a medical tool, the cystoscope, to examine the inside of jet engines without going to the significant expense of dismantling them; his personal test of a parking lot sweeping machine to determine whether its utility justified its cost; and the purchase of $80 in door hinges from a hardware store that replaced $110,000 in parts that Douglas had recommended to fix a bathroom problem on the DC-10 (to which a Douglas executive responded, "What can I say? . . . Every once in a while we need a swift kick to put us back in the proper perspective.").

Outsiders marveled at Northwest's minuscule budgets for public relations and advertising—at 1 percent of annual revenues, the lowest in the business—as well as Nyrop's disdain for the expense of trade associations and activities (Northwest in 1974 became the only carrier from a non-Communist nation to withdraw from the International Air

By 1974, desktop computer terminals had arrived in Northwest's reservations center.

Transport Association), his refusal to allow traveling executives including himself to displace paying customers on flights, the low salaries of the company's executives (although Nyrop's own pay was at one time the highest in the industry), its longtime use of a single standardized coach seat in its planes to cut expenses, and Nyrop's removal of painted U.S. flags from the tails of Northwest aircraft when he found out they cost $50 to touch up. Other airlines complained of the company's stinginess in giving the customary free tickets to competitors' officials. People started using the nickname "Northworst" during the 1970s in response to the airline's meager staffing of customer service areas, and allegations circulated that Northwest intentionally "boozed up" passengers to lull them into complaisance with poor service.

Even Northwest's Minneapolis headquarters, once a proud symbol of the airline's growth and success, came to stand for parsimony. *Fortune* magazine described it as "a dowdy, hangarlike building that has no windows, no pictures on the walls of offices, and no doors on men's toilet stalls." Eliminating windows controlled heating and air-conditioning costs, and the doorless stalls supposedly discouraged idleness. (The *Wall Street Journal* used similar language to describe the building, labeling it "a bleak, hangarlike, windowless, largely uncarpeted structure.") The building's cost of operation was one-fifth that of the headquarters of Northwest's competitors, which Nyrop noted by boasting, "There's no way that they are five or six times more productive than we are." (Measured by employees per revenue dollar, in fact, Northwest's people were the most productive.) "Northwest is so profitable primarily because of cost control, which is Nyrop's middle name," a business publication observed.

Visitors to Nyrop's office received coffee in paper cups. "You already have an annual report," he once said, reaching for a company publication in the hands of a reporter. "Give back the one I just gave you. They cost 44 cents." His laughter left the reporter uncertain how serious he was.

His seriousness showed in the company's financial results. Despite an economically volatile decade in which prices, especially the cost of fuel in a time of OPEC cartel embargoes and reduced U.S. government allotments, steadily rose, Northwest continued to make money at a pace that no competitor except Delta could approach. The airline set a record for profits, generating $64.7 million from an impressive $759 million in revenues, in 1974. The following year, six of the nation's top eight airlines

A Northwest employees basketball team, circa 1974.

lost money, but Northwest led them all by earning a profit of $43.4 million. By 1977, Northwest hit $1 billion in revenues and $93 million in profits. That marked the company's twenty-sixth straight year of profits and twenty-second consecutive year of dividends for shareholders. There is no mystery behind famed air pirate D. B. Cooper's selection of a 1971 Northwest flight to stage his skyjacking and ransom demand—everyone knew the airline was rich.

Northwest's astounding success explains why, at a 1976 observance of the fiftieth anniversary of Northwest's founding, Continental Airlines' board chairman and former president Richard Six, then the senior executive in all of commercial aviation, told the celebrants, "Northwest is first in profit as a percent of revenue in the airline industry . . . first in profit for four of the last eight years, first in retained earnings, first in shareholders' equity relative to airline size . . . and adds multi-millions per year to the Minnesota economy, a majority in the payroll. These figures mark a triumph of ingenuity and application, of zeal and of judgment." Six attributed those characteristics to the entire Northwest workforce, but most people knew they applied particularly well to Nyrop. Under his management, debt, number of passengers needed to break even, operating expenses, and administrative expenses all stood at the lowest in the industry, and profit as a percentage of revenues ranked highest. *The Wall Street*

A Hong Kong junk pressed into service as a billboard, 1974.

THE AIR PIRATE

Four decades after D. B. Cooper's parachute getaway from a Northwest airliner—the first such air hijacking in U.S. history—Florence Schaffner was still upset and afraid. The former Northwest flight attendant and receiver of the hijacker's written demands had taken a long leave of absence after the crime, routinely checked beneath her auto for planted explosives, and feared for her life. Someday he might come looking for her, she thought, or want her out of the way. Those who had turned Cooper into a folk hero—the sellers of T-shirts bearing his wanted poster, makers of commemorative belt buckles, and writers of countless songs in his honor—could not understand how much he had endangered her life and the lives of others. To Schaffner, Cooper, whoever and wherever he was, was no hero.

America's most notorious instance of solo air piracy began on Thanksgiving eve 1971 aboard Northwest Flight 305, which was flying thirty-six passengers to Seattle-Tacoma from Portland. The aircraft, a short Boeing 727, was one of the few in the airline's fleet with an entrance and exit ramp built into the tail end. A middle-aged customer dressed in a raincoat and suit and tie, who had bought his ticket under the assumed name of Dan Cooper—a reporter later erroneously referred to him as D. B. Cooper—occupied coach seat 18F, at the rear

FBI sketches of D. B. Cooper. This remains the only unsolved case in American air piracy.

of the plane. Schaffner was working the flight, and right at takeoff Cooper gave her a note. She sometimes received unwanted propositions from male passengers, so Schaffner shoved the note into her purse. He urged her to read it, though. "I have a bomb in my briefcase. I want you to sit beside me," it said.

Another flight attendant, Tina Mucklow, relayed this information to the cockpit as Cooper stated his terms. He demanded $200,000 in used $20 bills, stuffed into a knapsack, and four parachutes—all to be ready when the flight landed in Seattle. "Has bomb in briefcase and will use if anything is done to block his request en route to Seattle," stated a Northwest memo relaying information received by phone. Cooper would let no passengers leave the plane in Seattle until he received what he wanted. The plane circled outside Seattle while it took two hours for Northwest officials to gather the cash from several banks and supply the parachutes. Nobody on board panicked, and, despite his murderous threats, Cooper remained calm and pleasant. In Minnesota, president Donald Nyrop and other officers followed the unfolding events.

After the flight landed and rolled to a halt in a well-lit area of the airport, law enforcement officers stayed clear of the ship. Mucklow pulled in the waiting money and the parachutes, and Cooper agreed to let the passengers go, as well as Schaffner and a third flight attendant, Alice Hancock. Only Cooper, Mucklow, pilot William Scott, and first officer Bill Rataczak remained aboard. Cooper offered to give the crew members a cash tip, which they refused.

Cooper then demanded that the 727 take off again, heading to Mexico City at an altitude of ten thousand feet. Scott warned that the fuel supply would not last that long, and Cooper agreed to let the plane stop for more fuel in Reno. Because of the parachutes, everyone expected Cooper to jump out using the rear exit soon after takeoff. As the plane cruised over the Willamette River valley, the exit stair light illuminated in the cockpit. About an hour later, in the wee hours of Thanksgiving morning, Scott landed the plane in Reno with the stairs still down. Cooper had departed, leaving two parachutes behind and strapping the money, which weighed twenty-one pounds, to his body with nylon cords. At the time, it was the largest ransom ever pirated from a U.S. airline.

Bank workers had recorded the serial number of each of the ransom bills, but few knew that the airline had inadvertently cheated Cooper in the ransom knapsack. "Cooper may still be looking for me—I shortchanged him $40—or I should say, the bank couldn't account for serial numbers on two of the $20 bills!" Northwest Seattle employee George E. Harrison wrote in a memo.

The FBI issued a wanted poster that described Cooper as a white male in his midforties, five feet ten inches to six feet, 170 to 180 pounds, with low ears, olive skin, and possibly brown eyes, and with dark brown or black hair, parted left and combed back. A federal grand jury indicted Cooper in absentia for air piracy. Over the years, campers and hunters found some of the marked bills and debris possibly blown out of the plane. (Nyrop unsuccessfully tried to buy some of the recaptured bills from the government to bestow as gifts to give to friends of the airline.) DNA testing in 2011 of Cooper's necktie, left aboard the airliner, produced no matches.

The FBI's file on the hijacking now measures more than forty feet long, and the agency considered more than a thousand suspects. Spurious deathbed confessions and the rediscovery of repressed or imagined memories lengthen the suspect list every year. Did Cooper survive his leap? Nobody knows. The manhunt has never officially ended, although only citizen investigators now keep it alive.

New safety procedures were the most satisfying outcome of the Cooper hijacking. Eastern Airlines devised a lock that prevented the opening of rear exit doors in flight. Northwest bought a supply of them. •

First Officer William Rataczak, Captain William Scott, and stewardess Tina Mucklow meet the press after their encounter with D. B. Cooper.

Fragments of "D. B. Cooper cash" found by an Arkansas man along the Columbia River in 1980.

A RATTLER OF A CEO

When a young Steven Rothmeier was interviewing for a job with Northwest in the early 1970s, a decade before himself rising to the position of CEO, he arrived for a meeting with the company's chief executive. By that time, Donald Nyrop had led the company for twenty years, but he still stood tall and was energetic in his movements. "He had a large office, and he was sitting behind his desk," Rothmeier recalled. "He was wearing glasses that magnified his eyes. During the interview he threw at me questions about management and leadership. But at one point, he stood up and walked to an anteroom that connected with his office. It was his private bathroom. He used the bathroom and kept asking questions. Then he flushed the toilet and came back." The wily CEO scrutinized the young interviewee to determine if he was rattled.

"He looked at me forever to see what I would do, how I would respond. This was what we called a 'stress interview,' a test in which you didn't know what you would get."

Many Northwest employees found it stressful to work with Nyrop, but the experience variously struck others as enlightening, oppressive, ennobling, and puzzling, depending on the circumstances. Fast-talking, autocratic, taciturn, charming, and possessing a smile that quickly lit his face and just as suddenly vanished, Nyrop professionalized Northwest by making air travel safer, more profitable, and more efficient. He pioneered the management of the modern airline and in his distinctive top-down style led his company for a very long time—so long, in fact, that as the industry's senior leader his once-innovative style of management grew outdated.

Born in 1912, Nyrop grew up in a remote midwestern corn-and-cattle town where his father was the banker and everyone knew everyone else. "Two 747s would just about carry the entire population of his native Elgin, Neb.," Northwest historian Kenneth Ruble observed. Clearly some of his later corporate values inoculated him at a young age. "Our father knew the value of money," remembered his sister, "but he wasn't a penny pincher. He insisted we turn off the lights not being used, but we had the best croquet set money could buy because it was made better and would last longer." She also recalled a family dictum that good works "should be given through the use of intelligence rather than through emotionalism."

Nyrop graduated from Doane College in Crete, Nebraska, spent a year as a schoolteacher to pay off his college debts, earned a law degree at George Washington University at night while working by day as an auditor for the General Accounting Office, and entered the world of aviation as a lawyer for the Civil Aeronautics Board. America's entry in World War II moved Nyrop to the Air Transport Command, where he planned the nationalization of U.S. airline fleets for the war effort and rose to the rank of lieutenant colonel. After the war he joined the Civil Aeronautics Administration as operations administrator and chaired

Northwest CEO Donald Nyrop's leadership approach combined fiscal conservatism, hard-nosed decision making, and reserved geniality to produce some of the biggest profits in the business.

the Civil Aeronautics Board at the age of thirty-nine, the youngest head of a federal agency.

At the CAB and other agencies, he sometimes visited crash sites and witnessed the charred bodies and wrecked aircraft. In his mind, safety was the most important goal of any airline. He gained notoriety as a dogged saver of taxpayer dollars.

Unnecessary agency automobiles were among his favorite budgetary targets, and he once slashed the CAB car fleet in Minneapolis. "He came to the Twin Cities to do a walk-around inspection of the agency's facilities," Steven Rothmeier recalls the story. "He arrived at the office early, before anyone else was there. He found out that the last snow had been two days earlier. One agency car was covered with snow with no wheel tracks behind it. 'It looks abandoned,' he said, and he cut a car from the budget."

He was in the private practice of law when Northwest, after repeated attempts to lure him out of Washington, hired him as president in 1954. By that time he was married with four children, including month-old twins, and he wanted to raise them in the Midwest. He called his family his "chief hobby"—he volunteered as a statistician for his son's high school hockey team—and did not take a vacation during his first three years at Northwest. (When he finally did take trips with his family, he often conducted station inspections en route.) His other hobbies included fishing and collecting American Western art.

Northwest was then financially ailing and had a poor safety record. Nyrop typically worked weekends and responded to the many problems he inherited as challenges to be assessed and eliminated one by one. He spent much time traveling Northwest's route system, and he devoted some of his hours in airports scrutinizing the operations of the competitors. Declaring his intention to "apply the basic philosophy of running a good farm to running an airline," he compared operational problems to large rocks in the field that must be removed. But his rigid convictions of efficient and inefficient, right and wrong, fair and unfair, led him to frequent conflicts with the airline's unions. During one eleven-year stretch during the 1960s and 1970s, he faced five strikes—more than any other airline.

And of course, his reputation for cost cutting grew even more at Northwest. "On my second day as chief financial officer," Roth-

meier remembered, "Mr. Nyrop told me to sit down in his office, and he pulled out a pair of washable work gloves from our maintenance area. He pointed out that we had 752 pairs of them in storage. 'Let's get rid of them,' he said. 'They're washable!'" Rothmeier was also present at a meeting in which Nyrop described his interest in the behavior of first-class passengers when flight attendants offered them a choice of five different flavors of ice cream. Only two customers selected pistachio, which he used as evidence that Northwest should simplify its in-flight food menu and realize gains from the standardization.

Yet there was an undeniable warmth to Nyrop's leadership. In 1966, he introduced a decidedly minor investor, a teenager who owned a small amount of NWA stock, to the assembled audience of the annual shareholders meeting and presented the youngster with a large model of a red-tailed 727 jet. He quietly gave his own money to employees hit by illnesses or other personal catastrophes in their families. Though not always loved, he was often respected.

During the 1970s, the Northwest board waived its requirement that executives retire at sixty-five to keep Nyrop on. By this time, Nyrop's hair had whitened and his face had weathered. He finally stepped down as CEO and board chairman in 1978 because of health problems and the sentiment that he was a hindrance to labor harmony. He remained a member of the board until 1984. When he died in 2010, an aviation legend at ninety-eight after a retirement in which he never commented publicly on Northwest's affairs, the airline had just been swallowed up by longtime competitor Delta Airlines. He may have felt proud that Northwest made the ultimate sacrifice of subsuming its very identity to the hope of improving profitability and efficiency. •

Journal crowned Nyrop "the Vince Lombardi of airline executives. . . . He has instilled a philosophy of hard work, simplicity of organization, careful deployment of fiscal resources and most conspicuously, rigorous cost control."

Nyrop always explained his airline's financial success as a triumph of strict management. "The differences in airlines are not the differences in equipment," he said in 1975. "The differences really are in two specific areas: the way in which they handle their equities and financing, and their cost controls. Those who haven't done a good job of handling the capital accounts are today paying higher interest charges than those who did. The basic reason our debt is low is that in the 1960s, when the value of all airline stocks was up substantially, we took advantage of the opportunity three times to go out and sell stocks so that we didn't have to borrow so much money. That's what you call capital management of the corporation."

Most of Northwest's competitors were cash poor, debt ridden, and clumsily managed by comparison. In 1978, the profits that TWA had accumulated over the previous ten years could buy only a single Boeing 747 plus spare parts. Nyrop relished opportunities to pull out his spreadsheets before an audience and decimate his rivals through detailed explications—speaking in "a voice dry as an airport announcement," noted a reporter witness—of why they could not make money and Northwest could. "We've paid out more dividends than the entire retained earnings of Continental, Western, Pan Am, and of course Eastern," he declared during one numbers extravaganza for the press. "We have the best quality fleet of any airline in the United States today, and by far."

How did Nyrop spend Northwest's accumulated earnings and more? Mainly on aircraft: By the middle of the 1970s, the company had forked over some $1.4 billion to amass its fleet of 113 newer jets, "including more roomy, wide-bodied aircraft for NWA's size than any other carrier," company historian Kenneth Ruble observed. But in Nyrop's hands, aircraft generated money as well. Beyond the tax benefit of depreciating the value of the planes, Nyrop continued to actively broker his company's aircraft, selling 141 of them (compared with 223 purchases) between 1954 and 1976. The sold airplanes often commanded prices above book value because of Northwest's practice of maintaining them exceptionally well and improving them. Nyrop, for instance, had his mechanics add noise-reduction features to his Boeing 747s, even though that aircraft was already quieter than most ships in the sky. Mostly one at a time, he sold off the company's Boeing 720Bs and 320s throughout the 1970s, keeping them as revenue-producing members of the fleet until just before disposing of them. So the very steps Nyrop undertook to make his airline one of the most competitive in the business also directly added to company profits.

After its service ferrying Northwest passengers, the Boeing 720B generated money for the company as President Donald Nyrop sold the planes off one by one.

The Boeing 727, Northwest's first three-engine aircraft in decades, carried countless passengers during the 1960s and 1970s.

M. Joseph Lapensky proved a worthy successor to Donald Nyrop. He was not flashy, excelled as a financial strategist, and was devoted to the company.

FINDING A SUCCESSOR

Toward the end of the 1970s, *Fortune* took note of Nyrop's financial wizardry and the big shoes he left for any successor to fill: "Nyrop is immensely proud of the way he has positioned Northwest to face the future. He tells friends that even if a successor started making bad decisions as soon as he took over, it would take years for him to run down the company. Nyrop obviously does not want to let go. The airline has been his life for nearly a quarter of a century, and so active a man could hardly spend much of his time or energy pursuing his other loves. . . . The NWA board, which already has waived the sixty-five year retirement rule for him, is unlikely to force him out." After all, Nyrop had lifted Northwest to reliable profitability and unusual success. He was the company's largest individual shareholder, as well.

But *Fortune* was wrong. In the end, if Northwest's board did not exactly force Nyrop out, it encouraged his departure.

As Nyrop neared the airline's normal retirement age of sixty-five in 1977, employees and company watchers wondered how Northwest would handle the succession to the presidency. Nyrop himself often answered the question with, "We've got a dozen well-seasoned men around here who could run this airline just fine." An airline trade periodical scored a bull's-eye with its prediction of the succession path: "If we were to make a guess, he won't step down but rather sort of sideways into the chairmanship to observe his hand-picked successor, one of those dozen men who could do the job, for perhaps a year just to make sure that the individual has learned well all that Nyrop has been telling him for the last 22 years."

That was Nyrop's exact plan when he picked M. Joseph Lapensky to follow him as president. Lapensky's employment with Northwest even predated Nyrop's; he had joined the company's accounting department in 1945 and worked his way up to a spot on the board and a position as treasurer and vice president of economic planning. For the first time, Northwest had selected a president from within its own ranks. Lapensky had spent twenty-two years under Nyrop's tutelage. Like his mentor, Lapensky stood aloof from the Twin Cities business community, avoided contact with the press, and knew his numbers. A financial analyst called him "cut from the same cloth" as his predecessor, and, like Nyrop, Lapensky frequently won the accolade of "financial wizard."

THE DEREGULATION STORM

Lapensky's orderly nature served Northwest well as the company approached a tradition-shattering event in the history of commercial aviation: the end of many of the government's regulations on routes and pricing. Supply and demand would dictate what domestic

AIRLIFTING PROPELLER SHAFTS AND SILKWORMS

Within a few years of its founding, Northwest launched a scheme to airlift freight to rail connections, where the cargo could continue by train to its destination. Although that coordination of air and rail schedules did not last long, it gave the airline a hint of the money-making potential of moving merchandise. In the years to come, trans-porting cargo would grow into one of the airline's most profitable activities.

Northwest's freight-hauling business greatly expanded with the opening of its routes to Asia in 1948. Goods shipped across the Pacific on Northwest airliners ranged from thirteen-thousand-pound naval propeller shafts to silkworms, and the amount of airlifted cultured pearls alone could "make a strand 200 miles in length," a company press release claimed in the early 1960s. Domestic freight hauling also accelerated; in 1957 the airline began a service called Sky Truck that pooled its planes with the resources of nineteen trucking firms to connect shippers in the Pacific Northwest and Midwest with their customers in the East.

Handling cargo became a truly big business for Northwest in the 1970s, with the company's purchase of several Boeing 747 freighters specially designed for moving goods. These flying beasts could each haul 235,000 tons of material. In his early years with the company as manager of economic analysis, future CEO Steven Rothmeier was part of a team that calculated how to feasibly fill these gargantuan craft and market their services. Focusing on cross-Pacific shipping, the

Nose cone raised, a Northwest cargo plane yawns emptiness.

A Northwest stewardess escorts a load of air express boxes, circa 1948.

A shipment of Japanese pearls en route from Tokyo to New York City, circa 1950.

team discovered that opportunities awaited in transporting such goods as fresh produce, fish, cars, and industrial equipment. The company formed a freight division, Northwest Cargo, in 1975 to manage the operations of this fleet, whose planes had been retrofitted with extra-large loading hatches to accommodate cargo the size of automobiles. Between 1972 and 1985, the airline's freight revenues multiplied twelvefold, and they nearly doubled again by the late 1990s. That growth made Northwest the largest cargo mover of any American airline, and the fourth largest in the world.

Over the years, Northwest cargo planes carried 190-foot-long oil pipes, boiler tubes weighing a ton each, and many other goods seemingly unsuitable for air travel, but the company gained the most attention for its shipping of live animals. Miss Bell, a half-ton Asian elephant flown in 1955 aboard a Douglas DC-4, arrived safely for a circus appearance in Anchorage. Bertha, a Beluga whale shipped to an aquarium in New York in 1958, had been spared a death sentence for raiding prized salmon runs in Alaska. (During a stop on her flight, handlers in Grand Rapids, Michigan, noticed that "Bertha looked a bit peaked around the mouth and nostrils, so she was rushed to a zoo here and put in the seal tank," a newspaper reported.) Northwest transported Japan's fleetest racehorse, Hakuchikara, to Seattle to began a season of racing in the United States. In 1988, two pandas bound for the Toledo Zoo from China traveled with three attendants. "Copies of the bears' papers have been sent to Chicago's customs office and are believed to be in order," a Northwest memo confirmed. •

A full-sized automobile in the cargo hold in 1976.

A train of freight awaits loading into a Northwest cargo plane, circa 1975.

Stewardess Kathleen Cusick comforts a beluga whale passenger.

A Northwest staffer entertains two small monkeys before their flight in 1950.

The shah of Iran's German shepherd travels in the cargo hold, circa 1955.

airlines offered, and at what cost. Fears arose that devastating price wars, bankruptcies, and the harmful elimination of unprofitable routes would result. (In 1975, Nyrop had addressed the concerns about route eliminations by telling a reporter, "If the airline doesn't happen to go to Keokuk, Iowa, I don't think the people in Keokuk are being denied a Constitutional right.")

The Airline Deregulation Act went on the books in 1978. New airlines without the responsibilities and burdens of union contracts jumped into the battle for customers. At the same time, aircraft fuel began a steep price increase that squeezed established airlines as they fell into unaccustomed competition for passengers. Nevertheless, most airlines welcomed deregulation as a chance to easily place new sections of the country on their route maps. During the 1970s before deregulation, Northwest had added routes serving Boston, New Orleans, and other cities. Northwest's domestic destinations, however, still largely remained in the top half of the United States, with a web of flights connecting to Florida and Hawaii. The airline wanted to break out of this grid to carry passengers along the East and West Coasts and through the southern states. At the same time, Northwest added transatlantic service to Copenhagen and Stockholm—after a struggle to point out to the Civil Aeronautics Board that Pan Am had long let these routes wither on its line—and eventually expanded its European map to include London and Frankfurt. Under Lapensky's guiding hand, Northwest remained profitable well into the era of deregulation.

LABOR DISPUTES BRING NYROP'S FAREWELL

Meanwhile, Nyrop retained control of the company by hanging on as chairman of the board. In that position, he observed Lapensky and maintained an iron grip on Northwest, and one reporter compared him to "a bronco rider of old . . . willing to dig in his spurs and take his lumps in order to stay on top of everything that affects his beloved bottom line." A plaque hanging in his office gave an easygoing message: "Along the way . . . take time to smell the flowers." Tellingly, however, the plaque faced visitors and did not admonish the man sitting behind the desk.

Late in 1978, Lapensky took Nyrop's place as board chairman. Although Lapensky and others on the board called "hogwash" any suggestion that they had forced out Nyrop, most board members were more than happy to see the company patriarch go, due to Nyrop's long legacy of rancorous and disruptive labor relations. His impersonal, unbending, and unemotional approach to negotiations—which intentionally or not suggested that Northwest's people were of equal value to the company as its planes and parts—incensed the unions. "We were part of the equipment," one former flight attendant lamented. With his focus on cost control and efficiency through standardization, he built a company culture that challenged and confronted unionized employees at every turn.

By the end of Nyrop's tenure, his fellow board members had come to believe that continual conflict with unions was not good for the company. A pilot involved in his union's contract negotiating committee predicted that Nyrop's disappearance would "boost morale one million percent." Many in the company felt such relief. "The ducks stopped lining up at his command," the *Minneapolis Star* observed. "Enough board members finally recognized the extremely dangerous dimensions of Northwest's labor problems."

The danger became clear in a series of disputes that shut down the company repeatedly during Nyrop's last years, including an injurious pilots' strike in 1978 that lasted 109 days. That year Northwest worked under a backlog of 640 labor grievances. "Someday," observed J. J. O'Donnell, president of the Air Line Pilots Association, "Mr. Nyrop is going to leave Northwest and some employee group—I'm not saying it will be the pilots, but some group—is going to have its pound of flesh for all the abuse Nyrop has heaped on employees all these years."

Overall, Northwest's scorecard of labor unrest was not the industry's worst, but the vitriol of the airline's conflicts made impressions on people outside the company. "He's taken the strongest and firmest positions with regard to labor negotiations of anyone in the business, and it's damned hard to be critical in light of the results he's achieved," former United Airlines president George Keck had said of Nyrop in the early 1970s. "Let's face it—the name of the game is profits and, in the final analysis, that's what he'll be judged by." But that take on Nyrop's leadership eventually lost currency. Northwest's competitors, who through the industry's mutual aid pact funded a money pool that assisted airlines targeted for strikes, began to resent Northwest's frequent dipping into the pot.

Nyrop's jousting against unions had long divided Northwest, and many in the airline yearned for a reconciliation between management and workers. At last, they hoped, the company could heal. Waiting in the wings was a Northwest executive who hoped he could someday bring the company and its unions closer together. Steven G. Rothmeier—seemingly an analytic and unemotional Nyrop clone who the old president had once predicted could someday lead the company—had made his mark early by figuring out how to fill the new 747s with enough cargo to turn a good profit. In 1979 at the age of thirty-two, Rothmeier become Northwest's chief financial officer, the youngest such executive in the airline business. If he were in charge of all of Northwest's operations, he would handle the unions a little differently.

CHAPTER 7

ONE WHAMMY
AFTER ANOTHER

On a July day in 1985, in a quiet district of Copenhagen, Denmark, near the Tivoli amusement park and the city's downtown railway station, a bomb erupted. The bombers targeted Northwest's ticket office—the only such office of any American airline in Copenhagen. The bomb killed one person and injured twenty others, including three people inside the Northwest office, whose interior was "gutted," news agencies reported. A nearly simultaneous explosion at a Copenhagen synagogue injured seven people.

Four years later, a Swedish court convicted four men (Mohammed Abu Talb, a grocer and video store owner; two of his brothers-in-law; and Marten Imandi) for their involvement in the crimes. Talb and Imandi received life sentences, and police also suspected Talb of complicity in the 1988 bombing of Pan Am Flight 103 at Lockerbie, Scotland, which killed 270 people.

International terrorism had invaded Northwest's world. Unlike the plane hijackings of the 1960s and 1970s, the Copenhagen bombing resulted from the work of many conspirators with political motives. Their attack came suddenly and without warning, leaving wreckage and death behind.

The repercussions of many events of the 1980s, especially the lingering aftereffects of airline deregulation, hit Northwest like the shock of this bomb blast. Some of these events were predictable, others unexpected. Profits wavered, competitors came out slugging and faltered, old leaders stepped back as others advanced, unwanted suitors appeared, and self-proclaimed saviors with questionable motivations took control. No other decade in Northwest's history produced so many jolts.

In the air over Copenhagen in the 1980s.

A NEW WORLD OF COMPETITION

Airline deregulation, which began in the late 1970s, continued to produce some of the whammies. The old practice of establishing set fares for first class, business class, and coach gave way to a complex tangle of ticket prices that changed daily. The planes of new, low-overhead airlines like People Express filled the skies, and many unprepared airports grew congested. At Minneapolis–St. Paul International Airport, Northwest's home base, the number of airlines more than tripled in the seven years after deregulation, and the number of passengers carried went up by 50 percent.

Braniff—which rumors incorrectly pegged as a takeover target by Northwest—set a standard for recklessness by opening up ports of call in eighteen different cities in a single day. Meanwhile, the early 1980s ushered in a deep financial recession, record-high fuel prices, and President Ronald Reagan's controversial dismissal of striking air traffic controllers, all of which, with the competitive pressures of deregulation, helped slam air carriers with $1.4 billion in losses during 1980 and 1981 and spun forty-nine airlines into closing or bankruptcy.

Among the wounded who would soon take on overwhelming debt were Eastern, TWA, and

Northwest airliners cluster around a terminal at Narita Airport in Japan.

First-class china table setting, 1980.

Pan Am. Continental Airlines had accumulated losses since deregulation that totaled nearly half a billion dollars. After bankruptcy, Continental restarted without union employees, much of its workforce, and most of its former destinations. Even Delta Airlines, Northwest's chief rival for domestic customers and the annual top ranking for profitability, suffered unaccustomed losses and slashed employee wages. Yet Continental and Delta had the resources and experience necessary for survival. Rather than clearing a path for upstart new airlines, deregulation had decimated the ranks of small carriers and handed the large companies even more of the air traffic than they previously enjoyed.

Throughout this turmoil, Northwest did well. It took a cautious approach to the opportunities of deregulation, staggering its introduction of service to new domestic destinations over several years: St. Louis, Las Vegas, Orlando, Phoenix, Fort Myers, Denver, Dallas–Fort Worth, Omaha, Kansas City, San Diego, West Palm Beach, and Grand Rapids, among others. In the international market, it faced a mix of victories and setbacks. During the early 1980s, Northwest received the Civil Aeronautics Board's permission to add its first European destinations—cities that other airlines had ignored or given up on—by inaugurating flights to London, Hamburg, Glasgow, Copenhagen, Shannon (Ireland), Dublin, Oslo, and Stockholm. Despite the high cost of starting up these European routes, which *Business Week* in 1980 criticized as "a huge minus" to the airline's operations, Northwest had most of them running profitably within a few years.

In 1980, Northwest lost to Pacific enemy Pan Am in its effort to become the first U.S. commercial passenger carrier since the civil war of 1949 to serve the mainland of China. (Northwest had flown two aircraft to Beijing in 1973 to assist in a U.S. diplomatic mission. In 1980, it undertook another flight to bring U.S. officials to China for a trade exhibition.) It still retained its decades-old authorization to fly to China, along with a list of Chinese destinations it had planned to serve but never could in the 1940s: Beijing, Nanking, Harbin, and others. Northwest finally won permission to add that populous nation to its routes in 1984.

The inaugural flight to Shanghai, carrying 150 people, took about nineteen hours

Smooth flying over ocean waters in the 1980s.

from its takeoff in Minneapolis–St. Paul, about one-third the time Northwest's last flight to China thirty-five years earlier had required. Business relationships with China had not yet developed, so the airline mainly carried American tourists, 120,000 of whom would visit in 1984. Service to China helped Northwest overcome a serious threat from United Airlines, which bought the Pacific routes of struggling Pan Am in 1986. After more than forty years, the airline had become the undisputed leading American carrier to serve Asia and the Pacific.

THE PRICE OF SUCCESS

By the mid-1980s, Northwest's network of routes, serviced by fifteen thousand employees, reached fifteen thousand miles from west to east, stretching from Malaysia to Sweden. Through Airlink—a partnership with the regional airlines Mesaba, Big Sky, America West, Fischer Brothers Aviation, Simmons, and Express Airlines—the company funneled in connections from thirty-eight new cities. (In return, the regionals received easy entry for their customers to Northwest's growing assortment of domestic and international destinations.) Northwest in 1985 also joined the tour wholesaling business with its purchase of MLT, which offered travel packages through thousands of travel agencies. MLT came with a passenger-carrying affiliate, Sun Country Airlines.

Such business moves helped the company remain profitable; earnings settled at $10.5 million in 1981, 25 percent more than the previous year, leaving Northwest as one of only four airlines in the black. Those profits would rise eightfold by 1984 as the nation's economy recovered from recession. Among the major U.S. carriers in 1986, Northwest stood alone in making a profit for each of the previous ten years. Consistent profitability enabled the company to keep its level of debt low—far lower than did most other airlines. Even so, earnings were barely enough to build the enormous pool of money Northwest said it needed to continue modernizing its fleet.

These planes came at a steep cost. While Northwest could buy seven Boeing 727s for $50 million during the 1970s, that sum paid for only one 757 ten years later. Paying more brought important advantages: The 757 carried 40 percent more passengers and consumed one-third less fuel than had the 727. The airline bought twenty of these costly leviathans early in the decade and borrowed money to order ten more of the 184-seat 757s in 1985.

Hoping to generate hometown support, Northwest named its first two 757s "The City of Minneapolis" and "The City of St. Paul." It also bolstered its Pacific fleet by rushing to become the first airline to order a technologically improved version of a familiar model, the Boeing 747-400. Powerful onboard computers allowed a crew of only two to fly the 747-400, and the plane could move 450 passengers on one-fifth less fuel than the previous

747, allowing easy nonstop flights from the eastern United States to Asia. By this time, Northwest was flying more 747s than any other American carrier. Later in the decade, Northwest deviated from its reliance on Douglas and Boeing aircraft to acquire planes from the European manufacturer Airbus.

NEW RULES OF BUSINESS

While deregulation handed Northwest many of the same difficulties as it dealt to other airlines—fierce competition, the need to lower labor costs, pressures to economize and keep fares as low as its new bare-bones opponents—it produced a transformation unique to Northwest. For decades since its founding, the airline had advanced and often thrived under a triumvirate of forceful chief executives: Lewis Brittin, Croil Hunter, and Donald Nyrop. These men had stamped Northwest with their personalities, brought their personal strengths to bear on the airline's problems, and collectively given Northwest a reputation as a scrapper—an airline capable of leading the industry in innovation, use of technology, and forward thinking. They could successfully do so in decades when airlines and the risks of failure were relatively small.

The era of deregulation, however, changed the playing field. Already the major airlines had grown into corporate mammoths, more comparable in size to General Mills and Chrysler than to the modestly sized regional airlines whose planes shared runways with theirs. And suddenly, without government regulations keeping fares artificially high and closing domestic routes to all comers, those tenacious qualities that formed the Northwest brand became less important. With competitors on all sides lowering fares, no airline could afford to focus on innovation, technology, and thinking far ahead. Northwest had to become, like everyone else, a low-cost airline. It did not need leaders to captivate employees and the public with their personality. It did not even necessarily need leaders experienced in directing airlines. It needed managers who could keep the airline sailing ahead as less deftly supervised competitors failed to cut costs, failed to keep fares low, and foundered.

Through this evolving environment rose Steven Rothmeier. At the age of thirty-nine, he became America's youngest airline boss when the Northwest board elected him chief executive officer in 1984, just a year after his ascent to the company's presidency. M. J. Lapensky stepped aside to become board chairman. (Rothmeier replaced Lapensky as board chairman in 1986.) Unlike Lapensky, who often displayed a dry wit, Rothmeier was "not in the humor stage yet," said a financial analyst who followed the company. Maybe experience in the CEO seat would develop Rothmeier's sense of humor, or perhaps destroy it. The Northwest he took over was the nation's second-oldest airline that had maintained

CHANCE FAVORS THE PREPARED MIND ⏱

Steve Rothmeier recalls that his introduction to Northwest Airlines came by chance. While finishing his MBA in 1972 at the University of Chicago, he heard from a professor at his undergraduate alma mater, the University of Notre Dame. The professor had just met Donald Nyrop at a hockey game and learned that Northwest was looking for a couple of smart young business graduates. Rothmeier, who had written a paper on airline fares in deregulated markets, tried to get an interview with Nyrop, but a pilots' strike had shut down Northwest and he could not schedule an appointment.

Rothmeier was just starting a job with General Mills months later when the phone rang in his new office. "I didn't want to answer it," Rothmeier said. "I even walked out of my office and went into the hallway, but something made me go back inside. It was Northwest's director of personnel, who told me that Mr. Nyrop wanted to see me at the end of the week." Rothmeier ended up interviewing not only with Nyrop, but with seventeen of the other eighteen officers of the company. At last, Northwest offered him a job, and his prospects of advancement would be good as one of the airline's few young MBAs. "I was making more money at General Mills, but I couldn't resist the opportunity," he said.

He joined Northwest as a financial analyst at the age of twenty-seven. Few people at his new company knew that he had set himself a goal to lead a major corporation before he turned forty. After growing up as the eldest in a family of three boys in the Minnesota cities of Faribault and Mankato, Rothmeier in high school had to confront the catastrophe of his father's death in a car crash. He kept the family's propane gas business going and soon negotiated its sale to the Phillips Petroleum Company, a notable achievement for a young man barely out of his teens. At Notre Dame he played football under the legendary coach Ara Parseghian. He went on to volunteer for the army in the Vietnam War, ran a petroleum-supply team and directed a graves registration group, and returned home as a lieutenant to earn his MBA.

Right away it became clear that Rothmeier's talents in finance and long-term planning would carry him far at Northwest. He could crunch figures and forecast financial outcomes with the best, and he believed that numbers-based information could effectively guide all business decisions. "I think Louis Pasteur said, 'Chance favors the prepared mind,'" he was fond of quoting. "I have always sort of believed that." He was promoted to vice president of finance and treasurer at thirty-two and moved up to executive vice president of finance and administration, with a seat on the board of directors, at thirty-six. Less than two years later the board elected him Northwest's president and chief operating officer in 1983. Nobody was surprised when the airline named him CEO at the age of thirty-nine, ahead of his long-held goal and by far the youngest chief executive in the airline business.

Rothmeier's personality aided his decade-long rise to the top of Northwest. Understated, focused, and wary of moving in new directions without the justifying numbers, he differed from his airline's CEO predecessors by entrusting lower managers to carry out his plans the way they thought best. Far from easing his own burdens, however, this decentralization of decision making did not stop Rothmeier from keeping his own counsel, working seventy- to eighty-hour weeks, and feeling his responsibilities around the clock. To relieve the stress, he built a famously large four-bedroom man-castle for himself near the company's headquarters in Eagan, where he lifted Nautilus weights, read military history, enjoyed German wines, and listened to classical music. He often read business reports between weight-lifting sets. That same use of personal and business time had led college classmates to nickname him Sparty, after the rigorous preparations and disciplined living of the Spartans.

To achieve the complex merger of Republic and Northwest in 1986, he entrusted no less than thirteen committees with the task. Customer service, baggage handling, employee morale, and flight scheduling temporarily suffered—and Rothmeier required all Northwest managers to be at their desks by 8:00 A.M. every day to find solutions—but he believes the worst snafus of the merger arose from pay scale differences, seniority complications, and union problems. "We ended up with the most unionized airline in the world," he said, "95 percent union, and pilots and meteorologists were the only ones represented by the same unions in both companies. The other groups were put together for the first time in efforts involving thirteen unions. The unions were fighting, and there was deliberate sabotage of ground equipment. But there was no danger to passengers, and once things settled great things happened."

Al Checchi and Gary Wilson, engineers of the 1989 Wings buyout of the company, greatly exaggerated the financial problems of Northwest at the time of their purchase, he maintains. As the purchase moved ahead, he feared that the Wings bid of $121 a share was far too high and would leave Northwest with horrendous debt. Rothmeier could have stayed on to lead the company, but he left with many top managers a few months after the purchase. "We figured out these guys didn't know anything about running an airline," he said of Checchi and Wilson.

He remembers that one morning in October 1989 he heard that the Wings group wanted to bring in McKinsey and Company consultants to give their opinion on the airline's business strategies. That was the final straw for Rothmeier. "We had brought Northwest to the num-ber one share in the Pacific, and we knew you couldn't leverage an airline," he said. "We built it over twenty-five years. They wanted to bring in outside consultants for a jillion dollars. . . . They wouldn't listen to us, and if there were problems, we would be the fall guys. That wasn't going to happen. Five of us left on the same day."

After leaving Northwest, Rothmeier presided over a Twin Cities venture capital and merchant banking firm before founding Great Northern Capital, a St. Paul private investment company. He still has an office there, and on a clear day he has a view of planes taking off from Minneapolis–St. Paul International Airport. He is most proud of the people he hired during his time as chief executive of Northwest. What does he miss? "Not a lot," he says. "I did it every day for fifteen years, and during that time I did thirty years of work." •

one name—Western Airlines was the oldest, although some aviation historians disqualified it because it had briefly operated under a different name during the 1930s—and stood alone as the only major U.S. carrier to earn a profit for the previous ten years. Rothmeier was a reserved and bespectacled financial planning specialist who had served Northwest as chief financial officer just as the company was adjusting to airline deregulation. He represented a new generation of Northwest leaders who had earned their promotions in the aftermath of deregulation.

The cool and impersonal Rothmeier would not be the sort of CEO who, like his forebear Donald Nyrop, personally made aircraft purchase decisions and directed the interior design elements of plane cabins. He would break from that Northwest tradition and delegate decisions to managers. "To use a football analogy," wrote company historian Kenneth Ruble during the new CEO's tenure, "Rothmeier—as head coach—establishes the play book, then it's up to his assistant coaches to execute the strategy and produce results." Nyrop, in contrast, would have sewn the football and run it into the end zone himself.

Rothmeier, who played as a linebacker at the University of Notre Dame, could have originated this gridiron analogy; he often mentioned football in media interviews and followed a weight-lifting regimen under the guidance of the strength-training coach of the Chicago Bears. He liked to tell a story of a young assistant coach whose career goal was to become head coach by the age of forty—a goal Rothmeier transferred to the corporate realm—and he described the inspiration he drew from Notre Dame's coaching staff: "I lived in the residence hall that was next to where the coaches' offices were. It was always amazing because you could come back late at night and the coaches' office lights were still on, and you knew they were still in there working. You get up on Sunday morning, before you got out for breakfast or to mass, and the coaches were already in the office, working on next week's game plan," Rothmeier said, concluding, "I probably fall into the workaholic category."

Rothmeier established his managerial independence in multiple ways. Northwest's corporate headquarters, the dull structure that Nyrop had built practically inside Minneapolis–St. Paul International Airport—a home whose design rejected windows as a distraction, a needless expense, and an invasion of privacy—did not please the new man in charge. In its place, Rothmeier approved a 267,000-square-foot building situated on a landscaped, 138-acre tract in Eagan, a suburb near the airport. "They like the seclusion," said construction consultant Robert Ritchie of Rothmeier and his top aides. "They like the ponds, the rolling hills." The new four-story headquarters, which opened in 1986, bathed in sunlight that poured through walls of glass. (Northwest demoted the old headquarters to service as a maintenance facility and opened a new hangar for 747s, as well as a tower for technical and additional administrative employees, nearby.) In addition, Rothmeier borrowed large sums of money to enable Northwest to compete, a practice Nyrop likely would have disliked.

One of Rothmeier's MBA professors at the University of Chicago had appraised him as "dedicated and self-disciplined, and he's a tough s.o.b.—not afraid to make a decision." Rothmeier once explained how he delegated decisions to his eight-member executive management team. "If I should make a proposal and . . . eight are opposed to it, my vote breaks that 8–0 tie," he said, hastening to add, "But that's never happened." He was sensitive to accusations that he acted like an impersonal dictator, countering, "That's part of having high visibility, of making tough decisions."

Rothmeier made clear what his leadership of Northwest would emphasize. "Our individual standard of living and our corporate standard of living depend on winning the battle for market share," he declared to Northwest employees early on. "Each one of us is competing directly with his or her counterpart at all the other carriers—and the pie is not all that big, because there are 13 more jet operators today than when deregulation took effect." Another time, he told of his preference for simple decision making over too-rigorous analysis: "When you talk about management, you're really talking about five things: planning, organizing, staffing, directing, and controlling an activity, whether it be a football team or a school or a university or a parish or a corporation. A lot of airlines make things more complicated, as if you have to study the hell out of this or that. And that's not really the case." He challenged employees to become "winners," which he defined as people who could continue earning profits in an era of difficult competition.

An open atrium with hanging vines symbolized the differences between the company's new headquarters in Eagan, Minnesota, and its former coldly efficient offices at Minneapolis–St. Paul International Airport.

Despite a mechanics' strike in 1982, labor relations had already improved after Donald Nyrop's departure from the CEO's desk. Lapensky shocked employees in 1979 by paying bonuses for extra stresses they suffered from additional work during a strike that shut down United Airlines, and the following year, for the first time in a quarter century, Northwest came to a contract agreement with its pilots in advance of the expiration of the old agreement. Rothmeier continued this softening of the relationship with Northwest's employees, much different from Nyrop's view of workers as interchangeable in value with such assets as planes and equipment. An official of the International Association of Machinists commented on the thaw in 1985: "I perceive a more realistic attitude in bargaining with us on their part, which in turn generates a more realistic attitude on our side," he said. "I see that as beneficial to both sides." Rothmeier initiated a program called Operation Breakthrough, which encouraged employees to take part in operational decisions, and he made the unusual decision to accept the invitation of the Air Line Pilots Association to speak directly to an assembly of hundreds of Northwest captains—the only time in memory that a company CEO had appeared before the group that had gone on strike against the airline four times in twenty years. It was a gutsy move in a period when some Northwest aircrew salaries had tripled during the previous decade and airline executives frequently blamed labor for their financial woes after deregulation.

On Rothmeier's watch, the company began communicating more directly with employees; workers received thank-you notes from the airline for exemplary customer service, and Northwest even asked flight attendants for their opinion of new uniform possibilities. "This was not a democratic decision, mind you," cautioned a company official after the uniform had been selected, "but we did solicit their input. After all, they're the ones who were going to have to wear the uniforms, not me." Ultimately Northwest was able to craft budget-saving agreements with its unions that established two levels of salaries: one that preserved old pay tiers for current employees, and another that set lower pay for future workers.

THE GROWTH IMPERATIVE

Neither charismatic nor domineering, Rothmeier understood that Northwest's current profitability would mean nothing in the rough and tumble years ahead. He knew that the nation's seventh-largest airline could not match the rock-bottom labor outlays of the low-cost carriers. That left one other course to follow if Northwest were to continue to make money in the 1990s and beyond: find the economies that come with size and sales volume, preferably by combining with another airline. Without that growth, Northwest faced a friendly or unfriendly absorption by another major airline intent on expansion. Northwest's earlier efforts to merge with Northeast and National had failed, yet Northwest had survived. Getting bigger was not then essential for profitability. But by the mid-1980s, although the airline had steadily grown for sixty years without a merger, Northwest might not make it far without combining with another carrier.

Rothmeier and his board so strongly believed that a merger was crucial to Northwest's future that he approved on Labor Day in 1985 a secret proposal to Delta to purchase the Atlanta-based airline. The offer was $53 per share. Three times Northwest's size, Delta had huge reserves of cash, which, combined with Northwest's Pacific routes, would produce an internationally powerful carrier. "They said no," Rothmeier recalls of Delta's response. "They couldn't see being acquired by some Yankee operators." (A year later, Delta acquired Western Airlines.) With that possibility gone, the field of good merger partners looked slim. But few people realized that Rothmeier had a kindred spirit just a few miles from Northwest's executive offices in Eagan, the head of a feisty competitor with a good record of success but an uncertain future in the era of deregulation.

In the middle of 1985, Stephen Wolf, the popular and crafty chief executive officer of Republic Airlines, took the initiative to telephone Rothmeier to arrange a conversation that would forever change the two airlines. Over the next several weeks they met again at hotels around the Twin Cities, and they resolved to keep talking in the months ahead. Republic had begun thirty-nine years earlier as the tiny regional carrier Wisconsin Central Airlines. It had changed its name to North Central Airlines in 1952 and relocated its offices to the Twin Cities. A 1979 merger with Southern Airways, right after deregulation went into effect, created Republic and vaulted it to greater prominence. Its route network spiderwebbed the Upper Midwest, East Coast, and South while reaching as far west as Denver.

Rothmeier and Wolf continued meeting beyond the end of 1985, both keeping their advising teams small to keep news of their secret merger negotiations from spreading. "Everyone on the two merger teams gulped when Minnesota Governor Rudy Perpich, fearful that thousands of Minnesota jobs might vanish if either Northwest or Republic—or both—should become a takeover target, publicly suggested that the two merge," recorded Northwest historian Kenneth Ruble. Wolf's team tried to throw newshounds off the scent by dropping hints that Republic was reaching an acquisition deal with Delta or American.

Northwest's January 1986 meeting of its board of directors was nearing, but the two airline leaders lacked an agreement on the price per share of Republic stock that Northwest would pay in an acquisition. Finally, on the day of the meeting, Rothmeier proposed a purchase price of $17 per share, or a total of $884 million for an outright cash purchase of Republic. Wolf agreed, and the boards of both companies quickly signed off. The purchase price was an impressive consideration for the patience of Wolf and Republic shareholders,

Stephen Wolf, Republic's chief executive who worked with Steve Rothmeier to pull off the industry's biggest merger.

THE WONDROUS FLIGHT OF HERMAN THE GOOSE

When Northwest acquired Minneapolis-based Republic Airlines along with Herman, its blue goose logo (initially a mallard duck) in 1986, it mixed into its veins the blood of nearly a dozen earlier airlines with historical stakes in Republic's operations. Unlike Northwest, which had lasted sixty years without a previous merger or name change, Republic's past featured a tangle of company combinations and mountains of obsolete letterhead.

One branch of Republic's past originated in Clintonville, Wisconsin, the World War II–era birthplace of Wisconsin Central Airlines. The young company began by ferrying executives of an automobile parts company to

A Republic Airlines 727-200 during that company's growing years of the 1970s.

Chicago and Green Bay, and evolved in 1946 into a carrier that served several Wisconsin cities. A year after its founding, the airline was lucky to hire a young, former TWA executive named Hal Carr, who contributed to the rejuvenation of the small fleet and the building of new routes into neighboring Minnesota. By 1949, Wisconsin Central had more than two hundred employees and was flying thirty-two thousand passengers annually.

Only six years past its founding, the company moved its base of operations to Minneapolis and renamed itself North Central Airlines. Financial problems led to Carr's resignation, but he returned as a thirty-three-year-old president just as the airline was facing bankruptcy in 1954. Carr presided over a reinvention of the airline, expanding North Central's route map beyond the limitations of most regional airlines, covering thirty-four hundred miles and reaching as far east as New York City. By 1960, it was carrying more passengers than any other regional airline in the United States.

North Central ordered its first jets in the mid-1960s, a time of great growth. Now carrying more than three million passengers a year, it opened new headquarters at Minneapolis–St. Paul International Airport in 1969. A series of fatal crashes marred this expansion, but North Central held on to remain profitable through most of the 1970s. One of its venerable DC-3 aircraft was retired in 1975 as the world's high odometer leader with 84,879 hours flown—equivalent to ten continuous years in the air—since its manufacture thirty-six years earlier. With airline deregulation at the close of the decade, North Central was flying to ninety-three cities in nineteen states and provinces, but it needed the efficiencies of increased size to remain competitive.

Meanwhile, Atlanta-based Southern Airways faced a similar predicament—and Southern represents the second historical branch of Republic. Founded in 1936 by pilot and former Delta employee Frank Hulse, Southern began as a charter carrier serving eight southern states during the 1940s. It launched scheduled service in 1949 and widened its web to seventeen cities by the end of the 1950s. Southern endured a bitter pilots' strike in 1960 that led to the establishment of a competing airline, but managed to survive into the jet age with route expansions and new equipment. Some notoriety in the 1970s came from smiley-face decorated noses of its aircraft and the risqué uniforms of its flight attendants, who willingly or not donned hot pants and black stockings.

Without more capital, Southern could not upgrade its fleet and quickly lost ground in the era of deregulation. A merger with North Central received federal approval in 1979, producing a newly named entity, Republic Airlines, with a network of routes connecting New York, the Grand Cayman Islands, Denver, and Winnipeg, as well as an extensive list of destinations in the airlines' strongholds of the South and Upper Midwest.

Here a third stream of tradition merged with the multicultural Republic. In 1952, Seattle-based West Coast Airlines multiplied in size with the acquisition of Empire Air Lines, which also served the Pacific Northwest. It merged with Bonanza Airlines and again with Pacific Airlines in the late 1960s. This last combination produced Air West, a wide-ranging airline that came under the ownership of the eccentric billionaire Howard Hughes and his Hughes Tool Company in 1969. Headquartered under this new management in San Mateo, California, Hughes Air West adopted an eye-popping all-yellow color scheme and cast its reach into the Midwest. The airline was fast taking on debt and losing money, however—a turn of events Howard Hughes's mysterious death prevented him from witnessing. Hughes's holding company and estate sold the airline to Republic in 1980 for $38.5 million, giving Republic an impressive new total of fifteen thousand employees and 207 destinations bounded by the Carib-

bean, Mexico, Canada, and New England, more cities than any other U.S. airline.

The early 1980s were not easy times to operate such an extended system. Losses accumulated to $220 million during the early years of the decade, and the company's share value plummeted to $3.00. On the verge of bankruptcy in 1983, Republic survived because of employees' willingness to trade wage concessions for stock ownership. A new CEO, Stephen Wolf, who arrived in 1984 with previous experience at Continental, Pan Am, and American, was able to generate a profit of $177 million his first year. He did not believe it was possible to sustain Republic's health, though. Wolf initiated merger discussions with Northwest's CEO, Steve Rothmeier, in 1985, and the acquisition took effect the following year. At its end, Republic was the nation's ninth-largest airline. "Wolf did a wonderful job of trying to fix Republic," Rothmeier says. "He couldn't do it, though, because he didn't have enough money."

For years after the Republic-Northwest merger, people reported sightings of Herman the Goose on old signs in the airports of Minneapolis, Detroit, Memphis, and other cities. They are long gone now, although the memory of Republic remains strong among former passengers, retirees, and employees still working for Delta and other airlines. •

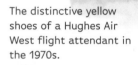

The distinctive yellow shoes of a Hughes Air West flight attendant in the 1970s.

A tombstone for Herman the Goose was planted on the lawn of Republic's headquarters in Minneapolis–St. Paul in 1986.

many employees among them, who a few years earlier had seen their company's stock drop to one-fifth that value when Republic's financial woes dragged the airline to the brink of bankruptcy. But Republic had recovered, and its 1985 earnings exceeded Northwest's by 242 percent.

Rothmeier hoped that the airlines could merge operations in time for the busy summer flight season, but the U.S. Department of Transportation set evidentiary hearings too late to allow for that ambitious schedule. The agency especially wanted to air the concerns of the Department of Justice that the merger might reduce airline competition in Minneapolis–St. Paul. Ultimately the Department of Transportation discounted that prediction. "By combining the two carriers' complementary fleets and route systems," the agency asserted, "this acquisition will address these long-term needs of the two carriers: Northwest will get an existing domestic system and a fleet of more efficient two-engine, two-pilot aircraft; Republic will have a trunk and international route system to feed, and the larger aircraft to operate more efficiently." The agency concluded that any loss of competition in the Twin Cities, Bismarck, Fargo, and Grand Forks would be offset by cost savings that would benefit the traveling public. The hearings, attended by all the interested parties and some two dozen attorneys, concluded in the late spring of 1986. Then came the recommendation of an administrative law judge, the filing of final briefs from all the parties, and the unchallengeable decision on the merger from Transportation Secretary Elizabeth Dole.

So, nine months after the announcement of the proposed merger, the deal finally became effective with the combination of the airlines' flight schedules in October 1986, after winding through this long process and winning the approval of the companies' shareholders. (The formal financial transaction, the wiring of hundreds of millions of dollars to Northwest's stock transfer agent, took place in the company's headquarters. Almost simultaneously, Rothmeier's title changed from president and CEO to chairman of the board and CEO, with John F. Horn assuming the duties of president.) The merger delighted most Minnesotans, who realized that however Northwest decided to absorb Republic's organization and operations, the new and larger company would not abandon the state. On the very month of its sixtieth anniversary, Northwest had shown that an elderly carrier (in aviation years) could still execute surprising maneuvers. Time would tell whether the company's bold move to ward off the pressures of airline deregulation would work.

MERGER COMPLICATIONS

The Northwest-Republic combination was then the largest airline merger in history. All at once, Northwest gained Republic's 168 aircraft, sixty-five new destinations (including locations in Mexico, eastern Canada, and the Caribbean), and 13,400 employees. The new Northwest would have 30,000 employees and a fleet of 312 planes—and now ranked among the five largest U.S. airlines in operating revenues and the top three in route miles.

Ahead lay the gigantic task of merging the two companies. The terms of the deal had relieved Wolf of future involvement, so the task was in Northwest's hands. Rothmeier publicly called the undertaking "a unique opportunity to mesh the best of two cultures, to take the strongest aspects of two systems and combine them into one very large and competitive operation." In a special series of newsletters Northwest published to inform employees of the progress of the merger, he added, "I am convinced that in the new combined operation, that is, the new Northwest Orient, there will be an attitude and spirit based on people, pride and performance that will further enhance your professionalism and provide opportunities for new and exciting personal and professional growth. We are convinced that, in the new Northwest, we will identify and focus on one basic concept, and that is that we will be one company with one purpose—long-term success." Privately, he and his top managers must have felt their stress rising, because Republic and Northwest were in some respects mismatched companies. In the end, many aspects of the combination went poorly and damaged Northwest's reputation for years.

Difficulties immediately arose from attempts to fuse the two airlines' labor forces, pay scales, schedules, and routes. Northwest was forced to invest millions of dollars in new hardware and software to correct snafus in its computer systems. Longtime employees often had to relocate or change jobs. These sorts of setbacks are normal in a large merger, but what Northwest most underestimated was the difficulty of mending a cultural divide in their approaches to business management and labor relations. Northwest tried to acquaint the workforces with

After the merger Republic's name was removed from its Minneapolis–St. Paul overhaul base.

An airliner with the markings of both Northwest and Republic sums up the confusion of a merged company in transition.

"I WILL ALWAYS REMEMBER THAT YOU WERE THE FIRST"

In the spring of 1988, unusual print advertisements began appearing in the domestic markets that Northwest served. "On April 23," the ads said, "Northwest will become the first airline to stop smoking on all flights in North America. We want to be the first because we're committed to giving you what you want: a smoke-free environment. So if you don't smoke and you don't like it when others do, Northwest is behind you all the way. No butts about it." The advertisement included a map of North America with the headline, "This is our no smoking section."

Northwest's move came amid mounting evidence during the 1970s and 1980s of the dangers of smoking and breathing secondhand smoke. Since 1975, Minnesota's Clean Indoor Act had prohibited smoking in many public and private places. Forty-one other states had since passed similar legislation. Just a year before Northwest's ban, the Mayo Clinic had directed its employees to stop smoking on the job, and many hospitals had banned the habit in their facilities.

Months before Northwest's announcement, President Ronald Reagan had signed legislation ending all smoking on domestic flights of two hours or less. "Coming from such a long clean air tradition, Northwest Airlines officials are confident that the same enthusiastic response will be echoed aboard the North American flights, where the ashtray may soon become as outmoded as the brass spittoon," predicted the airline's promotional literature. Northwest's surveys showed that 85 percent of its customers did not smoke, and 70 percent preferred smoke-free cabins.

Not all passengers were jubilant over the airline's announcement. "As a three-pack-a-day smoker, I would rather be whipped through the streets of Los Angeles than fly free anywhere in the U.S. on your airline," a Californian wrote in a letter to Northwest, adding, "When you shunned me and my business, I did the same to you!!" Another angry correspondent observed, "Even if the other airlines make similar rules, I will always remember that you were the first." Supporters expressed their delight as well: "Please send me a Northwest frequent flyer membership application and KEEP UP THE GOOD WORK," one wrote.

"In going far beyond the new Department of Transportation ban against smoking, our objective is to create a smoke free environment that passengers and employees will find pleasant and helpful," the airline declared in a letter to employees. As it turned out, however, Northwest had more than health benefits in mind. The company had engaged the Rowland Worldwide public relations firm, whose publicity of the no-smoking program and monitoring of customer response made it clear that Northwest hoped the smoking ban would bring substantial marketing advantages. Media coverage was overwhelming and almost entirely positive. Such health advocacy organizations as the American Cancer Society, the American Lung Association, the American Heart Association, and the Center for Disease Control had endorsed the policy. Northwest increased its total passenger revenue miles by 1.5 percent during the initial year of the ban despite several route cutbacks. Rowland's consultants concluded that the campaign "now occupies a secure place in the annals of creative marketing; it has become an example of how to turn a potential liability into an asset, and a necessity into a marketing coup."

Federal law eventually eliminated smoking sections on the domestic flights of all airlines. Only Northwest earned so much praise for following this inevitable course. •

one another by giving employees from each airline the chance to travel free on the other's routes. Northwest hoped that employees would make friends, learn about destinations and ways of doing things, and observe services cross-company. Unfortunately, the differences lay deeper than mere procedures and personalities. The old Northwest under Rothmeier had been cost-conscious, streamlined, and above all focused on continuing its run of profitable years. Employees may have rankled under the demands those emphases had imposed, but stockholders appreciated them. Republic, on the other hand, felt smaller, looser, less severe, and more inclined to give employees a measure of independence.

Widely perceived before the merger as an efficient and well-managed airline doing a good job of operating safe flights, directing baggage, treating passengers courteously, resolving complaints, and satisfying customers, the post-combination Northwest slipped to the status of a customer-service delinquent in the court of public opinion. Just a year after the merger, Northwest suffered a stunning acceleration in the number of passenger complaints tracked by the federal government, ranking worst among the major carriers. In the minds of many passengers, the new Northwest had become America's worst airline.

Even Continental Airlines, the large surviving carrier that the storms of deregulation had buffeted the most, had registered fewer complaints. To make matters worse, Northwest's customer service agents reportedly told passengers that everything was running normally. "A lingering perception of ineptitude and labor unrest doesn't help," *Forbes* noted. The airline responded by investing nearly $100 million in improvements to the primary customer-used facilities in its four biggest destinations: ticket counters, ramps, baggage facilities, and moving walkways.

More alarming than customer dissatisfaction, records of the Federal Aviation Administration detailed how Northwest pilots were following a trend of making poor decisions and increasing numbers of errors in flight. The number of near collisions attributed to the mistakes of pilots more than doubled, for instance, from two years before the merger to eleven months after it. In one bizarre incident during the merger, a Northwest pilot meandered a flight 190 miles off course over the Pacific Northwest. Some pilots attributed the safety decline to the accumulating pressures and confusion that the merger delivered. The merger threatened the employees in the cockpit "because pilots spend years learning their skills," a reporter analyzed, "then find themselves worried about job security and seniority in a rapidly changing industry. . . . Their jobs are tied up with their self-concept." The horrible crash of Northwest's Flight 255, which killed 156 people soon after takeoff from Detroit on August 16, 1987, only deepened the perception of danger. This was the airline's first fatal accident in twenty-four years. The accident also produced an unnecessary public-relations disaster beyond the tragedy when Northwest reportedly docked a Detroit employee for time he took away from his usual duties to assist in accident cleanup. That made headlines around the country.

THE END OF LIVES

Out of the tens of millions of passenger-carrying Northwest flights between 1927 and 2009, only about thirty ended in crashes. Most of those accidents occurred during the early 1950s and before, when aircraft safety design and weather forecasting had not yet reached modern standards. Overall, passengers have been remarkably safe flying the airliners of Northwest and virtually all other U.S. carriers. Northwest's safety record after 1970 was especially good, with only four crashes during those decades and none after 1993. Among airlines of comparable size, its accident rate was the second-lowest, bettered only by Southwest Airlines.

Nevertheless, crashes change and end lives. Northwest's accidents remain vivid in people's memories, and here are a few of the most tragic.

Investigators examine the wreckage after a Northwest Airlines crash in Winona, Minnesota, in 1948.

Investigators at the crash site of a Northwest plane in Tell City, Indiana, in 1960.

The scene at Northwest's first crash in 1929, which killed pilot Eddie Middagh.

ST. PAUL, MINNESOTA, 1929

In its first two years Northwest carried passengers a million miles without an accident, but that streak ended on a short jump from the St. Paul Airport to Wold–Chamberlain Field in Minneapolis when pilot Eddie Middagh crashed his Ford Tri-Motor into the bluffs above the Mississippi River in Mound's View Park soon after takeoff. The steward and six passengers emerged alive from the wreckage, but Middagh was killed.

MINNEAPOLIS, MINNESOTA, 1950

One of four Northwest Martin 202 aircraft that crashed between 1948 and 1951, the plane started a conflagration at 9:02 P.M. on a windy and snowy March evening when it plunged into a residential neighborhood near the airport. All ten passengers, three crew members, and two children on the ground died. The airliner, which began its flight in Washington, D.C., had aborted a landing attempt and struck a flagpole at Fort Snelling National Cemetery before limping ahead another half mile and demolishing a house in an explosion that lit up the night sky. Amazingly, three people in the wrecked house survived. A memorial for those killed was dedicated across the street from the crash site in 2011.

LAKE MICHIGAN, 1950

Just three months after the Minneapolis crash and the day before the Korean War began, a Northwest DC-4 along with its fifty-five passengers and three crew members vanished while flying over Lake Michigan, on June 23, 1950, en route from New York to Seattle with several stopovers. Air traffic controllers heard from Flight 2501 at about mid-

The catastrophic aftermath of the Northwest crash in south Minneapolis in 1950.

Only ruins remain of a house on West Minnehaha Parkway in Minneapolis after the crash of March 1950.

night near Benton Harbor, Michigan, when the crew asked for permission to drop in altitude. A line of thunderstorms was passing through the region. The request was denied because of other aircraft in the area. The plane, failing to appear for a stop in Milwaukee, was never seen or heard from again. A search of Lake Michigan began the next morning. Searchers found only a few floating signs of a crash—luggage, pillows, and cabin lining—and no survivors. In the days that followed, parts of bodies, along with clothing and the personal belongings of passengers, washed up along the lakeshore. The death toll was the world's worst at the time from an aviation accident. The fuselage has never been recovered—although search teams have tried to locate it in recent years—and the cause of the crash is still unknown.

THE PHILIPPINE COAST, 1960

A Northwest DC-7C, flying from Tokyo to Manila, lost power in one engine. Then a fire started when a propeller broke off and sliced into the nose section of the fuselage. Before ditching into the ocean, pilot David Rall was able to radio the plane's position to authorities in Manila. Fifty-eight people were aboard, including a group of school teachers on vacation. The nighttime water landing, accomplished under poor visibility in a storm, was violent and started an onboard fire, but everyone got out and into life rafts. Passengers credited their escape to small lights attached to their life vests. Four hours after the plane went down, U.S. military rescuers arrived. Everyone was safe except one passenger, who died from a heart attack. Stewardess Yuriko Fuchigami received the Imperial Order of the Sacred Crown from the government of Japan for her heroism in aiding passengers. "She and I were the last ones to leave the sinking plane after having tried in vain to open the very rear emergency exit," passenger Charles Monroe wrote to Northwest. "Certainly no one could have done more to help others, including using her stockings to bind Captain Rall's leg, than she did. Her attitude of comfort and her kind words were most reassuring to many people who were feeling mighty low."

THE EVERGLADES, FLORIDA, 1963

On February 12, 1963, Flight 705 set off for Chicago from Miami with thirty-five passengers and eight crew aboard. The Boeing 720 jet encountered a fierce squall that took it down in a rocky area of the Everglades soon after takeoff. The crash produced a thunderous explosion heard for miles around. Rescuers found a horrifying accident site. "The fuselage is busted up," one reported. "It's been consumed by fire. . . . The tail was broken off. Other major components were scattered around." Another emergency responder noted that "little blue cups, some with handles broken off, were strewn in the sawgrass. All contained lettuce and shrimp." The only survivors were a group of tiny tropical fish discovered inside a plastic bag that held an inch of water. Investigators found flight recorder data suggesting that elevator control difficulties were to blame for the crash.

DETROIT, MICHIGAN, 1987

Northwest had gone twenty-four years without a crash when Flight 255, bound for Phoenix from Detroit, dipped after takeoff and struck light poles and other obstacles. The DC-9 then broke into pieces, slid along the ground, and caught fire. The lone survivor was Cecilia Cichan, four, who was still buckled into her seat but seriously burned when help arrived. In what was then America's second-worst air disaster, five crew members and 148 passengers, plus two people on the ground, died. The National Transportation Safety Board's review of the accident concluded that the crew's failure to follow a taxi checklist to properly position the flaps and slats before takeoff was the cause of the crash; in addition, a takeoff warning system failed to alert the crew that the plane was wrongly configured. (Thirty-one airline flights crashed that year, the worst safety record since 1974.) Cecilia Cichan, who lost her parents and brother in the accident, received skin grafts for her burns and spent fifty-four days in the hospital before going home with her aunt and uncle. She graduated from the University of Alabama in 2006 with a degree in psychology.

DETROIT, MICHIGAN, 1990

In an early December fog two Northwest aircraft, a DC-9 going to Pittsburgh and a 727-200 on its way to Memphis, collided on the runway, killing eight people and injuring twenty-four more. Asked for his position, the pilot of the DC-9 had replied, "We're not sure. It's so foggy out here, we are completely stuck here. Looks like we're on 21-center

Wreckage and bodies cover the area after a Northwest flight to California via Phoenix crashed after takeoff in Detroit on August 17, 1987.

here—that would be dangerous, the takeoff runway." The controller said, "If you're on 21-center, exit the runway immediately, sir." Five seconds later, the 727 hit the other with its right wing as it lifted its nose in takeoff. All the deaths were aboard the DC-9, which caught fire and filled with smoke. The government's investigation of the accident blamed it on poor crew coordination aboard the DC-9, with slow air traffic control direction, poor signage, and inadequate training by Northwest contributing to the tragedy. •

Emergency workers battle a fire that erupted aboard a DC-9 when it collided with another Northwest plane at Detroit Metropolitan Airport on December 3, 1990.

Even the company's traditional supporters in the business community could not ignore the airline's decline. "You know what they call it now: Northworst," observed a director of community development for the Minneapolis Chamber of Commerce. Rothmeier was the target of public criticism that attacked the company's declining profits, as well as his remote demeanor and communications style, and examples of some of his testy memos leaked to the press. He sometimes responded defensively to the flack—and especially to complaints of Northwest's low stock valuation. "We have been very candid and very straightforward since the Republic acquisition as to what the prospects were for the shareholders," he told the *Minneapolis Star Tribune*. "We said in effect that the synergy and resulting profit to the shareholders was actually pushed back about two years."

By the end of the merger, Rothmeier could look back and say it was all worthwhile. "If we had not acquired Republic, neither Northwest nor Republic would be around today," he observed three years later. By that time, the airline's earnings had recovered from the tumult of the merger, hitting a record $135 million in 1988. The worst of the forced integration of two large airlines was far behind, profits poured back in, and a new drama awaited.

A FLUTTERING OF WINGS

At the start of 1989, a Northwest mystery was brewing. Rumors flew that somebody was targeting the company for takeover. The airline's stock price rose and fell as different wooers came under speculation. In March, partly in response to these rumors, Northwest's board adopted a "poison pill" policy, which protected the investment of shareholders during a hostile takeover attempt. If any company bought or said it would buy 15 percent or more of Northwest's shares, the board could activate a provision that multiplied by one hundred the value of outstanding shares, making the hostile buyer's task of acquiring stock much more costly.

Passengers are silhouetted against a Northwest advertising mural in 1989.

There was more than rumor behind the board's maneuvering. A shareholder who owned 4.9 percent of Northwest's stock had indicated its wish to pursue a friendly takeover of the airline. (Any acquisition of 5 percent or more would have required a public disclosure of the owner's identity, so staying under that threshold gave that shareholder highly valued privacy.) Northwest would not publicly disclose the name of the friendly suitor, and it said it was not interested in hearing more from the prospective buyer. That hopeful purchaser, however, was Wings, Inc., an investment group run by Los Angeles businessman Al Checchi. "We were crestfallen," Checchi later wrote. "Our six-month quest to acquire Northwest Airlines was over before it started." Or so he thought.

Meanwhile, on March 30, 1989, Rothmeier's office received a faxed letter from Marvin Davis, a businessman who had made billions in oil wildcatting before turning his attention to real estate development. Holder of 3 percent of Northwest's stock, Davis had earlier acquired Twentieth Century Fox and tried to buy CBS and Resorts International. Davis, lacking any previous experience running an airline but professing a desire to keep the current Northwest management in place and not break off the airline's assets, offered to buy the company for $90 per share, a total of $2.72 billion. At the same time he faxed the letter, Davis issued a press release telling the world of his offer. Another investment group's proposal to acquire Northwest, he said, had sparked his interest in the airline. He had formed a partnership called NWA Company to follow through on the acquisition. "Our study has left us with a high regard for the company and its business opportunities," he wrote. By 6:00 P.M., a reporter called Rothmeier for comment—the first of more than ten thousand such inquiries that Northwest would field from the press during the next five months.

Northwest's stock immediately shot up to over $100 a share (from $40 nine months earlier), but few within the company were enthusiastic about Davis's proposal. "We heard about his past business dealings," read Northwest's 1989 annual report for employees, recounting events months later. "We learned that his track record didn't exactly jibe with his words. And with knowledge came concern. What would Davis do to Northwest? Does he really want to run an airline?" Worries over Davis's intentions intensified. "My major concern with Marvin Davis was the fear he would buy Northwest and sell us off piece by piece," said Trudy Moore, a customer service agent in Memphis. "And there would go our careers and futures." Industry analysts were skeptical that Davis could pull off a purchase of Northwest without canceling or reducing $350 million in aircraft purchases over the next three years that the airline needed to upgrade its fleet.

Checchi had a surprising response to Davis's intrusion. "Northwest management, employees, and the Minnesota political establishment were horrified; we were relieved and

SOARING EAGLE ◐

In 1984, Northwest created its Airlink program, a combination of regional airlines intended to feed passengers to the large carrier's major hubs in the Twin Cities, Detroit, and Memphis from smaller outlying destinations. Mesaba Airlines, the first company to join Northwest in this scheme, already had its own deep roots in the Upper Midwest.

With just a single plane, Mesaba (named after the Ojibwa word for "soaring eagle") began in 1944 when pilot Gordy Newstrom began ferrying employees of the Blandin Paper Company from its home base in Grand Rapids, Minnesota, to the Twin Cities. Under new ownership and after years of gradual growth, Mesaba offered scheduled air service between small Minnesota towns in 1973. Soon after joining the Airlink confederation, it moved its headquarters from Grand Rapids to Minneapolis–St. Paul International Airport. Mesaba grew alongside Northwest, expanding in the late 1980s to provide feeder service to Detroit from outlying regions.

Mesaba had fifteen hundred employees and fifty-five aircraft by the mid-1990s. In 1996, with its operation of a fleet of sixty-nine-passenger Avro aircraft leased from Northwest, Mesaba gained distinction as the nation's first regional carrier to sell first-class tickets. Just a year later, the airline again expanded its operations to serve communities outside Northwest's hub in Memphis. Mesaba moved to a new headquarters—in Eagan, Minnesota, the same home as Northwest's—but suffered a terrible financial wallop in 2005 when Northwest declared bankruptcy. Left without most of its aircraft and customers, Mesaba followed its patron into insolvency the following year.

By the time Mesaba emerged from bankruptcy in 2007, its employees were working on lower wages, its fleet was shrunken, and its future as an independent airline was uncertain. Northwest bought Mesaba that year. As a Northwest subsidiary, Mesaba merged into Delta Airlines with the combination of Delta and Northwest in 2009.

The sixty-five-year history of Mesaba was about to take a new turn. In 2010, Delta sold Mesaba for $62 million to one of Delta's regional feeders, Pinnacle Airlines. Pinnacle—reneging on an earlier promise not to move Mesaba—shut down its Eagan headquarters in 2011, moved its administrative operations to Memphis, and laid off 193 employees. Mesaba remains the nation's oldest regional airline, but its history has been fractured. •

thrilled," he later recalled. "The price of Northwest stock soared on Davis's offer. Not only would we profit from our Northwest investment, we were back in the hunt."

Northwest's board dismissed Davis's offer, claiming it undervalued the company. In his rumbling low voice, the notoriously determined Davis said he would "proceed aggressively" to become Northwest's new owner. He then circumvented the board to try to drum up proxy vote support and seize control of the company. Northwest rebuffed this hostile activity by putting the company up for auction, opening its books for inspection, and accepting friendly new offers from all comers, with the condition that the new suitors refrain from soliciting proxy votes, negotiating with the airline's labor unions, and scooping up shares of Northwest stock. Those offers could take many forms: an outright sale of Northwest, the introduction of new partners to the company, or a refinancing of Northwest that would retain the current management. A motley assortment of potential buyers stepped forward, and Davis had no choice but to give up his proxy shenanigans and step in line.

"Although it is unbelievably under-recognized in Minnesota, Northwest ranks as the most financially sound and the best managed of the major airlines," the *Star Tribune* stated in an editorial about the importance of keeping the company intact and in Minnesota. Any sell-off of Northwest would greatly damage the region's economy and the health of Minneapolis–St. Paul International Airport, the newspaper explained. "As many as 73,000 jobs are directly or indirectly related. About $2 billion of revenues are generated annually, of which 6.7 percent represents personal income to Minnesota citizens." To the newspaper, Northwest already seemed half-dead as a contributor to the economy of the region: "If new owners are in the future, we should be prepared to work with them to attempt to preserve as much as possible of a viable airline serving the Twin Cities."

By this time there were seven possible bidders in the mix, including Davis. Checchi's group was the front-runner because it had offered $115 a share for Northwest and could put down a large sum of cash to augment its financing. Checchi was working closely on the deal with former Northwest board member Gary Wilson, former Marriott Corporation executive Fred Malek, and KLM Royal Dutch Airlines, which was adding $400 million to the equity kitty. The addition of KLM to the buyout team was a major coup for Checchi. KLM "was one of the world's largest passenger and freight carriers, and its management clearly understood the value of international route authority, particularly Northwest's," he observed. "They had broached the subject of creating an alliance with NWA the year before, but had been dismissed" by Rothmeier. When Checchi, inexperienced with commercial aviation, met with KLM's representatives "who by my reckoning had over 250 years of airline experience, I felt not only presumptuous, but more than a little ridiculous."

Also in contention was the takeover specialty firm Forstmann Little and Company, which had previously revived Dr. Pepper and would likely finance its proposal through loans from corporate pension funds. Another takeover specialist in the mix of suitors, Kohlberg Kravis Roberts and Co., had earlier bought RJR Nabisco, Beatrice Companies, and Safeway. These were heavy hitters.

Nobody was surprised that Twin Cities businessmen Carl Pohlad and Irwin Jacobs appeared among the prospective buyers—their names appeared seemingly every time a large Minnesota company was on the auction block. Pohlad's advantage was his earlier service on the board of directors of Texas Air Corporation, the owner of Eastern Airlines. The International Association of Machinists, Northwest's largest union, also plunked down a bid for Northwest. They would pay with cash and the sell-off of nonessential company assets, such as Narita International Hotel near Tokyo, which Northwest had built in 1978 and ten years later had rejected an offer of $200 million to sell. A desire to keep the airline out of heavy debt and to avoid layoffs motivated the union to join the bidding. (Northwest's pilots later threatened to strike if the sale of the company burdened the new owners with large debt.)

Among the most surprising of the bids came from old Northwest nemesis Pan Am, now financially sickly and burdened by debt. "The unsettled situation at Northwest presents us with a window of opportunity," Pan Am's chairman, Tom Plaskett, explained to his airline's likely flummoxed employees. "The linkage of two airlines with virtually no overlapping routes into a single global carrier would create a formidable U.S. challenger to the rapidly expanding foreign megacarriers. The combination is especially significant given the international heritage and inherent employee strengths of both carriers." It sounded like the Northwest-Republic saga all over again, but this time Northwest was the hunted.

If he ever felt he was on shaky ground, Rothmeier did not follow the usual course of seeking assistance from the government to avoid an unfriendly takeover. "Indeed, Gov. Rudy Perpich and U.S. Representative James Oberstar had difficulty getting Rothmeier to even return their telephone calls," the *Star Tribune* reported. Nevertheless, Perpich wanted to save Minnesota jobs, and he pledged his support to the airline. "It depends on Steve Rothmeier," the governor said. "If he decides he wants to put up a fight, we'll be there." Rumors, ultimately shown to be inaccurate, circulated of Rothmeier rounding up his own team of investors to save the company from unwanted buyers. Or perhaps, as one airline analyst speculated, he was drawing inspiration from the character Clint Eastwood played in the spaghetti Western *The Good, the Bad, and the Ugly*, who emerged alive from a gun battle simply because his enemy ran out of bullets. At the close of Kenneth Ruble's 1989 history of Northwest, with the outcome of the buyout drama still unresolved, the company historian wrote, "It was unclear whether Rothmeier would retain control of the company."

With all the bids in hand, Northwest made an across-the-board rejection. None of

Northwest employees gather and chant against the uncertainties of the company's takeover.

the bids was "sufficiently more attractive than the others," Northwest's board announced. All bidders were invited to submit new proposals within two weeks that avoided the shouldering of huge debt and included a payment to Northwest if the deal was accepted but later unraveled. Checchi was furious. He felt certain that his group's offer was the best and most sensibly financed that Northwest had received. "There was substantial support among our group to drop out of the bidding process altogether and sell our shares to the winner, at a significant profit," he later remembered. "After much discussion, however, the sentiments that had driven us to express interest in NWA in the first place prevailed."

At least six bidders sent in new proposals before the end of the two-week deadline. Northwest made its choice within three days: the Checchi group, Wings Holdings, which in the end offered $121 per share, or $3.6 billion. After hectic hours of negotiations to seal the deal, Checchi at last went to bed. "It was 5:30 in the morning," he recalled. "As I lay in the sudden darkness, I felt a rush of fear mixed with exhilaration: 'My God, I'm responsible for 40,000 people.'" He soon met with Rothmeier—their first time together beyond a quick introduction weeks before. "He was neither cold nor hostile; neither did he seem anxious or comfortable," Checchi declared. "He was like a black hole, emitting no light." Soon enough, Rothmeier's unreadability would again perplex him.

CHANGE OF OWNERSHIP

It was the largest ownership transfer in U.S. aviation history. Leveraged to the tune of $3.3 billion through bank loans (but without relying on the junk bonds that formed the foundation of many of the era's corporate acquisitions), it gave Checchi's Wings group 45 percent ownership in Northwest's common stock, control of 61 percent of the voting stock, and three seats on the new seven-member board of directors. Suddenly Northwest's debt burden had soared from the second lowest in the industry to the second highest.

News of Checchi's successful bid produced an ominous feeling among many Northwest employees. "There have been so many rumors, we're numbed by the whole thing," Ben Monk, an inspector in Northwest's engine overhaul shop, told a newspaper reporter. "I can't say anyone is really happy about it. There was no euphoria. . . . We feel a little bit like pawns in a chess game. We have no control over our situation, and it's not a comfortable feeling." Trudy Moore, the Memphis customer service agent who had distrusted Marvin Davis's intentions, felt similarly unsure of Checchi's motivations "because he was notorious for putting deals together and had no experience running an airline."

Checchi, working from an improvised office in a former conference room at Northwest's Eagan headquarters, tried to dampen down such fears. His team of thirty financial experts had combed Northwest's financial books, and he declared that the company had a healthy cash flow that could easily service the debt. He predicted a doubling within five years of Northwest's annual revenues to $11 billion. Praising the airline's current leadership, he asked CEO Steve Rothmeier and his management team to stay on, and they said they would. (The purchase deal paid Northwest's management more than $39 million for their stock shares and options, including $10 million that went to Rothmeier.)

"Our business plan is to strengthen the airline and build on its recent successful operating performance," Checchi said after the announcement of his successful bid. He would avoid layoffs, a sell-off of the airline's assets, reductions in service, and cuts in wages, he said. Going ahead, Northwest would pursue "a program of substantial growth, including all of the new aircraft purchases contemplated by NWA's management. . . . We intend to maintain NWA's headquarters in Minneapolis–St. Paul and to retain all of its existing hubs and routes." The *St. Paul Pioneer Press Dispatch* was hopeful of the buyout's prospects: "As long as the economy stays healthy and the [company's] growth plan stays on track, the deal has a good chance of working, especially considering signs that the Checchi group and Northwest unions can find common ground."

The wealthy Checchi, then forty, had worked his way up the corporate ladder to his unlikely position as Northwest's de-facto head. With a grandfather who owned a Boston fruit shop and a father who worked as a fish inspector and later as a supervisor for the U.S. Food and Drug Administration, Checchi had seen his first business success as an executive for Marriott Corporation. He then became an associate of the Bass family investment group of Texas, and he had engineered the Bass purchase of 25 percent of the shares of Walt Disney stock that had helped that company fight off a hostile takeover. Later, he advised Disney executives on how to financially reinvigorate the company. During consulting he performed when the government was considering selling the transportation entity Conrail earlier in the 1980s, he made a good impression on representatives of the International Association of Machinists, an important union in Northwest's operations. That background, plus his partnership with KLM Royal Dutch Airlines, had given the Northwest

This branded alarm clock made on-time flying a little easier.

board confidence in his ability to manage their airline despite no previous experience in the industry.

Problems lay ahead. Among the new management's first tasks was to guide through a $5.2 billion order from Boeing for eighty new 757s and ten 747-400s. The airline had never before made such a large aircraft purchase. Northwest's five thousand pilots declared an impasse, with a future strike possible, after twenty-eight months of negotiations with the company to settle a new union contract. Even worse, Checchi found a chill of rigidity and fear in Northwest's headquarters. "The atmosphere seemed a throwback to the 1950s: hierarchical, militaristic, and closed. It was not a fun place." When he flew home to Los Angeles, he learned why so many people referred to his company as Northworst: "The plane was filthy. The flight attendants looked dowdy in their cranberry-colored outfits. Service was terrible. The gate agent was surly. . . . We would have to change a culture."

To improve communications with employees, Checchi embarked on a tour of Northwest stations around the world. During his stop in the Philippines' capital city of Manila, rebels launched an overthrow attempt against the government of President Corazon Aquino. Checchi and several dozen Northwest staffers were trapped inside their hotel as street fighting raged outside. "Soldiers on the ground were exchanging fire with those on the roof above me. Although I was never in any real danger, I was unable to communicate with the United States for several days," he noted. Checchi did not yet know it, but surviving an armed revolt would seem easy compared with the conflicts of the months ahead.

Two months after the acquisition, Checchi was shocked to hear that Rothmeier and four other top executives were taking advantage of golden parachute exit privileges they had negotiated, and were leaving the company. "We prevailed upon them to at least finish the week," Checchi recalled. "I don't think I need say what we thought of this lack of professionalism. Airlines may be the most complicated business[es] in the world. The livelihoods of 40,000 people were directly tied to this one, as were the economic prospects of countless other businesses and whole communities." The sudden exit of Rothmeier and his team "seemed inconceivable."

Despite the tumult of 1989, Northwest finished the year with profits of $290 million, up 48 percent from the previous year. According to John Dasburg, the company's vice president of finance and administration, who would soon step up to a larger role with the airline, Northwest had plans for these earnings. "Generating this type of profit," he said, "enables us to purchase new aircraft, invest in service improvements and retire long-term debt." The to-do list for the next few years went on and on.

CHAPTER 8

THE DECADE THAT LASTED A LIFETIME

In the days after the successful bid for Northwest by his Wings group, chairman Al Checchi beamed optimism over his company's prospects. "It'll be a whole lot more fun for employees," he said. "One thing I've learned about the service business and service employees is they want to serve—they want to make customers happy. And if you can give customers better service, you'll have employees who are much more excited." Checchi spent $422 million to make employees and, by extension, their customers more satisfied: scrapping dowdy uniforms, giving better free flight privileges, improving training, redesigning communications, and creating new charitable giving programs. "We even instituted the industry's first recycling program," Checchi remembered.

He fostered a benevolently paternal view of employees, once advising a flight attendant of the long-term consequences of participating in a nude *Playboy* photo shoot. (He prohibited her from appearing with her uniform or anything suggestive of Northwest, and she took his advice to forget about the whole thing.) After pilot Norman Prouse and two other crew members flew from Fargo to the Twin Cities in March 1990 the morning after a drinking spree and while still legally intoxicated—a much-publicized incident—Checchi allowed Prouse to return to work after completing alcoholism treatment, working as a counselor in a chemical dependency program, and proving his sobriety. "This is a man who did something terrible," a Northwest spokesman said. "The company paid a price. He paid a price. He has demonstrated his recovery, and this is a company that recognizes its relationship with its employees."

These efforts to improve Northwest's employee relations and quality of service produced measurable improvement. In 1990, the airline ranked first among the major carriers in on-time performance, a distinction Northwest retained for many years, and it soon won

A 747 awaits takeoff in 1990, a year of uncertainty for Northwest.

record-high grades in the Federal Aviation Administration's surveys of air safety. Meanwhile, Checchi moved out of the conference room that had served as his temporary office in the airline's headquarters. He decorated his new corner office with expensive furnishings and oriental carpets. His workspace was an office representative of an executive who commanded an invigorated and responsive organization.

THREATS ON THE HORIZON

The trouble was that financial pressures already threatened the airline, preventing other Northwest executives from undertaking similar office remodels emblematic of success. "In the board room nothing had changed except the directors and the airline's solvency," wrote Gail MarksJarvis of the *St. Paul Pioneer Press*. "The scratches in the table were deeper; the green walls looked dingy." Cracks also appeared in the company's leadership. Frederick Rentschler, named Northwest's new president and CEO in June 1990 to replace temporary chief Fred Malek, was gone by November. Into his place stepped John Dasburg, previously the airline's vice president of finance and administration and Checchi's friend from their years at Marriott. At Marriott, Dasburg had served as president of the company's lodging group and executive vice president of the corporate parent, with more than a hundred thousand employees reporting to him.

Dasburg went through a tough introduction to chief executive responsibilities—describing his first ten weeks on the job, which included a Northwest airliner's runway collision in Detroit that killed eight people and left twenty-one injured, as a period that stretched "like a lifetime"—but rebounded to earn the regard of many employees. He proved especially good at working with Northwest's unions. In a company and industry

Pilot Norman Prouse *(center)* emerges from a courthouse to face the cameras after flying intoxicated in 1990.

Cochairman Gary Wilson, a quiet behind-the-scenes force during Northwest's tumultuous times during the 1990s.

Temporary president Fred Malek *(left)* and cochairman Al Checchi *(center)* introduce new Northwest president Frederick Rentschler, who survived only four months in office in 1990.

John Dasburg, the Northwest CEO who flashed humor and frankness during deeply troubled times for the airline.

with no shortage of stressed and self-important leaders, Dasburg stood out for flashing humor and frankness. When a reporter once inquired about the meaning of a painting in his office that showed an abstract representation of an airliner, Dasburg wryly observed that it nicely symbolized the chaos that reigned in the industry. He later recalled that the many dramas he faced at Northwest "trained me in negotiating and reaching a common goal, but not always in the most elegant way." His job was often thankless—focused on shrinking the number of employees while maintaining operating and service standards—and he worked in the shadow of the flamboyant and voluble cochairman Checchi.

Dasburg's unique contribution to Northwest came in his advocacy of the practice of routing passengers through a small number of busy hubs. The idea came to him not long after he became CEO. "I got a call at home from a young executive describing the core of a turnaround strategy that he was convinced would work," Dasburg recounted in the book *How to Run a Company: Lessons from Top Leaders of the CEO Academy*. "It had been a long day, but the young man insisted I hear him out." They spoke for four hours, well into the evening. "He convinced me that we could turn Northwest around by abandoning the prevailing strategy of developing or acquiring as many hubs as possible (at the time referred to as 'ubiquity') and instead focusing on only three hubs: Minneapolis–St. Paul, Detroit, and Memphis, Northwest's historic hubs." When Northwest followed this course, Dasburg's peers at other airlines were puzzled because the common wisdom called for carriers to try to serve all its destinations approximately equally. In later years, this routing strategy saved money and generated earnings for Northwest. While many competitors still maintained route systems that passengers could use to fly directly from one airport to another, Dasburg helped build Northwest into "a network airline, not a point-to-point airline. Our business is selling a ticket from Fargo to Hartford," he said, with customers passing through one of the main hubs.

That success, however, lay years ahead. During the early 1990s, a series of financial mishaps, some predictable and some not, dimmed the effects of Checchi's optimistic programs to raise Northwest's service level. An economic recession settled over the country within months of the arrival of the Wings principals. Air traffic fell 15 percent in the United States and dropped up to 50 percent in other regions of the world. Soon 650 empty airliners would occupy the desert in the U.S. Southwest, unneeded by their owners because of low demand. Then the Gulf War of 1990 set Iraqi and Kuwaiti crude oil equipment aflame, along with oil prices. The cost of aircraft fuel rose 140 percent. Northwest's traditional domination of such markets as Minneapolis–St. Paul, Detroit, Seattle, and Tokyo no longer guaranteed healthy earnings. Vanishing profits forced the airline to cut back on its aircraft orders from Airbus and others, and relations between the airline and its suppliers grew strained when Northwest had to ask for loans and delayed payment concessions. Within a few years the fleet—once Northwest's pride and distinction—would be the second oldest in the business, with an average age of sixteen years. Rumors flew that Northwest would soon have to sell off its valuable landing rights at O'Hare Airport in Chicago.

The airline lost more than $300 million in both 1990 and 1991, its first full years under Wings management. Northwest laid off some workers and tried to renegotiate its contract with the pilots union, a process that under the best of circumstances would have progressed slowly. Compared with the disasters that some other carriers suffered, however, Northwest did well just by staying aloft—Pan Am, Midway, Eastern, American, TWA, America West, and Continental all either declared bankruptcy or went out of business. In desperation, American Airlines introduced new fares that slashed its previous prices by as much as half. The other major airlines believed it essential to keep money flowing in from ticket sales, and they all followed suit in cutting prices to levels sometimes below American's. Rising expenses quickly caught up with these new fares, slashing the industry's revenues by almost $2 billion. Even though this hopeless race to rock-bottom pricing lasted only a few months, it damaged Northwest's credit rating and made it more difficult for the airline to borrow money.

THE DANGERS OF STATE HELP

Financially, 1990 and 1991 had been the worst two years in the history of U.S. commercial aviation. Northwest's financial troubles continued along with a growing recognition of its unique position in the region as an economic bulwark of the community. If Northwest sank, what else in the Upper Midwest would sink along with it? Twin Citians had long feared some economic catastrophe that would set in motion a decline making the metropolitan area culturally indistinguishable from such lesser cities as Omaha and Des

Northwest employees demonstrate at the Minnesota capitol in support of a state aid package in 1991.

Moines. Was Northwest's financial stall, with its potential for a collapse of the company, the dreaded event? Checchi perceived the widespread concern and found a way to turn it to his company's advantage.

Given its importance, could the privately held Northwest successfully win public investment funding? Would the taxpayers go along? It was worth a try. Northwest asked Minnesota to kick in a huge aid package to keep the airline afloat, a move Governor Arne Carlson supported. The state would contribute construction financing for a new facility in Duluth for the maintenance of Northwest's Airbus airliners (three hangars and a thousand new jobs) and an engine overhaul facility in Hibbing (five hundred new jobs). The Metropolitan Airports Commission (MAC), a government entity that since 1943 has managed the operations and development of the Minneapolis–St. Paul International Airport and several other regional airfields, would contribute a $270 million loan to the airline. (MAC had a strong interest in keeping its facilities busy and generating money.)

To receive the package, the airline promised to keep its corporate headquarters in the Twin Cities, which would remain a major Northwest hub, and to hold steady on its current number of employees in the Minneapolis–St. Paul metropolitan area. The deal also required Northwest to keep its corporate net worth above $1 billion and to make the state a preferred creditor if the airline defaulted on the loan. Only half of the loan could be used to reduce debt from the Wings leveraged buyout.

Mark Dayton, then the Minnesota state auditor and a future governor, jumped into the controversy. In letters to concerned citizens, he wrote, "To my knowledge, this proposal would constitute an unprecedented use of . . . funds for an economic development purpose. Thus it is an enormous precedent, and one which should be approached with the greatest of caution." He went on to assure Minnesotans that he would insist that any investment in Northwest meet low-risk standards. In addition, Dayton pressured the airline to publicly release its recent audited financial statements and issue information on its creditworthiness.

Giving the state aid package required the approval of the Minnesota Legislature. "I took [the legislature's approval] to be pro forma," Checchi remembered. "This proved to be the most naive action of my business career and almost destroyed Northwest Airlines." Lawmakers who opposed the package were roasting the airline, and Checchi's leadership in particular, in public. Checchi objected to any characterization of the state aid as a "bailout" and viewed it as an offer similar to the financial lures to relocate coming to Northwest from other states. He faced a storm of skepticism and hostility when he testified in Minnesota legislative hearings deliberating the aid package. He remembered one public exchange with state senator Charlie Berg as "truly amusing":

"Mr. Checchi, I think you are a lousy businessman," Berg said.

LIKE IT OR NOT, THE FACE OF NORTHWEST

Although Northwest nearly always had intelligent and savvy leaders at its helm during its history, these men generally shied away from media attention or seemed too colorless to merit much press. Al Checchi was different. In his four years as the airline's cochairman, his oversized personality dominated press coverage of the company, and reporters focused on such personal attributes as his shoes and his lifestyle. By turns warm, vengeful, thoughtful, egotistical, principled, greedy, and naive, he resisted easy categorization. Whatever people thought of Checchi, they never failed to form a strong impression, although they sometimes underestimated him.

Born in 1948 as Alfred Atillio Checchi to an Italian American family in Boston, he attended Amherst College and earned an MBA from Harvard. After seven years at Marriott Corporation, he worked for investment genius Les Rainwater, who was in the process of building the fortunes of the Bass brothers of Texas into a $5 billion empire. Checchi helped the Bass companies make several investments, including a 25 percent stake in the Walt Disney company. When he formed Wings Holdings in his bid to acquire Northwest, he was operating his own investment and acquisition firm in Los Angeles, where he lived with his wife and three children.

Checchi's best skill was his enthusiasm for assembling strong teams of partners who could contribute money, management experience, industry smarts, reputation, or whatever a deal needed for successful completion. Because Checchi was energetic, fun, and full of original ideas, teammates flocked to him. In the acquisition of Northwest, he gathered a remarkable crew of partners that included former NWA board member Gary Wilson, former Marriott executive and Nixon admin-istration staffer Fred Malek, corporate law expert Bob Friedman, and the shrewd executives of KLM Royal Dutch Airlines, among many others. "Many days," he later observed, "I have looked back with wonder at all this assembled excellence and leafed through the impressive documentation that we produced."

Part of this documentation, the agreement to purchase Northwest, allowed members of the airline's crucial management team to leave their jobs and still receive substantial payments. "We had been given no reason to believe that management would not want to continue in place, since we intended to build the business, not liquidate it, and we had no intention of managing the business ourselves," Checchi wrote. Steven Rothmeier, Northwest's CEO, never had confidence in Checchi and his team, however, and he and his top managers walked away. "Somewhere flying over Ohio en route to the closing party, as the partners grappled with the challenge of producing management succession for Rothmeier and his team, I became chairman and, by default, leader of an airline. . . . My life would never be the same," Checchi recalled.

Now in charge, he began a long round of trips to visit fifteen thousand Northwest employees at their stations around the world. It was an exhausting year for Checchi, and at the close of it he wrote in Northwest's annual report, "1989 was a year of change—you may be sure that 1990 will be more of the same. As a noted American often says, 'You ain't seen nothing yet!'"

Even when anticipating change, Checchi had no way of expecting the abuse he would face a couple of years later as the airline accepted a low-interest loan of Minnesota state funds in return for his promises to finance the construction of maintenance plants around the state. "In the hands of politicians," he observed, "the bipartisan transaction that *they* had presented to us was distorted into a 'bailout' that *we* were requesting from them. . . . Like it or not, I was the face of Northwest, and before this was over, I was transformed by political foes of the transaction into a wolf—literally."

Checchi's personal reputation similarly bled in 1993 when he assumed responsibility for negotiating concessions from workers and lenders to keep the company solvent—"there was no escaping this, and no one else wanted the job." Union members ridiculed Checchi and his cochairman Gary Wilson as fat cats unwilling to make the same sacrifices they demanded of workers. Some of Northwest's investors and lenders "viewed Checchi and Wilson more as financial dealmakers than airline executives," the *St. Paul Pioneer Press* reported.

Checchi's cochairmanship ended that year, although the financial restructuring he helped achieve and the later sale of Northwest stock to the public earned him hundreds of millions of dollars. He spent $40 million of that fortune in an unsuccessful bid for the Democratic nomination for the governor's office in California in 1998. The following decade, after starting his own investment portfolio management firm, he formed and served as chairman of Join Together America, a nonpartisan organization devoted to the addition of common sense to the political process. •

"Why do you say that, Senator?"

"You ordered those [Airbus] planes and you hadn't built the maintenance sheds."

"That's correct, Senator. We don't need them for another two and a half years."

"Well, I'm a pig farmer. And I want you to know that when I buy pigs, I've already built the pens."

Years later, Checchi concluded, "Here I was, left speechless again. . . . I was alternatively described as a 'leech,' a 'parasite,' and—a personal favorite—a 'mugger in Gucci shoes.'"

During the last six months of 1991, Northwest spent $820,000 to lobby in the Minnesota Legislature on behalf of the aid package—reportedly the largest sum an organization had ever invested in one legislative issue in such a short span of time. (The total included $6,500 to buy food and drinks for legislators and aides.) Governor Carlson signed the financial package, reduced in value during the legislative process from $838 million to $761 million, into law in March 1992. Soon after, Northwest announced that it would push back by six months its schedule for the construction of the maintenance facilities in northeastern Minnesota. (A 1994 renegotiation of the financial deal greatly reduced the size of the Duluth plant; the changes in the state aid agreement also replaced the Hibbing engine repair facility with a new reservations and service center in Chisholm.)

This delay in the construction schedule, as well as reports that Northwest had lost $239 million in the first five months of 1992, scrambled into action auditor Dayton, still the gadfly, who continued to seek financial disclosure from Northwest. "The picture of financial health you painted for the taxpayers of Minnesota is in sharp contrast to the stark economic realities in your letter last week to all Northwest Airlines employees," he wrote to CEO John Dasburg in June 1992. "Since the taxpayers of Minnesota now have a deep financial stake in the success of your company, you owe it to them to fully explain the financial difficulties faced by Northwest Airlines. I urge you to make a full and honest disclosure to the citizens of Minnesota about the present financial condition of Northwest Airlines and its future prospects." Dayton suggested that the airline hold the MAC loan funds in escrow until the new facilities and jobs actually materialized.

Governor Carlson did not follow Dayton's repeated recommendation to convene government officials and Northwest executives to discuss the airline's contingency plans. If Northwest defaulted on the loan, Dayton asked Carlson, "What collateral is available? What is the current value of that collateral? How could it be secured? What remedies could be pursued in the event of a default? What would be the impact of such a default on the MAC's operating capabilities and its underlying financial condition? What financial impact would a default have upon [Twin Cities] metropolitan-area taxpayers?"

Edward Stringer, Carlson's executive director for cabinet affairs, challenged Dayton to show evidence that Northwest was trying to fleece the taxpayers. "The notion that there can be a meeting that puts all the concerns to rest simply does not recognize the reality that this is an ever-changing situation," Stringer wrote. "Northwest's finances obviously change week to week. . . . Clearly, there are a host of people with a vested interest in this issue, and it is simply unworkable to bring this large group together as you suggest, on a regular basis, to keep them up to date on these matters. We thank you for your suggestion but we do not believe it is workable."

The records of the State Auditor's office do not include a reply from Dasburg, if he made one, but Northwest's true financial condition was soon enough known to everyone through news accounts, and the *Minneapolis Star Tribune* editorialized that Northwest's financial projections for the state "had turned from roses to weeds." The state's aid could not keep Northwest going. Without willing lenders, the airline could not refinance its crushing debt of $4 billion that, along with mounting losses, would soon propel Northwest into bankruptcy without immediate action. The company's cash reserves were low, and banks demanded that Northwest cut its annual expenses by $300 million before there would be any restructuring of debt. Characteristically, Checchi took a corrective course different from that of other airline leaders. "Although every airline in America immediately began laying off workers to reduce costs, I decided to hold off," he later declared. "I went to labor, explained our situation, and said we had a chance to do something different."

AT THE BRINK OF BANKRUPTCY

Checchi had in mind an across-the-board 10 or 15 percent reduction of wages. He and cochairman Gary Wilson spent months trying to convince Northwest's unions, lenders, and suppliers to agree to wage cuts, the loosening of loan payment terms, and the liberalization of purchase agreements. No one was persuaded, and one banker told Wilson that any slack cut on loan repayments would come over his dead body. The mechanics' union had turned away the chairmen's proposed concessions package, even though it gave the union part ownership of the airline through stock that the chairmen and other shareholders would surrender. "At times their efforts had become desperate," a reporter observed. "Checchi was moved to tears during bargaining with the pilots. Both men wangled with other shareholders over who would give up the most stock in Northwest." Checchi and Wilson were under tremendous pressure and criticism from nearly everyone working with or analyzing their business to get results and avoid the bankruptcy that had subsumed so many other carriers.

It was an odd twist of events for Northwest: Its board chairmen—in the past a succession of reserved and conservative business figures such as Nyrop, Lapensky, and Rothmeier, leaders almost never targeted for criticism or ridicule—were now subject to public scorn and heckling. Creditors were outraged that Checchi and Wilson had pocketed

DEATHS IN THE FAMILY 🕛

On September 13, 1992, Northwest ramp supervisor Susan Taraskiewicz took a break from her overnight work at Logan International Airport in Boston to pick up sandwiches for herself and a couple of coworkers. She had not been seen again for thirty-six hours, when police found her car in the parking lot of a nearby car repair shop. Taraskiewicz's body was in the trunk; she had been stabbed and beaten. Investigators believed the murder was the work of more than one person, and they have never tracked down the culprits.

This had not been the only recent murder of a Northwest employee. In February 1991, flight attendant Nancy Ludwig checked into the Hilton Airport Inn in Romulus, Michigan, after finishing a work shift. In her room, an assailant stabbed, tortured, raped, and killed her. Years later, DNA evidence led police to Jeffrey Gorton, who was convicted of the murder in 2002 as well as the earlier rape and murder of a Michigan music professor.

Every year on the anniversary of her daughter's death, Marlene Taraskiewicz arrives at the airport holding a sign accusing Northwest of inadequately assisting in the search for Susan's killers. Just a month before Susan's slaying, a team of ten Northwest baggage handlers had been accused of stealing credit cards and making illegal purchases with them, and her mother suspects those people may have feared Susan would turn them in. Susan's diary, discovered after her death, told of harassment she had received from other Northwest workers, including one involved in the credit card thefts. Her coworkers never reported her as missing, and they even punched her time card to give the impression that she had returned to work.

Although unsolved, the case remains an open investigation. Travelers often give Marlene Taraskiewicz coffee and support as she holds up her sign in the airport. •

$38 million in management fees during the company's economic travails. Once respected as tough negotiators, the cochairmen now faced attacks for antagonizing the very people they needed to persuade. Some board members wanted them removed from future negotiations with the airline's partners. "I was the public face of Northwest—there was no escaping this, and no one else wanted the job," Checchi remembered.

Northwest suffered a mammoth loss of $1 billion in 1992. Observers reasoned that the airline never used to find itself in this kind of potentially lethal financial pinch, so the guys in charge, Checchi and Wilson, must be responsible. Which they were, in large part, for leading a takeover so dependent on borrowed funds and the necessity of steadily increasing revenues to keep up with the debt payoff schedule. One and a half billion dollars in loan payments were due from Northwest in 1994, which was impossible for the airline to fulfill. For engineering this financial fiasco, the chairmen "are really in dreamland," one board member believed. "Checchi and Wilson were watching their power base erode," the *Pioneer Press* perceived. "They still have loyal allies among some key shareholders, but Dasburg was gaining a significant following of his own, including KLM Royal Dutch Airlines, Northwest's largest single investor. Friction also existed within the company. According to a board member, the cochairmen were being nudged toward bankruptcy by some of their own top managers, who advised the cochairmen to ditch the management headaches and find a way to protect their investment in bankruptcy." Northwest's bankruptcy would also serve to punish the recalcitrant unions, which stood in the way of the airline's survival, some managers believed.

Toward the end of June 1993, the board of directors met in an emergency session at Dasburg's house to discuss the possibility of Northwest declaring bankruptcy. The board members soon learned from Dasburg that the pilots and mechanics would not grant wage concessions. Which type of bankruptcy lay ahead—Chapter 11, involving reorganization of the company, or Chapter 7, requiring the airline's liquidation? Board member Walter Mondale, recalling the "smell [of] death on the plane" he had experienced on a flight operated by bankrupt Pan Am, argued against following that path at all. If Northwest failed, the entire region would suffer a loss of financial health, prestige, jobs, and security. Mondale, granted a seat on the board to represent the public interest, urged his colleagues to give up more to the employees whose wages the airline needed to reduce. And employees had to really understand, he maintained, Northwest's danger of going bankrupt. The former U.S. senator and presidential candidate, aided in his arguments by fellow public-interest board member Melvin Laird, at last persuaded the others to put the brakes on bankruptcy, at least temporarily, and return to the bargaining table with all the groups needed to craft a fast solution—for time was running out. Surreptitiously, though, members of the board leaked information to outsiders about Northwest's preliminary bankruptcy court filings, hoping to pressure the airline's partners. Many people knew, for instance, that Northwest's attorneys were scheduled to appear in bankruptcy court on July 6, 1993, to move ahead with the proceedings.

Although these information leaks may indeed have pressured the targeted groups, they also alarmed creditors and suppliers, many of whom embargoed the company. Cash, supplies, and parts suddenly grew scarce. "At one especially low point, the company's

Members of Northwest's machinists union come together, after much dispute, to approve a concessions package that kept the company solvent.

stockpile of toilet paper at the Twin Cities airport ran out; managers went to Sam's Ware-house to buy some," Gail MarksJarvis reported. The company's cash reserves ebbed dangerously low.

RESCUED BY CONCESSIONS

At the last minute, one day before the airline's scheduled appearance in bankruptcy court, the Air Line Pilots Association agreed to a $365 million concessions compromise that handed labor 37.5 percent ownership in the company and three seats on the board. Northwest, still needing $521 million in concessions from its other unions, pushed back its bankruptcy filing by a couple of days. U.S. Transportation Secretary Federico Peña brought together company representatives and union leaders of the pilots, machinists, and flight attendants to forge some kind of agreement. Soon the machinists union local head, Tom Pedersen, faced an upset crowd of members outside a Northwest hangar in Minneapolis. He wanted to make the point that a bankrupt Northwest would benefit nobody. "Al Checchi's going to be a millionaire regardless of what happens," he told the assembly. "But Al Checchi is never going to miss a meal. Can you say that about yourself? It's time to start looking out for yourself." Some accused Pedersen of kowtowing to Northwest's owners, but Northwest's machinists ultimately agreed to support a concessions deal.

Northwest had received an astonishing $980 million, spread over three years, in salary and benefit reductions. Instantly, the company's annual operating expenses had dropped 3 percent—enough to keep the airline flying. The complex web of financial agreements that saved Northwest from bankruptcy reached completion when Airbus, the company's principal supplier of planes, agreed to relax the airline's payment schedules.

The unlikely team that gave financial concessions to Northwest—a coalition of one hundred banks, union workers, and suppliers—warned that the airline could expect no repeat performance in the future. The terms of these life-saving wage concessions required Northwest to acquire $500 million in new capital within a few years. "Key members of the coalition say that if Checchi and Wilson are to be credited with anything, it was stepping aside long enough to let chief executive officer John Dasburg—who has earned the unions' trust—take the lead in labor negotiations," the *St. Paul Pioneer Press* reported.

With all the concessions in hand and its daily expenses suddenly lower than those of its competitors, Northwest underwent one of the most abrupt financial spurts in aviation history. The company's operating earnings in 1993 increased by $964 million over the previous year, and in 1994 Northwest was able to report a profit of $296 million, the best in the business. Earnings kept soaring through the 1990s, with the 1996 profits of $536 million establishing a new record for the airline. Northwest topped those earnings by

10 percent the following year. Unimaginable only a few years earlier, Northwest ranked second in *Fortune* magazine's annual survey of the world's most admired companies in 1997. "The restructuring of Northwest was a success for all concerned," Checchi later wrote. "Northwest became the most profitable airline in the United States for the three years following the restructuring, even without the effects of the wage concessions. . . . The employees who invested an average of 12 percent of their wages received common stock that at its high was worth approximately three times their concessions." Many outsiders agreed with his assessment: "Northwest's cochairmen, Al Checchi and Gary Wilson, are being hailed in some quarters as savior-savants, polishing reputations that became tarnished soon after their brash buyout of the airline," the *Pioneer Press* observed.

With these successful results coming in, Northwest began a campaign to make investors receptive to a public stock offering, the first open sale of the airline's shares since the 1989 buyout. New advertising hammered the message that Northwest was a sound carrier and a sound investment. As part of that blitz, Wings Holdings was renamed Northwest Airlines Corporation. The stock offering in 1994 raised close to $1 billion for the airline.

Northwest's courtship of KLM Royal Dutch Airlines, its investment partner since 1989, had accounted for much of its financial recovery. As early as 1991, the airlines had run joint flights from the Twin Cities to Amsterdam. But the game changed in 1993 when the U.S. Department of Transportation granted Northwest and KLM exemption from certain antitrust laws. The aviation partners quickly took advantage of this benefit by expanding their intercontinental alliance. They set up a unique sharing of transatlantic routes, merging flights, schedules, prices, reservations systems, and advertising—the industry's first cooperative effort on such a grand scale. Within a year, they were jointly operating service to twenty-four European, African, and Middle Eastern destinations and to sixty in North America. The resulting efficiencies dramatically improved the profitability of the shared routes. In the process, KLM's center of activities in Amsterdam became an unofficial fourth hub for Northwest. The airlines deepened their alliance in 1997, with each gaining a seat on the other's board of directors, and their fleets bore a joint Northwest/KLM logo. At the end of the decade, Italy's Alitalia Airline became the third member of the alliance.

A similar agreement in 1998 with Continental Airlines sought to take advantage of the small overlap in route coverage between the two competitors. The alliance gave Northwest 14 percent ownership in Continental plus shared scheduling, reservations, frequent flyer plans, and other forms of cooperation. Another alliance, with Alaska Airlines, came the same year.

All was not happy within the revitalized Northwest Airlines, however. The airline's longtime weakness, poor labor relations, returned to haunt the company. Pilots, still unsettled by the wage and benefits concessions they had earlier granted, initiated a strike

BREAKING TO A HALT

Northwest did not have the industry's worst record of strikes and other labor stoppages—Eastern Airlines and TWA often claimed that dubious honor—but the company's shaky relationships with unions that prevailed from the 1960s into the airline's final decade gave it a poor reputation in managing labor relations. Donald Nyrop, the head of the company during much of that time, embodied the company's unyielding and chilly attitude toward workers' representatives when financial and competitive pressures grew strong. As much as employees

Northwest mechanics walk a picket line during the first nationwide work stoppage in U.S. airline history in 1946.

Pilots went on strike in 1978 to win pay increases.

respected Nyrop as president and as a man, they often felt embittered by the impassive approach he brought to labor negotiations. His peers among airline executives often applauded it.

Memories live long. Regardless of its effectiveness, Nyrop's unbending style during labor conflicts proved an obstacle after his departure when Northwest needed wage and benefits concessions from workers in the following decades to simply stay afloat.

But strikes had hit Northwest before Nyrop's arrival—including the first nationwide work stoppage in U.S. airline history. In 1946, mechanics walked off their jobs and formed picket lines for two days at airports around the country over wage, seniority, and other contract disagreements with the company. When ground crews and baggage handlers honored the picketers, the airline had to suspend its fifty-four daily flights. The International Association of Machinists ended the strike when President Harry Truman appointed a panel to help resolve the dispute. Mechanics later called two strikes during the 1960s. The first arose from a complex disagreement that smoldered from the anticipated arrival of jet aircraft during the late 1950s and erupted hotly in 1960. Northwest maintained that mechanic flight engineers could safely occupy a third seat in the cockpit if, as Northwest proposed, the engineers went through mandatory flight training. Pilots supported the mechanics' opposition, maintaining that only one of their own should sit in the cockpit. Eventually thirty-one flight engineers scheduled to fly on jets went on strike, grounding all the DC-8s, and soon all flight engineers joined the strike. The airline limped along with a shrunken flight schedule before suspending all domestic

Flight attendants authorized a strike in 1967 to end restrictions on their private lives, but changes in Northwest policy averted the work stoppage.

departures and had to push back its introduction of the jets. In the end, Northwest agreed to let instrument-rated pilots fill the third seat.

Another mechanics strike simultaneously planned against Northwest and four other airlines was held in 1966, and mechanics walked off the job for several weeks in 1982. They staged a marathon work stoppage in 2005–6 that proved unsuccessful.

Pilots mounted some of the most damaging strikes against Northwest and stopped their work five times between 1969 and 1998. For ninety-five days in 1972, they pulled the airline's schedule to a halt over disagreements with the company over the renewal of the union contract—and the dispute lasted longer when Nyrop insisted on returning the pilots to work only gradually. A 1975 pilots strike lasted three days but drew the wrath of government officials when Northwest used supervisory personnel to keep flights going from the Twin Cities to Chicago but canceled flights to North Dakota communities. Three years later, another strike prompted by a contract renewal largely grounded the airline for months. In dispute were such issues as pay increases and the accumulation of seniority and pension benefits during time spent on the picket line. The length of this strike, 109 days, helped end the industry's practice of financially assisting airlines when strikes disrupted operations, and it played a role in ending Nyrop's leadership of the company. The pay and benefits concessions that employees had granted during Northwest's fight for financial survival in 1993 paved the way for another strike by sixty-one hundred pilots in 1998. For more than two weeks during the normally busy summer months, the airline flew no flights.

Flight attendants struck less often. A strike that would have disrupted holiday travel—and would have marked the first stewardess work stoppage against a U.S. airline—was averted at the last minute in 1952, and flight attendants authorized strikes in 1967, 1969, and 1981. In 2000, Northwest accused flight attendants of staging planned sickouts, and in 2006 it mounted a successful fight in the courts, with the support of President George W. Bush, to keep flight attendants from going on strike after contract negotiations stalled and bankruptcy loomed ahead. •

Northwest flight attendants in red overcoats rally to gain the right to strike from the Federal Mediation Board in 2000.

that shut down Northwest for nearly three weeks during the busy summer flying season of 1998. Despite the record profits of recent years and the handsome rewards Northwest executives had received—especially in stock options—the pilots' pay had not significantly improved beyond the levels set during the concessions negotiations. "I thought that with the relationships that we had developed throughout the early and mid '90s, things would go much smoother," CEO John Dasburg confessed. "I was . . . certainly very surprised that the pilots struck."

With the shutdown and the events leading to it costing Northwest $600 million in lost revenues, the pilots won a return to the bargaining table, where they eventually gained pay, benefits, and job security improvements. The similarly afflicted mechanics, who turned down a contract offer from Northwest, and flight attendants watched the pilots with interest as their own contract renewals dragged on.

The Northwest pilots' strike of 1998 gave blissful noise relief to residents under the normally busy flight paths near the Minneapolis–St. Paul airport.

CHAPTER 9

BROKE AND VANISHING FAST

In the spring of 1953, in observance of the fiftieth anniversary of the Wright brothers' first flight, historians and aviation enthusiasts gathered in St. Paul for a meeting of the Minnesota Historical Society focused on the region's role in the development of air travel. There Leslie L. Schroeder, the state's commissioner of aeronautics, reflected on the future. "In 2003," he predicted, "a group similar to that meeting here today doubtless will assemble under the sponsorship of the Minnesota Historical Society to celebrate the centennial of man's flight. We may be sure that such a group will regard the aircraft of our day as relatively primitive. The greatest progress still lies ahead in man's conquest of the airspace to meet his requirements for improved transportation and communication."

No assembly of the Minnesota Historical Society gathered fifty years later to mark the hundredth anniversary of the Wright brothers' achievement, contrary to Schroeder's forecast. And although he correctly guessed that the Stratocruiser of his time would seem rudimentary compared with the airliner of the twenty-first century, he could not foresee the most important change in air travel to come in the next half century. Nobody in 1953 could have predicted it.

What would those mid-twentieth century devotees of flight have thought of the evolution of commercial airlines that took place over the next five decades? By the turn of the next century, airlines had evolved into extraordinarily complex businesses in many ways not different from such corporate giants as General Motors and Microsoft. Their foremost goal is not to profit by stretching the limits of travel, as may have been the case in the 1950s, but to survive from year to year by using their assets, even if that requires reducing them, to generate the greatest possible financial return for their investors. Only the most efficient of airlines—usually the largest—can reliably harness routes, aircraft, employees, and the behaviors of customers to make a profit. In an industry buffeted by security threats, rising fuel and labor costs, economic downturns, and cynicism among the hundreds of millions of passengers who now fly every year, airlines precariously balance profit against their role as the world's true circulatory system. If the centennial of the first flight of the Wright brothers seemed a yawner to some in 2003, it may be because the wonder of air travel is less present in our minds than the burden and anxiety of it.

RICHARD ANDERSON'S FIRST REIGN

In early 2001, John Dasburg left Northwest after eleven years as president and CEO, to take on the leadership of Burger King. Once trusted by Northwest employees who followed him into the concessions that kept the airline from bankruptcy in the early 1990s, Dasburg had grown aloof in his later years, and probably exhausted as well. He did not satisfyingly respond to workers who felt cheated when executives cashed in on stock options while employees continued to work for concession-reduced wages. To replace the CEO, the board appointed Richard Anderson, Northwest's chief operating officer, another of the executives who had benefited from the stock options. At the same time, Douglas Steenland was promoted to president.

Anderson, an articulate attorney not afraid to take risks, had first joined the airline in 1990 as deputy general counsel. He previously worked three years in legal affairs for Continental Airlines, and before that spent a decade as a prosecutor and judicial counselor in Houston. At Northwest he quickly advanced to a position overseeing technical operations, and he became executive vice president and chief operating officer and later president. As CEO, Anderson stepped easily into the role of public figure. "He is not inadvertently abrasive," observed a fellow NWA executive. "When he wants to tick you off, he's doing it deliberately." In the words of U.S. Representative James Oberstar, Anderson had "jet fuel in his veins" and was extremely knowledgeable about the technical aspects of operating an airline.

Interviewed soon after he became CEO, Anderson declared that Northwest was healthy. "Fundamentally, our strategy at Northwest is sound," he said. "We've done a lot of work over the last decade at Northwest. We have a new fleet plan in place. We'll be taking delivery of a new airplane every two weeks for the next five years. We started alliances in the airline industry back in the early '90s and we have the strongest alliance across the Atlantic with our partner KLM. . . . I believe we are in a very strong strategic position." He had no idea that everything would soon turn upside down and that he would quickly face the worst financial disaster ever to befall U.S. airlines.

Richard Anderson brought a calculated abrasiveness to his tenure as Northwest's CEO.

THE AFTEREFFECTS OF TERRORISM

Terrorists did not steer Northwest planes into targets during the sobering attacks in the United States on September 11, 2001, but like all of its competitors, the airline suffered in the aftermath. Airliners sat idle. Passengers stayed away. Security improvements confused passengers and cost millions of dollars. Pressure from low-cost carriers like JetBlue and AirTran forced Northwest to renegotiate union contracts, strive for greater efficiency, and struggle to adapt. Gone was the airline of a decade earlier that could expect record profits to roll in one year after the next. Suddenly even Northwest's eternally profitable Asian routes and cargo business were not bringing in earnings. Anderson characterized these calamities as evidence that the industry had hit its "third major shakedown" since deregulation. "It is part of the continuum of what deregulation set out to do: make legacy carriers more efficient producers," he said.

Ten days after the 9/11 attacks, Anderson announced that Northwest was eliminating ten thousand jobs. "The events of September 11th fundamentally changed our business and I believe significantly impacted the way we live our lives in the United States," he said. "It's always difficult, and next to watching the horrific events of September 11th on television, the next most difficult thing for all of us at Northwest is the impact it has

Grounded planes await activation after the terrorist attacks on the World Trade Center and the Pentagon on September 11, 2001.

on the people's lives at Northwest." For the next six years, the airline industry as a whole would steadily lose money.

Northwest had earlier avoided a mechanics' strike by negotiating a new union contract that increased workers' pay an average of 24 percent, leaving Northwest with the most burdensome labor costs of all the major airlines. Anderson had to find a way to lower wages. In 2003, the time came for Northwest to renegotiate its contract with pilots. The last time the airline and pilots had gone through this dance, a strike had shut down the carrier for nearly three weeks before Northwest changed its bargaining position. Hoping to save $950 million in labor costs, the airline persuaded the pilots to agree to a two-year pay cut of 15 percent. For Anderson, that was a fair start—but he needed another $700 million in salary reductions. "We must reduce them," he wrote to employees. "I don't like it any more than you do, but it's reality." He slashed executive salaries by 5 to 15 percent.

The company's financial results for 2003, a net loss of $565 million, did little to cheer shareholders, although Anderson had lopped off $1 billion in operating expenses since 2001. If the 2003 profit and loss statement alarmed them, the following year's loss of $878 million left them even more concerned about their investments in a company with such a seemingly bleak future. That year, another unpredictable event—the outbreak of severe acute respiratory syndrome (SARS)—had hurt Northwest's profits in Asia.

Few corporate leaders could endure awakening each day to a steady diet of beatings and dispiriting outcomes, and Anderson announced in 2004 that he was leaving Northwest to take a lucrative executive vice president position at the United Health Group medical insurance conglomerate. The decision shocked most Northwest employees and the airline's union representatives, who had no inkling that Anderson was considering leaving. His tenure as the airline's CEO was unusually short by Northwest's standards; so many of the company's previous leaders had held on for a decade or more. (But Anderson's departure fit a trend; he became the eleventh chief executive to move on from the eight largest carriers since the 9/11 attacks and was one of the longest-tenured airline CEOs when he stepped down.)

NEW LEADER, SAME PROBLEMS

Anderson's replacement as CEO was Doug Steenland, who had joined Northwest in 1991 as vice president and deputy general counsel after working as a lawyer for the U.S. Department of Transportation and in private practice. Within ten years, he rose through the ranks with Anderson and advanced to general counsel and executive vice president and chief corporate officer. In those positions, Steenland was deeply involved in the efforts to avert bankruptcy in 1993 and the negotiations that preceded the 1998 pilots strike. As president,

Northwest's Airbus maintenance facility in Duluth, created by the airline as part of its Minnesota state aid agreement of 1991, was on the decline by 2002, employing just 230 people.

MECHANICAL DERRING-DO

Along with ground workers, mechanics are the unsung heroes of airlines. The public rarely sees them, yet their efforts keep planes safe and functional. In Northwest's earliest days, mechanics boasted skills in fabric mending and carpentry, worked in a shop with a dirt floor and potbellied stoves, repaired engines in a lean-to, cleaned parts in a dishpan, chased stray dogs out of the hangar, and once pawned an engine to help the airline meet its payroll. One longtime mechanic, Lou Koerner, worked his entire first year without a day off—seven days a week—before earning a vacation.

In an oft-told incident from 1932, Eberhardt Heinrich and another mechanic drove from the Twin Cities to Rochester, Minnesota, on Christmas Eve to help extricate from a farmer's field a Northwest Ford Tri-Motor whose pilot could not find the airport in a snowstorm and had to make an emergency landing. With the temperature hovering around zero and the plane's engines dead-frozen from two days of inactivity, the mechanics draped a tarp over the plane, set alight two plumber's pots beneath the fuselage, and worked nine hours to coax the plane to takeoff condition. Then they flew back with the pilot and were home by bedtime.

Towering above these scenes of early mechanics' derring-do stood James "Big Jim" LaMont, an aviation pioneer who joined Northwest as mechanic in 1928. LaMont had previously captained a steamboat, worked with airplane inventor Samuel Langley, toured with stunt flyer Ruth Law, maintained planes for air legend Glenn Curtiss, and

A Northwest mechanic works on an airliner motor in the company's St. Paul shop in 1933.

Early Northwest mechanic extraordinaire Jim LaMont in 1929.

Inspecting jet turbine rotors in the 1980s.

A mechanics' training session in the 1950s.

built aircraft for the embryonic Russian Air Force. A bear of a man, he sometimes dressed up as Santa Claus to make Depression-era deliveries of presents to needy kids. When he retired in 1945, Northwest lost a valuable link to the earliest days of American aviation.

As aircraft evolved in their design and construction, Northwest's mechanics kept pace by learning how to work with sheet metal and much larger and more complex engines, climate control gadgetry, safety apparatus, and hydraulic and electric supply systems. Over time, the use of new imaging, electronic, and computing technology reduced the necessity of tearing down aircraft under maintenance to examine their workings. Northwest led the way in developing alterations that made aircraft quieter. And its maintenance workers gave the airline a

reputation for effective and frugal self-sufficiency by devising equipment and techniques for servicing airliners without passing them into the hands of third parties—a tradition that would come to an abrupt halt starting in the 1990s with the outsourcing of maintenance services.

By increasing competition, airline deregulation in the late 1970s encouraged cost cutting that pressured carriers to scrutinize maintenance expenses for possible budget cuts. Mechanics had to work better and more efficiently. Ironically, the federal deregulation legislation also included fine print that allowed Northwest and other airlines to discourage mechanics from taking advantage of state whistle-blower laws when they believed safety was compromised. One Northwest mechanic in the Twin Cities, Thomas Regner, was fired in 1998 and could not receive whistle-blower protection when he reported a series of repeated maintenance mishaps to the Federal Aviation Administration. The company denied that Regner's reports to the FAA led to his dismissal, and he later returned to work.

By that time, Northwest's mechanics were working under gloomy conditions. Along with custodians and cleaners, they rejected their longtime union representation, the International Association of Machinists and Aerospace Workers, after contract negotiations with the company had stalled. Mechanics believed that they had disproportionately contributed to the wage and benefit concessions of the 1990s that kept Northwest from declaring bankruptcy. So they voted to join a newer union, the Airline Mechanics Fraternal Association (AMFA).

In 2005, Northwest presented its mechanics with an astonishing request. Citing increases in fuel and labor costs, the airline wanted AMFA members to approve contract changes that would allow the company to lay off 53 percent of the workers, enabling Northwest to outsource heavy maintenance work to Hong Kong, China, and elsewhere. "The company has no choice," CEO Douglas Steenland told the mechanics. When they refused this demand on August 19, 2005, forty-four hundred AMFA members began the longest strike ever called against Northwest. The company hired replacement workers, and Northwest's other unionized work groups—pilots, flight attendants, and ground crews—crossed the mechanics' picket lines.

(Opposite): The work of Northwest mechanics grew increasingly complex after the 1950s.

Northwest declared bankruptcy the month after the strike began, and the airline inflamed mechanics by publishing a guide to financial survival that suggested that employees save money in hard times by shopping at thrift stores and searching garbage for usable goods. The strike seemed to many—even to the mechanics—a lost cause because Northwest was getting along without them. Finally, after 444 days, the strike ended in November 2006. Northwest refused to rehire AMFA members, four thousand of whom had remained on strike the entire time, and gave them ten weeks' back pay. The airline's maintenance workforce dropped from ten thousand to about eight hundred with the outsourcing of the mechanics' former duties. •

Northwest mechanics on strike in 2005.

Steenland had worked more behind the scenes than Anderson, focusing on government affairs, Northwest's alliances with other airlines, and labor relations. He and Anderson joined forces to cut costs and argue with the unions for labor concessions, so his rise to leadership did not signify a change in the airline's course. "It's unusual to have a 13-year relationship like that [with Anderson]," Steenland said when Anderson stepped down. "From April 2001 to today, I don't think we've had a fundamental dispute. We always reached consensus. It was a collaborative approach."

Steenland's inheritance as CEO had considerably degraded from Anderson's, however. Anderson's fundamentally sound airline had sickened since 2001. Yearly revenues were falling, and Northwest had accumulated $2.2 billion in losses during Anderson's forty-three months in charge. Even so, Northwest still possessed formidable assets: thirty-nine thousand employees, fifteen hundred flights each day to more than 160 domestic and international destinations, and the number four ranking among U.S. carriers. No other American carrier transported more passengers between the United States and Japan.

But Northwest was doomed unless Steenland could reduce labor costs as successfully as it had slashed other operating expenses. He made his case unemotionally, forcefully, and calmly—a numbers- and bottom-line-based approach that angered union leaders, who knew the livelihoods of members and the existence of their organizations were threatened. By the summer of 2005, the company raised to $1.1 billion the value of the wage concessions it required from workers to stay afloat. Two more unions agreed to the concessions, and the mechanics were next. The president of Northwest's mechanics union local said he was troubled to hear Steenland declare "everything else is running fine but we need to get labor costs in hand." Union leaders complained that although they could negotiate with Anderson, Steenland "presents more of an authority figure. His [approach] is more like, 'The world according to Doug,'" as one labor leader said. "Steenland has offered employees a stark choice," the *Star Tribune* reported. "Agree to his demands at the bargaining table for steep pay cuts and job losses or risk a Northwest bankruptcy filing and even deeper labor cutbacks in court."

Steenland wanted $176 million in cuts from the mechanics, and he had funds ready to train new workers if his current employees refused and went on strike. Convinced that the burden of financial relief did not have to fall on their shoulders, mechanics refused to consider those demands and began a

"Our labor costs are too high," CEO Doug Steenland tells Minnesota lawmakers in 2005.

Members of the Association of Flight Attendants rally in 2006 in support of their Northwest colleagues who wanted the right to strike during the airline's bankruptcy.

strike on August 20, 2005, rather than concede. The better-paid pilots, they said, could more easily accept pay cuts than could mechanics sometimes making less than $20 per hour. The strike dragged on for 444 days, and thousands of the strikers were left without jobs when Northwest permanently hired the mechanics who had crossed the picket lines.

INTO BANKRUPTCY

But worse was still to come for the airline. A week after the strike began, Hurricane Katrina smashed into the Gulf Coast, damaging oil rigs and refineries and dramatically raising the cost of air fuel. That was the last financial straw for Northwest, which missed a loan payment of $42 million and whose climbing debts left it one choice: a declaration of bankruptcy, which came a few weeks after the hurricane. This time, there was no avoiding the financial surrender that the airline had dodged through employee concessions a dozen years earlier. "We had developed a plan to restructure Northwest outside of Chapter 11 and have been implementing that plan," Steenland said. "Unfortunately, in addition to an uncompetitive cost structure, our efforts have been overtaken by skyrocketing fuel costs."

On the same day that Northwest made its financial desperation official, another large carrier was filing for bankruptcy. For the first time in its seventy-five years of operation, Delta—crippled by rising fuel and labor costs that had added $10 billion to the company's debt since 2001—filed for Chapter 11 protection. Northwest's longtime competitor laid off 15 percent of its workforce, and it reduced salaries of the employees who remained. Northwest and Delta joined US Air and United in bankruptcy, leaving only three of the country's seven largest airlines operating in the free and clear.

Northwest operated under bankruptcy for nearly two years, taking advantage of the financial protections to sell off unneeded aircraft, cut employee wages, and prepare for a survivable future. It also preserved the company's pension plans and gave employees a stake in the airline with provisions for profit-sharing bonuses. "We sort of re-said our vows," Steenland said. "We are blessed to have the opportunity to be an airline in the Twin Cities. It has a strong economy, and our customers here have been very good to us. We have no intention to do anything here but hopefully be able to grow the [Minneapolis–St. Paul] hub." These were modest hopes expressed by a subdued chief executive speaking on behalf of a humbled company.

DELTA'S COURTSHIP

Northwest exited bankruptcy protection in May 2007 and made a profit of $764 million that year. Steenland said, "Our focus is going to be on the customers and the employees."

Within six months after the bankruptcy ended, it was in close discussions with its competitor Delta, also newly free of bankruptcy, over a merging of the airlines. Much had changed since Delta's refusal of Northwest's offer to absorb the Atlanta-based carrier twenty years earlier. Delta was now reportedly in merger discussions with United Airlines to fend off an unwanted buyout by US Airways. There was a frantic scramble of airlines seeking to combine with other airlines, but Richard Anderson, Northwest's former CEO, who took the helm of Delta in August 2007, certainly knew what his company was bargaining for in NWA.

Northwest and Delta had flown parallel tracks over the decades. Each had created large spheres of influence—Northwest's in the northern states, the Pacific Northwest, and Asia; Delta's in the South, Far West, and Europe—and their route maps sometimes jostled one another's. Delta traced its origins to a crop-dusting firm formed in 1924 that soon evolved into a passenger airline serving the Mississippi delta region. (The Delta name goes back to 1928.) During the 1940s it headquartered in Atlanta and extended service as far north as Chicago. It grew rapidly during the 1970s and 1980s, often trading annual top-profitability honors with Northwest during those years, and cast its route web to the West Coast, Hawaii, and Europe. A 1986 merger with Western Airlines further diversified its U.S. destinations and leapfrogged it ahead of Northwest in size. Four years later, Delta acquired most of the transatlantic routes of nearly defunct Pan Am, including one connecting Detroit and London that Northwest sought. (Northwest ended up buying the route from Delta in 1995.) It expanded its reach into the Caribbean and Latin America through the 1990s but, like Northwest, suffered heavy losses and announced layoffs and proposals for wage concessions that produced employee dissatisfaction after 9/11. Northwest and Delta formed a cooperative marketing agreement in 2002 and watched each other descend into bankruptcy on the same day in 2005. Delta's debt amounted to $20.5 billion.

Eleven months after their merger talks began, on April 14, 2008, Northwest and Delta announced an agreement to merge in a transaction that would involve the combination of stock valued at $17.7 billion. Delta was to pay $2.8 billion to purchase all of Northwest's stock, and Northwest shareholders received 1.25 shares of Delta stock for every Northwest share they owned. Even though the newly merged entity, which would use the Delta Airlines name and be headquartered in Atlanta, planned to spend $1 billion to accomplish the merger, it expected that the transaction would generate $1 billion a year in more efficient use of aircraft, a bigger and well-diversified route system that would draw new passengers, lower overhead costs, and boosted efficiencies that would save money. (The company would be in no position to save money on fuel costs, however, which hovered around $3.60 a gallon when the merger was announced—an increase of 75 percent over the previous year.) The merged business would also be on a better footing to compete with the large international operations of such foreign airlines as Lufthansa and British Airways.

Former Northwest executives would not lose their headquarters, the merger managers promised, because there would be branch headquarters in Minneapolis–St. Paul, as well as in New York City, Amsterdam, Paris, and Tokyo. Only one employees' union, the Air Line Pilots Association local that represented Delta pilots, supported the merger, and its members would receive a small equity stake in the merged company. Northwest pilots—although ALPA represented them, as well—did not receive consideration in the merger agreement and wanted joint representation with their Delta colleagues. A host of other unionized Northwest employees, including flight attendants, customer service and reservation agents, and flight simulator technicians, would face an uncertain fate under the wing of Delta, where only the pilots and dispatchers had union representation.

Opponents of the merger pointed out that although the route maps of the two airlines did not overlap in most regions of the United States and the world, hundreds of thousands of travelers who visit a dozen domestic destinations would see their choices—and consequently cost competition—diminish after the merger. In these cities, Northwest and Delta directly competed to offer nonstop service to other locations; the list included Cincinnati, Minneapolis–St. Paul, Detroit, and Salt Lake City. Critics also feared that passengers who flew in and out of the seven domestic hubs that Northwest and Delta operated would soon see fare increases, a concern that numerous studies on pricing patterns in hub cities supported.

To the accusations that the merger would deal a serious blow to airline competition, Northwest and Delta counterargued that recent events had shaken up the old methods of anticipating degrees of competition. In the previous seven years, everything had changed. The most competitive players in the industry, the merger partners maintained, were no longer such legacy carriers as Delta, United, and American, but the low-cost airlines, which now included JetBlue, Southwest, and AirTran. Several low-cost carriers—ATA, Aloha, Champion, and Frontier among them—had recently gone out of business or reorganized their finances under federal bankruptcy protection, and many others did not serve the same destinations as the merged company, but Northwest/Delta still regarded their type of operation as the enemy.

When a subcommittee of the U.S. House of Representatives met to review the merger proposal, the chair, Representative Jerry Costello of Illinois, began the proceedings by noting, "I have grave concerns about airline mergers. Previous mergers have rarely produced the projected benefits and efficiencies promised. Mergers have been good for airline executives, but not so good for consumers or employees." Steenland and Anderson spent hours before the subcommittee answering questions and defending the benefits of the merger.

CEOs Doug Steenland and Richard Anderson answer questions about their proposed airline merger before the House Judiciary Committee on December 15, 2009.

In his opening statement, Steenland detailed the two paths that he believed lay ahead for Northwest. "One is to continue on the road now traveled, as a stand-alone airline, being whipsawed between rising oil prices, which will cost Northwest over $1.5 billion more this year versus last year, facing increased competition from domestic carriers that have now captured more than one third of the U.S. domestic market, and facing heightened international competition from large, well-funded foreign airlines that have been allowed to consolidate and are increasing service to the United States," he explained. "The other choice is to merge with Delta to create a single, stronger airline, better able to face these challenges. By combining the complementary, end-to-end networks of two great airlines, we will achieve substantial benefits and build a more comprehensive and global network."

Steenland added that the combined airline would be financially stronger, in a better position to maintain its jobs (although he acknowledged the certainty of some layoffs), and increasingly capable of offering the kind of air transportation that passengers want. He promised that the merged company would close no currently existing hubs, and that people in smaller communities would continue to receive service. Steenland predicted that "combining Delta and Northwest will offer customers greater choice, more competitive fares, and a superior travel experience." An unprofitable airline, he concluded, could do nothing to benefit shareholders, customers, or employees.

Anderson reminded members of the subcommittee that both Northwest and Delta had just come out of bankruptcy and "really cleaned up their strategies. If the Cincinnati, Memphis, Detroit, Atlanta—if any of these hubs were not viable, you can bet that the creditors' committee and constituents in the bankruptcy process would have required the carriers to reject the leases and the airplanes." He pointed out that given Northwest's route network in Asia and Delta's in Europe and Latin America, the combination of the airlines would give travelers access to "a global network that neither airline independently could offer." He promised that the enlarged Delta after the merger would bring benefits to employees through equity stakes in the company, increases in concessions-reduced pay to meet industry standards, and the maintenance of strong pension plans.

The CEOs met skepticism over the effect of the merger on competitiveness in the industry. Albert Foer, president of the nonprofit American Antitrust Institute, testified that the airline executives were probably exaggerating the efficiencies that the merger would produce. "If there is one thing that we have learned from the long history of antitrust, it is that efficiencies are easy to assert, difficult to achieve, and rarely of the magnitude that the parties—in their self interest—claim," he said. Although Steenland and Anderson both cited the rising cost of airplane fuel as difficulties in the future independent operation of their airlines, Foer maintained that no consequence of the merger would lead to lower fuel prices. "We see no reason to believe that the benefits of merger are due to efficiencies

Northwest's corporate markings disappear from a building at Minneapolis–St. Paul International Airport in 2009.

rather than market power and are therefore quite skeptical," he concluded. Competition usually weakens, he declared, when competitors merge.

Patricia Friend, testifying on behalf of the Association of Flight Attendants, which represented Northwest employees, told the subcommittee of her union's fear that the merger would lead to furloughs, base closures, layoffs, and outsourcing of labor. "Workers cannot, and should not, be left to fend for themselves in this situation," she said. "We did not bring these problems on ourselves. The federal government set this chain of events in motion with the passage of the Deregulation Act and its subsequent neglect in forming a rational aviation policy for our country. The airlines themselves have compounded the problems for workers with an almost endless string of cutbacks, bankruptcies, mergers and layoffs. Government and the airlines, then, bear the responsibility." Citing the uncertainty over whether flight attendants in the combined company would have union representation, Friend maintained that "the merger should not be permitted to become a vehicle for union busting" and accused the airlines of devising mergers to weaken the bargaining power of employees.

Delta CEO Richard Anderson introduces Northwest flight attendants to the Delta wine list in 2008.

THE UNDERWEAR BOMBER ⏱

On Christmas Day, 2009, Northwest Airlines had only six days remaining as an independent airline before officially losing its name and identity to Delta Airlines. That day Flight 253 from Amsterdam to Detroit, an Airbus A330-300 twinjet carrying 279 passengers and 11 crew members, was nearing its destination when a passenger rose to spend about twenty minutes in a lavatory. When he returned to his seat, he told fellow passengers that he was not feeling well and covered himself with a blanket. As the plane approached Detroit, people nearby heard a series of pops, smelled smoke, and saw a small fire erupt on the trouser leg of the passenger and a nearby wall. In the most notoriously felonious behavior by a Northwest customer since D. B. Cooper hijacked a plane in 1971, the inflamed passenger had been trying to detonate a bomb made from the compound pentaerythritol tetranitrate (PETN) sewn inside his underwear. It was the same substance that "shoe bomber" Richard Reid had tried to ignite on an American Airlines flight eight years earlier.

Another passenger, Jasper Schuringa of the Netherlands, pulled a burning object from between the legs of the smoldering traveler, and flight attendants used a fire extinguisher to put out the blaze. The bomber, severely charred on one leg, was handcuffed, isolated from other passengers, and arrested after an emergency landing at Detroit Metropolitan Wayne County Airport, with U.S. Customs and Border Protection officers awaiting the plane's arrival.

Authorities identified the bomber as Umar Farouk Abdulmutallab, twenty-three and a native of Nigeria, who had attended secondary school in Togo and had been an engineering student at University College in London. His friends had long known him as a religious extremist, estranged from his family, who frequently delivered impromptu and strident lectures on the teachings of Islam. After his arrest, Abdulmutallab allegedly claimed to have had terrorism training and access to bomb-making materials in Yemen, and it is possible that he was in contact with the al-Qaeda leader Anwar al-Awlaki. Al-Qaeda in the Arabian Peninsula took responsibility for the incident, it said in retaliation for U.S. attacks on militants in Yemen. A month after the attack, an audio recording purportedly by Osama Bin Laden praised Abdulmutallab's actions.

Abdulmutallab was charged with eight crimes, including the attempted use of a weapon of mass destruction and attempted murder. He pleaded guilty to all charges and was sentenced to life in prison in 2012. The incident prompted the start of more vigorous preflight screening in the United States of travelers from fourteen countries, including Nigeria.

A U.S. Senate investigation of the incident found that State Department, CIA, FBI, National Security Administration, and National Counterterrorism Center employees had made fourteen errors that enabled Abdulmutallab to board and attempt to destroy the Northwest aircraft. •

COMING TOGETHER

Ultimately the airlines received government approval to merge. They would continue to operate separately until the start of 2010, when Delta expected to receive one certificate from the FAA to run both operations, and Northwest's and Delta's reservations, ticket counters, gates, and control centers fully merged. To save money and adjust to dropping passenger demand for seats, Delta planned to trim the merged system by nearly 10 percent. Some of the biggest reductions came in Northwest's old hubs of Detroit, Memphis, and Minneapolis–St. Paul. Even so, the combination made Delta the world's largest airline with a fleet of 786 aircraft (not including the planes of its regional affiliate partners), seventy-five thousand employees, and around six thousand scheduled daily departures. It served over 390 worldwide destinations in 67 countries and gave customers access to 840 destinations in 162 countries through alliances with other airlines.

By the end of the first quarter of 2009, Delta signs and logos replaced all the Northwest signage in the hub cities of Minneapolis–St. Paul, Detroit, and Memphis. Flight attendants, pilots, gate agents, and ticket agents had abandoned Northwest uniforms for Delta's. The biggest changes came at Northwest's largest hub in Minneapolis–St. Paul, where on a quiet weeknight in March 2009 "crews removed the old Northwest signs that once lined the wide ticketing level nearly wall-to-wall, and replaced them with Delta signs," the *Minneapolis Star Tribune* reported.

The merger of Northwest and Delta required the marriage of twelve hundred separate company systems—ranging from frequent flier programs to procedures for awarding employee benefits. At Delta's headquarters in Atlanta, a wall-sized board in a conference room displayed hundreds of multicolored sticky notes, each listing a merger project that could demand the efforts of hundreds of employees to make thousands of changes.

Travelers still felt confused, however, because the airlines continued to issue separately branded tickets. Northwest's union contracts, still in force, maintained that only the airline's employees could assist the airline's passengers; Delta's nonunion workforce could not touch them. As a result, passengers holding Northwest tickets sometimes had to leave lines before Delta ticket counters and move to identically signed counters manned by Northwest staff. The workforces of the combined airlines could not yet mix.

AN INGLORIOUS END

As the airline sailed into its final days, it suffered from disarray. During the summer of 2007, thousands of Northwest flights were canceled because of crew shortages, often on short notice that left travelers stranded. Steenland observed that "new work rules didn't quite work the way we were expecting them." The pilots union issued a vote of no confidence

LIGHTS OUT

One of the first postmerger changes in what some people called the "Deltafication" of Northwest came in the refashioning of baggage claim and ticketing counters at the airports Northwest served. By the end of March 2009, Delta transformed these public areas and painted its colors on about 35 percent of Northwest's fleet; the figure had increased to 80 percent by the end of the year. At the same time, the interiors of the aircraft were redecorated with Delta's blue leather seats.

And by mid-2010, Northwest's website had shut down. For devotees of Northwest it was a dismal course of events, but the Associated Press found something good to report. "One benefit to travelers," it noted, "will be in the menu. Northwest dropped snacks long ago to save money. But people who fly the airline now will get their choice of peanuts or cookies."

Although Delta had committed to keep at least ten thousand employees in Minnesota as well as maintaining four hundred flights daily out of the Twin Cities through 2016, everyone knew that some workers would soon lose their jobs as a result of the consolidation. In 2010 the Minnesota Department of Employment and Economic Development began using a federal grant of $2.6 million to help 613 laid-off workers find new positions. More than half of a sample of such employees had worked at Northwest for more than twenty years. Some had never worked anywhere else.

Many of the employees who remained with Delta faced uncertain union representation. The Association of Flight Attendants (AFA) represented Northwest cabin workers at the time of the acquisition, while Delta's flight attendants were not unionized. The difference was resolved at the end of 2010, when the former Northwest flight attendants, totaling 26 percent of Delta's cabin workers, voted to discontinue their affiliation with the AFA after sixty-three years of collective bargaining. The AFA accused Delta of intimidating and coercing employees before the vote, an accusation the airline denied.

In the year following the completion of the merger, Delta was nearly $1 billion in the black—the largest profit it had earned in many years. Simultaneously a survey measuring airline quality by *U.S. News & World Report* named Delta the nation's worst carrier. If fares were not supposed to rise, there was little evidence in analyses of ticket prices. Competition was healthy for some routes, but by 2011, fares from Minneapolis–St. Paul, where Delta now controlled 89 percent of the gates in the main terminal, had jumped significantly for routes in which the airline had no competition.

"Among the effects of the merger has been a culture

Northwest CEO Doug Steenland and his predecessor and counterpart at Delta, Richard Anderson, worked closely to bring about the merger of their airlines.

clash between Northwest employees, accustomed to a Midwestern work ethic, and their Atlanta bosses, steeped in a Southern business style seen by some NWA veterans as paternalistic and inefficient," Tim Gihring wrote in 2011 in *Minnesota Monthly*. Said one longtime Northwest employee: "It's like the Flintstones took over the Jetsons."

Business gradually normalized. In early 2010, Delta opened its northern headquarters at Minneapolis–St. Paul International Airport in the old Republic Airlines building. A reduced staff of 760 worked there. Many of their colleagues had moved to Atlanta or accepted buy-outs from Delta. Later that year, Delta asked permission from the city of Eagan to subdivide Northwest's former property—site of the 266,000-square-foot headquarters building, largely vacant except for a few payroll workers, and seventy-two acres of land—to make it easier to sell. The asking price was $33 million. Delta continued to maintain a flight school and data records center in Eagan.

Unlike other some other merged airlines that left one or two aircraft from the acquired company unpainted in tribute to the vanished name, Delta made no plans to keep any aircraft in a commemorative Northwest livery. The last Northwest-painted plane, a DC-9, reportedly received its new colors in January 2011. With that, Northwest's visual presence faded away. Former Northwest employee Bill Lentsch, Delta's senior vice president for Minnesota operations, explained the company's approach to the maintenance of obsolete traditions. "The Northwest history is something that we're all proud of and we're all fond of, but I think the excitement that comes along with being part of the biggest and the greatest airline in the world is something that is just overwhelmingly positive and wipes all that other stuff away," he said.

Not everyone agreed. The acquisition made Northwest artifacts ranging from old promotional brochures to pilfered cabin silverware soar in price at flea markets and on online selling sites. Grab them while you can. •

in Northwest's leaders, and the Association of Flight Attendants demanded Steenland's resignation. Interviewed that summer on national television, Steenland exchanged remarks with interviewer Meredith Vieira:

VIEIRA: You going to promise me, guarantee me, that if I buy a ticket [at the] end of August, you won't cancel that flight?

STEENLAND: We—you are guaranteed.

VIEIRA: How about the rest of customers? Them, too?

STEENLAND: Well, there's always weather. You know, safety always comes first at an airline, so we always make sure that nothing happens with respect—

VIEIRA: But it won't be the fault of poor management, anyway.

STEENLAND: I—it better not be.

The constant crew shortages ended by autumn. Then a Federal Aviation Administration whistle-blower, Mark Lund, alerted government authorities that Northwest had developed inappropriately close relations with FAA managers and—contrary to the regulations of that agency—often avoided penalties for safety infractions by voluntarily reporting the problems to FAA officials. Lund charged that any FAA inspector who wanted to cite Northwest for safety rule infractions "has to typically fight through the FAA management chain" to properly register problems. A review of Northwest's compliance with FAA safety orders found twenty-two times in 2008 and 2009 that the airline was in violation of rules. In one especially egregious case, Northwest failed to follow guidelines in inspecting the landing gear of twenty-seven aircraft to prevent parts from falling off and potentially rupturing fuel tanks. The planes had to be grounded. A report by the Department of Transportation's inspector general's office concluded that "the status of Northwest's compliance with more than 1,000 [safety orders] is unknown."

In addition, Northwest in 2010 pleaded guilty to a felony charge of conspiring to fix the charges for cargo shipped between the United States and Japan from 2004 to 2006. The airline, according to the charges, colluded with other carriers in setting cargo rates in violation of antitrust laws. Northwest was one of sixteen airlines investigated by the Department of Justice for violations of cargo price fixing, and it paid a fine of $38 million.

If that was not enough, two Northwest pilots in 2009 became the subject of countless talk-show discussions and late-night TV jokes when they overshot their destination on a flight from San Diego to Minneapolis by more than a hundred miles because they were distracted while using a laptop computer in the cockpit. They were so inattentive that they did not notice the repeated attempts of air traffic controllers to reach them and find out what was wrong. The gag writers of TV host David Letterman devised a Top Ten list of "Northwest Airlines Pilot Excuses" that included, "According to our map, we only missed our target by half an inch," and "For a change, we decided to send luggage to the right city and lose the passengers." Commented late-night competitor Jay Leno: "Have you heard Northwest Airlines' new slogan: 'When we say nonstop, we mean it. Let's keep going.'"

The FAA revoked the licenses of Captain Timothy Cheney and First Officer Richard Cole, who never admitted that they had done anything wrong. The pilots challenged the FAA decision as too hasty and made under public pressure, and the agency relented by making it possible for them to return to work after undergoing additional training and testing. Ultimately, however, the question of whether the pilots would return to work for Northwest became moot when Cheney retired and Cole lost his job.

With these ignominious events fresh in everyone's memory, the FAA merged Northwest's and Delta's operating certificates on the final day of 2009, allowing Delta to impose its code on all Northwest's flights and officially remove Northwest's name as a government-sanctioned carrier. When the airlines joined their reservations systems two weeks later, Northwest Airlines finally and unalterably ceased to exist. The company that had begun eighty-three years earlier in a scramble for a borrowed two-seat plane ended as the second hand of a clock moved upright to complete the largest airline merger in history.

THE HISTORY OF NORTHWEST AIRLINES

1926 Colonel Lewis Brittin establishes Northwest Airways, with its operations base at Speedway Field, south of Minneapolis–St. Paul. The airline carries its first bags of mail.

1927 Byron Webster makes the first ticketed passenger flight aboard Northwest.

1928 Northwest begins coordinated air and rail cargo service between the Twin Cities and Chicago.

1929 Twin Cities investors purchase Northwest from Detroit businessmen and bring ownership of the company to Minnesota.

1930 Northwest installs its first radio navigational system.

1933 Amelia Earhart joins Brittin and Croil Hunter on a groundbreaking survey flight to establish the safety of passenger service to the Pacific Northwest.

1934 After the airmail scandals, the company reincorporates as Northwest Airlines, Inc. Founder Lewis Brittin serves a brief jail term and resigns.

1937 Croil Hunter ascends to Northwest's presidency.

1938 Northwest develops the first oxygen mask adaptable to commercial aviation.

1939 With its use of Douglas DC-3 aircraft, Northwest introduces stewardesses to its routes.

1941 The airline's revenues from passenger service exceed its airmail income.

1942 Northwest begins nearly four years of grueling involvement in the effort to win World War II.

1945 Northwest's first transcontinental flight wings from Seattle to New York.

1946 Northwest inaugurates passenger service to Alaska, a stepping-stone to the Orient.

1947 Northwest begins passenger flights to the Far East through Alaska.

1948 Aircraft begin flying with Northwest's distinctive painted red tails.

1949 The victory of Mao Tse-tung's Communist forces in China forces Northwest's evacuation from that country.

1949 Northwest begins flying the Stratocruiser and becomes the first U.S. carrier to offer alcoholic drinks on flights within the United States.

1950 The airline begins its involvement in airlifts during the Korean War.

1952 Northwest sells off the last of its Martin 202 aircraft, which had been involved in a series of serious crashes.

1953 After Croil Hunter's retirement as president, Harold R. Harris fills the job for just one year.

1954 Donald Nyrop, the youngest chief executive of an airline, starts his twenty-two years as president.

1957 Northwest meteorologists devise techniques to detect and avoid air turbulence.

1961 The company relocates its headquarters and maintenance facilities to Minneapolis–St. Paul International Airport.

1963 Northwest becomes the first U.S. carrier to operate a fleet made entirely of fan-jets.

1968 A hugely profitable year allows Northwest to lead the industry in earnings for the first time—a distinction it would keep for several years running.

1971 A passenger known as "Dan Cooper" hijacks a Northwest flight and escapes by parachute with a bag of cash, never to be seen again.

1979 M. Joseph Lapensky becomes Northwest's CEO after Donald Nyrop's transition to board chairman.

1983 Steven Rothmeier becomes president.

1984 NWA, Inc., is incorporated in Delaware as a holding company for Northwest Airlines.

1984 Northwest launches Airlink, a partnership with regional feeder airlines.

1986 Northwest purchases Republic Airlines, the nation's ninth-largest carrier, for $884 million.

1989 In a leveraged buyout, ownership of Northwest transfers to the Wings group, headed by Al Checchi and Gary Wilson.

1991 John Dasburg becomes president and CEO.

1992 Northwest receives a $772 million aid package from the state of Minnesota in exchange for the company's promises to keep jobs in the state and build new maintenance facilities.

1998 A pilots' strike shuts down the airline for nearly three weeks.

2001 Northwest's new CEO is Richard Anderson.

2004 Douglas Steenland succeeds Richard Anderson as CEO.

2005 Northwest mechanics, custodians, and cleaners begin a 444-day strike in opposition to the airline's plans to outsource heavy maintenance work overseas.

2005 Northwest declares bankruptcy and reorganizes, emerging from bankruptcy protection in 2007.

2008 Northwest and Delta Airlines announce plans to merge their companies.

2009 Alert passengers and crew avert disaster aboard a flight from Amsterdam to Detroit when the "Underwear Bomber" ignites an explosive hidden in his clothing.

2010 The Northwest–Delta merger is finalized, and all vestiges of Northwest's existence soon vanish.

ACKNOWLEDGMENTS AND SOURCES

My efforts to write this book would have stalled early without the valuable research resources of the Minnesota Historical Society. The manuscripts collection of the MHS includes the vast Northwest Airlines corporate archive as well as other collections of papers from Republic Airlines, the Metropolitan Airports Commission, and many people professionally connected with Northwest. The MHS's photography collections feature a wealth of images that offer a view into the history of Northwest and the regional development of commercial aviation. MHS staff members guided me through these archival holdings, whose deep and sometimes arcane riches form the backbone of this book.

Other authors followed this path before me, and I especially acknowledge the work of the late Kenneth Ruble, corporate chronicler extraordinaire. His book *Flight to the Top* includes the voices of Northwest players now deceased and presents the company's perspective on its own past and the context in which the airline grew. *Northwest Airlines: The First Eighty Years* by Geoff Jones and *A Pictorial History of Northwest Airlines* by Stephen Mills offer useful summaries of Northwest's history as well as informative galleries of images. I found an enjoyable collection of historical anecdotes in *Voices from the Sky* by Robert L. Johnson of the NWA History Centre. Finally, Al Checchi's book *The Change Maker: Preserving the Promise of America* is valuable for its window into the mind of an important Northwest figure, although other participants in the events he describes undoubtedly have different interpretations.

I am grateful to the many journalists who covered Northwest's every move over the decades, including writers for the Twin Cities daily newspapers, the *Wall Street Journal*, *USA Today*, the *New York Times*, and magazines such as *Minnesota Monthly*, *Corporate Report Minnesota*, the *New Yorker*, *Forbes*, *Fortune*, and many aviation trade publications. Their reporting gave color to events that otherwise would remain drab. Melissa Koch and Dawn Mikkelson's film documentary *The Red Tail* takes viewers inside the Airline Mechanics Fraternal Association's 2005–6 strike, a remarkable look at the tragic attempt of Northwest employees to take control of their lives while economic and business forces combined to overpower them.

I am deeply appreciative to many people and organizations who helped me with my specific or general requests for photos, information, and interviews: president Bruce Kitt and the wonderful volunteer staff at the NWA History Centre, the Public Affairs Department of Delta Airlines, Steven Rothmeier, Jay Rothmeier, Al Checchi, Sandy Clifton, Karen Hanson, Tammy Lee Stanoch, Charles Curry, Mary Curry, Phyllis Curry, Randy Dotinga, Ann Aronson, and Tracey Baker, among many others.

Finally, here's a toast to my editor, Todd Orjala, and to Doug Armato, director at the University of Minnesota Press. This book began in their heads, and they, along with their able staff, guided it to the final touchdown.

ILLUSTRATION CREDITS

Associated Press/AP images: page 176, AP Photo/Joe Migon; page 187 (*top*), AP Photo/Staff; page 187 (*bottom*), AP Photo/Nick Ut; page 219 (*right*), AP Photo/H. B. Littell; page 223, AP Photo/Dale Atkins; page 224, AP Photo/Lennox McLendon; pages 258–59, AP Photo/Jim Mone; page 272, AP Photo/Scott Applewhite.

Duluth News Tribune: page 261, photograph by Charles Curtis.

Library of Congress, Prints and Photographs Division: page 118 (*left*), LC-USZC4-12517.

Minneapolis–St. Paul Metropolitan Airports Commission (audiovisual materials, Minnesota Historical Society): pages 20, 46, 58 (*right*), 81, 120, 264, 265; page 216, photograph by David Galbraith.

Northwest Airlines, Inc., Corporate Records (Minnesota Historical Society): pages 5, 15, 16, 17, 23, 25, 28 (*top*), 30 (*top left and right*), 33, 37 (*bottom*), 39 (*both images*), 42 (*right*), 43 (*bottom*), 48 (*both images*), 49, 50 (*bottom*), 51, 52, 54, 55, 61 (*top*), 62 (*both images*), 70, 74 (*left*), 75, 77, 83, 86, 87, 88 (*all images*), 94, 95, 96, 101, 102 (*left*), 103, 107, 108, 109, 110 (*bottom right*), 110 (*top left*), 110 (*top right*), 114 (*right*), 116, 118 (*right*), 122, 123 (*both images*), 125, 128 (*bottom right*), 128 (*top right*), 134 (*left*), 135 (*top*), 136 (*all images*), 137 (*top left, bottom left and right*), 140, 141, 143 (*both images*), 145 (*bottom*), 145, 146, 147 (*all images*), 148 (*both images*), 149 (*both images*), 150 (*both images*), 158 (*left, and top right*), 159, 161 (*both images*), 163 (*left*), 166 (*bottom left, top right*), 169 (*left*), 170, 171, 172, 173 (*both images*), 174, 180, 181, 183, 184, 185, 188, 192, 193 (*left*), 194 (*bottom left and right*), 200, 201, 203, 211, 212, 215, 216, 219 (*left*), 221 (*left*), 262 (*left*), 263; page 73, photograph by Ralph Vincent; page 100, photograph by George Miles Ryan Studio; page 115, photograph by Don Berg Photography; page 167, photograph by John Kreissler; pages 145, 195 (*top left and bottom left*), photographs by Forde Photographers; pages 19, 60 (*bottom*), 78, 119, 121, 142, 158 (*bottom*), 194 (*top*), 195 (*right*), photographs by Robert R. Blanch Photography.

INDEX

Jack El-Hai's books include *Lost Minnesota: Stories of Vanished Places* (Minnesota, 2000) and *The Lobotomist: A Maverick Medical Genius and His Tragic Quest to Rid the World of Mental Illness*. He has written about business and history for the *Atlantic*, *Scientific American Mind*, *History Channel Magazine*, *American Heritage*, and *Utne Reader*.